David McCue was born in North Cheshire. After atte[...] spent his national service in the Sudan and Ethiopi[...] Egypt. In 1959 he returned to Africa, joining the [...] Force. Developing a keen interest in sudden, violent worked in Choma and then Livingstone as a detective assistant inspector. It was this work that inspired him to write *The Bodies Man*.

In 1967 David retired from his position as detective chief inspector in charge of CID Lusaka Central and returned to England. He gained a degree in education at Manchester University, married and spent the remainder of his working life teaching in the largest junior school in Trafford, where he was quickly promoted to deputy head teacher. In 1994 a specialist informed him that he had less than nine months left to live. He retired from teaching, but obviously he is still here!

For Tim,

With my very best wishes.

David McCue

THE BODIES MAN

THE BODIES MAN

David McCue

SilverWood

Published in 2017 by SilverWood Books

SilverWood Books Ltd
14 Small Street, Bristol, BS1 1DE, United Kingdom
www.silverwoodbooks.co.uk

ISBN 978-1-78132-632-9 (paperback)
ISBN 978-1-78132-633-6 (ebook)

British Library Cataloguing in Publication Data
A CIP catalogue record for this book is available from
the British Library

Page design and typesetting by SilverWood Books
Printed on responsibly sourced paper

Contents

Prologue

I was in the enquiry office when I received news of an accident about seventeen miles south of Choma on the main road to Livingstone. A motorist reported having seen a crashed car in the bush on the west side of the road, and from what he could see from his car, the driver appeared to be dead.

At this period in Northern Rhodesia's development, with possible independence for the country looming sometime in the near future and the political picture showing a very restless and unsettled African population, there was a general practice among car drivers not to stop in the case of an accident. A number of drivers had been attacked by angry crowds after stopping to help, and so they were advised to report the accident to the nearest police station, and this he had done.

I looked in the station yard for a vehicle but every vehicle was in use except for a force motorbike. I put my first-aid kit with my camera and measuring instruments in one of the bike's two pannier bags and set off, zeroing the milometer as I did so. I started looking for signs of the accident from sixteen miles out and found the crashed car just about where the man who had made the report said it would be.

I put the bike on its stand and walked to the car to check the driver. He was half-out of the car and was lying with his chest on the bonnet. His body, from the waist down, was draped over a shattered steering wheel. The upper part of his body had been flung through the windscreen and had come to rest with the head twisted completely round, his eyes staring at the sky. He was very obviously dead, but I had had to check. I found that the head had been almost severed from the body but was still attached by a piece of flesh on the left side of the neck. He had not been using a seat belt but in those days it was rare to come across one in a car.

I searched the car for any useful evidence and carried a heavy travel bag back to my bike. On examining the car I found that the nearside front tyre was badly damaged, and examination of marks in the dirt of the road showed evidence to suggest that there had been a high-speed blowout. After the car had left the road it had skidded for about twenty yards into the bush and had then hit the trunk of a large tree, causing the damage to the vehicle and the death of the driver. It had then spun to a stop a few yards further beyond the tree. I checked the road for signs of another vehicle being involved but there were none.

Fairly straightforward, I thought.

I carried out all the required measuring and took photographs, but as I did so I became aware of a rustling sound. I looked around quickly but saw nothing to alarm me until I noticed movement of the long grass about thirty yards away. Before I could worry about lions or leopards, the answer appeared on the bonnet of the car. Ants! Scouts were running ahead of the main army, which in turn, was obviously causing the movement of the high grass further back. I decided that I would have to remove the body and protect it for forensic examination.

My first problem was the head. It was not really a problem in the physical sense, but I wondered what the magistrate would think of what I was going to do. I saw that bushes closer to me were now beginning to wave and rustle, and this made up my mind for me.

Using the knife I always carried, I sliced through the remaining flesh joining the head to the body and quickly went and put the head in the empty pannier bag on the motorbike. I ran back to the car. The driver's door had come open in the crash so, with great difficulty, I dragged the now-headless body back through the shattered windscreen and out through the door. I found myself gasping for breath. The hardest part was yet to come. I had to remove the body from the scene or the ants would make a mess of it, not to mention any carnivores within scenting distance. I decided that I would have to remove it on the motorbike.

I dragged the poor guy to where I had parked the bike. By now the car was covered by an army of ants. It took all my strength to lift the body and sit it on the rear end of the motorbike's seat. I then had to lift my foot over the front of the seat whilst balancing the body behind me. The only way that I could do it was by placing the body's right arm over my shoulder and hanging on to it as I got on to the saddle. Once seated, it was a fairly simple task to pull his hands around my waist and handcuff them together and we were ready to go.

I drove carefully on the way back. I didn't want to skid on the loose sand of the road. As I neared Choma a car came up from behind me and started to overtake, but then, upon seeing my headless passenger, dropped back and followed me into the town. It left me when I turned into the lane to the mortuary. I made my passenger comfortable in one of the fridges with the help of Dr George's handyman. I then went back to the police station to write my report, entered the details of the afternoon's work in the occurrence book and signed off duty.

The other officers had left for dinner in the hotel so, after a much-needed shower, I followed on. As I entered the dining room there was a sudden silence and my fellow officers and the other diners all stared at me. News had travelled quickly in this small town. That was the day I was given the nickname "Bodies", which stayed with me for the remainder of my time in the Southern Province.

1

The War Years

My name is David McCue and I was born in July 1933. My brother John followed me in November 1934, and my sister Jill in November 1939. The baby of the family, Jane, arrived in April 1946, a celebratory baby sister at the end of the war.

My father worked for the Warrington Electricity Board, being steadily promoted into more responsible positions. When the electricity industry was nationalised at the end of the war Dad went to work at MANWEB HQ in Cheshire. My mother had given up work upon marrying and took on the work of raising four children as we came along. Not the easiest job in wartime Britain.

My earliest memories are of infant school at Stockton Heath Council School. I remember being given a peg for my coat and my bag, which was full of the usual stuff youngsters need when they first start school.

Most children of my age sensed that something bad was happening, but Mum and Dad didn't say much in front of John and me. I learned to read very quickly, as did John, and at every opportunity we read the daily newspaper. Other friends at school offered bits of information that had been overheard and we put together a picture of the war that was about to explode into our lives. Rumours abounded. A favourite one was that all the children were to be sent to Canada. However, it never happened to us.

As time passed, we saw that the land at the rear of the school was being dug up and air raid shelters were being constructed. Most of us were excited by this and began to plan how we would fight the Germans if they invaded Britain. John and I had made friends with Roland and his younger brother Patrick, two new boys at the school. Their father was a major and, during his life in the army, had collected all sorts of weapons which he displayed on the walls in his house. We felt that we could hold off a German attack if we used these weapons. We discussed and planned where and how we would hold out against the enemy. We decided that our base would be in the woods at the top of Hill Cliff, which was a steep hill overlooking Warrington, which lay away to the north of us.

Things started to become more real to us when, as a family, we trooped down to the village, as we called Stockton Heath, to be issued with gas masks. We kids hadn't even thought of the possibility of gas attacks. Jill, my baby sister, was fitted into an all-embracing baby's gas mask. She looked as though she was sitting in a miniature submarine. She wasn't very happy. The rest of us tried on our masks and I for one hoped that we would never have to wear them.

Eventually, war broke out. Our army was sent to France to help stop the German advances, but every day seemed to bring bad news. Eventually the British Army was forced to withdraw to Dunkirk, a town on the French coast, and most of the soldiers were only saved by the heroism of the sailors in all types and sizes of ships and boats. Unfortunately many lives were lost. Harvey Upton, who was the son of our next-door neighbours, was in a truck in France which was hit by a German bomb and barely escaped with his life. The other soldiers in the truck were all killed. All this seemed so far away to our young minds. The warm, rather dry, summer days passed quietly but we soon started to get a flavour of things to come.

One Saturday morning, John and I went into Warrington. We suddenly heard loud whistles and shouts to lie down. We were in Bridge Street at the time and it was here that we heard our first air raid siren, a loud up-and-down wail. All traffic was stopped and officials were directing everyone to lie face down and close to the walls of buildings, with our hands on the backs of our heads. It struck me, even at my age, that to lie against a building would not be good if that building was hit by a bomb. Still, I suppose they knew what they were doing.

We waited for some time, listening for the sound of enemy aircraft. At last the long blasts of whistles, and gesticulations from officials, brought us to our feet. John and I dusted each other's coats and looked around. This had only been a practice. The funny thing was that nobody seemed to be angry at being made to lie down in the street. It might have been different had it been raining and the pavements wet.

The summer days passed slowly, but not much seemed to be happening so far as we kids were concerned. At school, the air raid shelters had been dug out in the field at the back. Instead of just going back into school at the end of playtimes, martial music was played loudly and we all proudly marched to our classrooms, keeping in time with the beat.

We eventually had to practise what to do if the air raid siren in the middle of the village was sounded. We were taken out of our classrooms and our teachers were shown which shelters each class would go into. We then practised moving

15

quickly but quietly from our classrooms and into the shelters. There was great excitement when we were each given a small tin, which, we were told, contained emergency rations. These were called "iron rations" and were to be used only if we were in the shelter for a long time, and then only when instructed to do so by our teacher.

Nobody asked what we would do if we needed the toilet, but many of us wondered. Later we realised that behind curtains at the far end of each shelter were buckets, which would have to do as toilets. The shelters were dark and damp but that didn't seem to matter. We had a number of practices over the months that followed but I can't remember any real need to use them. Most of the air raids happened at night.

In class we learned to knit. Boys learned as well, and several times a week we spent an hour or so knitting scarves for the sailors of a corvette of the British Navy. We were encouraged to write letters to the sailors of our corvette, and many of us did so. By this time I was seven years old and had moved up from the infants to the junior section of the school.

Night attacks on British towns and cities began on the 7th September 1940. An anti-aircraft gun, pulled by a truck, was parked in the street each night, directly outside the front door of our house. Several times a week, when there was an air raid, the gun fired shell after shell into the sky until the air raid siren sounded the all-clear. Each time a shell was fired the whole of the house shook.

We were fortunate to live where we did. Bombs did fall nearby, but these were probably not aimed at us. They were most likely to have been dropped by enemy planes getting rid of bombs that they had not been able to drop on their intended targets, which were Manchester and Liverpool.

Whenever we had been awake all night, as German bombers had been constantly overhead, we were only required to go to school in the afternoon the next day. This often happened. If we looked out of the back bedroom windows at night we could see a red glow in the sky. This was Liverpool burning, twelve miles away to the west. When we looked out of the front bedroom windows there was also a red glow in the sky as Manchester and a large area around it burned. We didn't get away completely untouched. A house fairly close to us received a direct hit from a bomb and the front half of the house was completely blown away. German planes also dropped a lot of incendiary bombs (firebombs), and I remember one dropping on the roof of the house directly across the road from us. The incendiary bomb smashed through the roof and ceiling of an upstairs bedroom and landed on the bed of a little girl we often played with. The bomb bounced off the bed and on to the floor. All the family were downstairs, with the children sitting under the table, as we were in our

16

house. They suddenly realised that smoke was pouring down the stairs and that the house was on fire. You couldn't throw water on to an incendiary bomb, as it would only add to the ferocity of its flames. Luckily everyone had been told this and each house had one or more buckets of sand outside the back door. Sand was eventually used and the bomb was rendered harmless. Unfortunately a lot of damage had been done by the water which had been used to put out the fire caused by the bomb.

After a bad night, when we had been awake, sitting under the table, we would spend the next morning collecting shrapnel. Shrapnel was the name given to pieces of shattered shells which, after being fired at the enemy planes, exploded into jagged lumps of metal, which then fell back to the ground. Many shells caused damage to the enemy planes and some were shot down and crashed to the ground, but none crashed near to us. We found lots of pieces of shrapnel in the roads, on pavements and sticking out of tree trunks. Years after the war had ended, gardeners digging up their gardens in the spring would find buried pieces of shrapnel. In wartime, metal was scarce, so what we collected we handed in to a place in the village where it was stored. When enough had been collected it was sent to be melted down and made into shells again.

We kids also collected waste paper. We were given large, empty sacks by the local vicar and it often took all day to collect a sackful. When we had done this we returned to the vicar's house, handed over the sack and waited excitedly for our reward. The vicar would return with a plate filled with sweets and we were allowed to pick one each. John and I usually picked a hard sweet because they lasted longer and we could suck them for a while before wrapping them in pieces of paper to be sucked again later.

The main bombing in the north had started shortly after the bombing in the south of the country. For our part of the country the bombing was mainly concentrated on the large cities of Manchester and Liverpool, but most areas were bombed to some extent. The worst example near to where we lived was the bombing of a garden fete, which was being held on the Thames Board Mills recreation ground in Warrington. The fete was well attended by families and friends and money was being collected for the Spitfire fund. The fund was to help buy more aircraft to defend us against the increasing bomber raids.

It was a beautiful Saturday afternoon and John and I were, as usual, in the woods at Hill Cliff, looking down on the Warrington area. We suddenly saw a column of smoke rising from somewhere near the River Mersey and close to the Thames Board Mills to the north of us. A few seconds later we heard the sound of an explosion. At the same time we saw an aircraft below us, which was climbing towards us at high speed. It was coming from the direction of the smoke. It passed about fifty feet above us and we had a good view of the pilot.

Simultaneously, we both shouted, 'It's a German!'

The crosses on the wings were clear to see. He was heading due south and seemed to be flying low to keep out of sight. We raced home to tell Mum and Dad what we had seen.

News of the bombing spread quickly through the area. Rumours of the number of dead and wounded varied depending upon who was speaking. Tales of body parts being fished out of the river and off the roof of the factory abounded. All I know is that the local press confirmed that two large families had been all but wiped out. Mothers and babies were reported killed. Also, a large number of people had been buried in the ruins of a refreshment building and had to be rescued.

Evidently two bombs had been dropped, but we had only seen the smoke and heard one explosion. That evening, German radio reported that the aluminium mills at Bank Quay had been bombed. I thought that mistaking a garden party for aluminium mills was something that even the Germans would not do. It must have been their intention to bomb the garden party when they spotted it.

The heavy bombing continued, on the big cities particularly, and in the north reached its height in December 1940. Over the three days before Christmas, Manchester and Liverpool were bombed by wave after wave of German bombers. In Manchester 684 people were killed and 2,364 were wounded. In Liverpool, a smaller city, not quite so many people were killed, although in one incident, 166 people were killed when a single bomb hit an air raid shelter.

By the end of 1940 the number of air raids in the north of the country gradually fell and then stopped. The German air force was losing too many aircraft and crews and Hitler, the German leader, realised he was not going to bring our country to its knees by bombing. Also, he had decided to attack Russia. This was the biggest mistake he would ever make. Air raids had largely stopped throughout Britain by May 1941.

When I think about it, we adapted to the scarcities and changes in our lives very quickly. Virtually everything seemed to be rationed except for local fruit, vegetables, fish and bread. The government encouraged the population to "Dig for Victory" by cultivating gardens and spare land to produce vegetables and even fruit. We all adapted to the situation. The general fitness of people was probably better than it is today. We were certainly a lot slimmer.

2

Grammar School and Beyond

I completed my primary education and left junior school in July 1943. I had taken my eleven-plus examination and had been awarded a grammar school place. Dad had now to decide whether he could afford to pay the required fees, but after we broke up for the summer holidays the new Labour government passed a law making secondary education free of cost, as was primary education already.

Dad now had to choose whether he would send me to the Boteler Grammar School in Warrington or to Lymm Grammar School about six miles away in Cheshire. He chose the Boteler, an all-boys' school. I think he thought that it would have better disciplinary standards than a mixed school such as Lymm. For me, it was an unfortunate choice. I don't blame Dad. He was not to know how it would turn out, but later he sent my brother and sisters to Lymm Grammar School. However, during the school holidays, I had a serious accident.

One day I went out with Mum. We went to the park in Stockton Heath. There was a steep slope leading down into a large field, which lay below the level of the bowling greens and park buildings. As Mum walked down the slope I jumped from the top side of it on to a deep pile of grass cuttings. As I sank into the grass I felt something solid shatter beneath me. This was followed by a severe pain in the inside of my right leg just below my knee. I looked down and saw blood pumping out of a gaping wound. I grabbed hold of the wound and shouted to Mum. I could see that she had turned pale and was running towards me. One of Mum's friends came running over as well. She helped get me into a pram in which she had been carrying her own child. Mum started to run with me towards our doctor's, over a mile away. By this time the pram was swimming in my blood. Luckily, a couple of men in the village saw her predicament and helped her to push me all the way to the doctor's surgery.

We arrived at the surgery of our local doctor, Dr Binns, and were rushed into a room with a long couch in it. The doctor stood there with a much younger man, whom he called Edward. Edward turned out to be the doctor's son, home from university where he was training to be a doctor.

I was placed on the couch on my back and given a rounded piece of wood to bite on. Edward and his father then began to pick pieces of glass out of the wound, which, at this time, had almost finished bleeding as my leg was held up. At last it was pronounced clear of glass and then it was flushed with water and painted with iodine, which added to the pain.

I shall never forget what happened next. Edward was to do the stitching. He held in his hand a needle, but was told to get a larger one. The one that was selected was shaped like a fish hook and looked large enough to land a shark. Mum held my hand and told me not to look, but even at that age I was curious about medical matters. In went the needle and the pain seared through me. I would have cried out but for the wood between my teeth. Worse was to come.

'No, Edward, deeper,' said his father.

Out came the needle, and then back in.

'Deeper, Edward.' And out it came again.

At last, on the fourth attempt, Edward got the right depth and the needle was pushed through and into the opposite side of the wound. From there it was pulled upwards until the stitch could be tied.

For a wound that started from the fibula, the inner bone of the two bones at the front of the leg below the knee, and passed out of sight to the back of the leg, he completed the stitching with only six thick stitches. Today, such a wound would have required an ambulance and an operating theatre, but these were war years.

Mum was told by Dr Binns to get someone to help carry me up to bed at home, where I was to stay until he called at the house to check on me in a few weeks' time. He told Mum that the district nurse would come in a couple of weeks to attend to the ridge of flesh which stuck out from the leg for about half an inch in between the stitches.

On returning home I was violently sick. I quickly adapted to the conditions, however, using a portable loo which poor Mum had to empty several times a day. I was forced to drink numerous cups of Bovril each day. This was supposed to restore my blood to the necessary level. After about four days I developed an extremely high temperature and began to hallucinate. The doctor was called and this time it was Edward's father. Once again I was given something to bite on. Dr Binns told Mum and Dad to hold me, pulled out a scalpel and made a deep cut at right angles across the wound. The stuff that seeped out of the now-opened wound had a horrible smell. The doctor cleaned it out and again used iodine in the hole. We didn't have antibiotics for civilians at that time. More stitches were required, but the needle this time was not as large. It was all rather hazy and I ran an extremely high temperature for about a week.

Some weeks later the district nurse began to make regular appearances and the torture began. The flesh, and there was a lot of it, which stuck out from the almost-healed wound was wetted and then bluestone rubbed on to it. Bluestone is copper sulphate in the form of a large crystal. The object was to burn away dead flesh which stood proud of the healing wound. The procedure was painful and unpleasant and I dreaded the days when it took place. It appeared that live flesh and dying flesh could not be separated, so she burned it all.

This continued for a number of weeks until the healed wound was flat. I bear the marks to this day and can run my first finger along the channel of the burnt area. I shall always remember the way the wound, when wetted and rubbed with the bluestone, bubbled as the flesh was slowly consumed.

The accident meant that I had to learn to walk again, and I did so with my mother in attendance, urging me to straighten up.

I arrived at grammar school in short trousers, which we all wore in the first year. I was heavily bandaged, and because of this I escaped the bullying that the rest the new boys endured. My injury was large and very obvious so I was left alone.

New boys were picked up by the legs and arms, lifted high into the air and bumped hard into the ground. After several bumps they were thrown as high into the air as their tormentors could throw them and left to crash down. Caps and school bags were routinely stolen and hidden, very often where they could not be found. Many of the newcomers were terrified. I remember that during these escapades schoolmasters were nowhere to be seen and prefects turned a blind eye. Bullying, in one form or another, continued throughout that first week.

All through my time at the school after my injury had healed I was routinely bullied by a boy a couple of years older than me, who was in the third year. I used to cycle to and from school, crossing the high level bridge over the ship canal. On a number of occasions he would wait for me there and knock me off my bicycle. He never gave a reason. I think he just enjoyed it.

Grammar school was not as I had imagined it would be. I was placed in the top class, the A class, which was made up, I was told, of boys who had scored highly in the eleven-plus examinations. The other three first-year classes, the B, C and D classes catered for pupils according to their eleven-plus results. Most of our teachers were obviously too old to be called up for active service and a number of them had already retired from teaching but had returned to do their bit for the country. Gowns were worn by members of staff during lessons and in the school dining room. At lunchtime, grace was recited in Latin.

The headmaster was a man called Nathanial Leonard Clapton. He was a large man with a threatening demeanour. Classrooms had windows looking out on to the school grounds and playing fields, and also windows looking inwards to corridors which extended for the full length of the school. Mr Clapton silently prowled the corridors and sometimes stood for some time at a window observing the class before being noticed. Discipline was hard and teachers, many of them past their best years, struggled to maintain order among boys used to air raids and wartime shortages, and who were perhaps acting older than their ages would suggest.

I found that most lessons were boring. I enjoyed English, art and religious studies, which I found interesting. I would have enjoyed geography and history had they not been so place and date-based. Lessons were largely fact-based, giving me little idea as to where they were leading. There was little or no continuity. Mathematics was largely the learning and applying of rules. Our work was invariably done in books. We rarely applied any of it to real-life situations. Theorems were learned by rote, lesson after lesson. Science was also taught on the basis of learning rules by rote, with little or no practical work.

One mathematics teacher whom I came to like and respect was an old man called Mr Moor. He had many stories of his experiences in the trenches in France in the Great War and could hold us spellbound. We tried every lesson to steer him towards his experiences, but he was a crafty old fox. We only heard more war stories if we had worked hard and had paid attention during the lesson. It was a strategy that I sometimes used in my own teaching career in later years.

Mr Pike, our history teacher, was another teacher whom I liked and respected. The poor man had suffered from a stroke, which had left the right side of his face paralysed. This side of his face sagged, leaving his mouth twisted and saliva often running on to his chin. A piece of wire, curved at both ends, was hooked behind his right ear. The other curved end was hooked into the top of the right-hand side of his mouth. The object of the wire was obviously to pull the drooping side of his face upwards. Despite the hooked ends being wrapped in tape, the pain must have been considerable. In my mind the man was a hero and I treated him with great respect. I'm afraid that some members of the class thought it was a laughing matter. It was not Mr Pike's fault that the history syllabus was so fact- and date-based and devoid of interest.

Apart from science and maths, both of which I felt were lacking in inspiration and vitality, I was reasonably interested in learning. However, the school seemed to be trying to be something that it could never be at that time in its history. The bombing was over, and the war gathered pace. We had no young teachers to inspire us. We had a sterile curriculum and an elitist structure. The headmaster, together with certain teachers, appeared to be trying to mould the school into a copy of a public school.

Some teachers could not control their classes. I remember our music teacher, who shall remain nameless, lining us up in the school hall for music class. We stood in a line and each of us, in turn, had to sing a verse from a song. We all sang the same verse and some of us, including myself, whose voices had broken were told to stand at the back of the hall and keep quiet whilst the remainder continued with the lesson. We stood there throughout every singing lesson.

One day we had a lesson in the classroom on learning the symbols used in writing music. Most of us were bored but dutifully copied what was written on the blackboard. One member of the class, however, yawned loudly. The music teacher, shouting incoherently, ran across the classroom and stabbed the back of the boy's hand with a pencil, pinning it momentarily to his desk. The classroom became deathly quiet apart from the sobbing of the stricken boy and the blustering of the teacher. One of the boys nearest to the door ran out of the classroom and into the one next to ours and returned almost immediately with a teacher. This teacher ordered the same boy to run quickly and fetch the headmaster whilst he examined the wounded hand. He left the pencil in the hand but cleaned the injury as best he could. As he was doing so, the headmaster arrived. He spoke quietly to the music teacher, who left the room.

The injured boy was taken to hospital, and after treatment he was sent home. He returned several days later and received a hero's welcome from the class. The music teacher was never seen in school again.

The main event that changed my attitude towards school life occurred outside school hours and concerned our French teacher. One evening it was decided by Mum and Dad that I could take my brother and sister to attend a performance of Handel's "Messiah" at the Methodist chapel in Heath Street. I was dressed in my school blazer and cap. On arrival at the venue we entered the hall, which was crowded, and I became worried when I couldn't see three empty seats where the three of us could sit together. As I stood looking desperately for a place where we could all sit, my school cap was gently lifted from my head. To my horror, in my search for seats I had completely forgotten that I was wearing it. In those days we were brought up to remove our hats or caps in church, raise our caps to any adult we knew when meeting them in the street and always to give up our seats on a bus to older people even though we probably didn't know them. It was called good manners and I regret its passing.

I turned to see a tall man smiling down at me and holding my cap. I apologised and tried to explain how, in my worry about finding seats for the three of us, I had forgotten that I was wearing a cap. He told me not to worry, and led us to three seats I had not seen. The three of us enjoyed the singing, especially of the "Hallelujah Chorus", which we all stood up for, as was traditional.

The following week, in the French lesson I was called to the front of the class. The teacher, who turned out to be a member of the Heath Street Methodist Chapel, then proceeded to harangue me for forgetting to take off my cap in the chapel. I tried to explain but was told to be quiet. With his voice rising in volume he told the class that I was not fit to be a member of the school and cast doubt upon my parents' ability to bring me up properly. He made many sarcastic remarks about my worthlessness and ended up calling me a guttersnipe. The classroom was deathly silent. I never spoke to or answered questions from that teacher again. In the School Certificate examinations I passed in all subjects except for French, as I did not attend the exams on principle and therefore failed, of course.

I had not enjoyed my time at the school. It was an elitist establishment and even in games, at which I could have been successful, the boys were left to pick teams themselves. Most of them lived in Warrington and of course they picked friends. The same groups formed school football teams. The rest of us were called "the leftovers", even by the teachers, and nobody came to coach us or referee our games.

When the Warrington Schools Athletic Championships came round in my second year, I asked the PE master, Mr Stobbs, if he would enter me for the high jump competition. He had already picked his athletics team but didn't have a high jumper, so he put my name down.

I won the event and eventually went with the Warrington Schools team to Belle Vue in Manchester for the Lancashire Championships. I got through several rounds in the high jump but finished fourth equal. I was mainly competing against older boys and had not yet developed my full strength. Word had gone around the school when it became known that I had won the Warrington Schools high jump, and thereafter I was known as "the frog man".

When the time came to leave school I was very thankful. However, it was made clear to me that leaving school did not mean lounging about at home. I was sixteen and it was time for me to get a job.

My Uncle John worked at Crosfields in Warrington. Crosfields made detergents, including Persil, and all sorts of chemical products. Uncle John was well thought of by the company. He had won the Distinguished Flying Medal for his flying in the defence of Malta in the war. He didn't talk about it but I am fairly sure his plane was shot down on one occasion. Some years later he was placed on the board of the company.

I was interviewed for a job in the chemical sales department and, after a short interview, was offered the job of keeping ledgers relating to the sales of detergents. I was told that my starting salary would be £1 per week, paid monthly. I know that this sounds very little for a week's work, but the average adult wage at that time was a little less than £5 per week. I was instructed to open a bank account into which my salary would be paid.

When I drew my wages from the bank on payday I always left a small amount in my account, which I watched gradually grow over the years. I then handed the money I had withdrawn to my mother and received an allowance of two shillings to spend as I wished. My parents still paid for my clothes and bus fares.

When a year had passed I decided that I would look after myself, buying whatever I needed. I asked Mum to tell me how much I should pay towards my keep and we arrived at an amount which seemed very generous on her part.

At last, as I neared my eighteenth birthday, I left my job and began to prepare myself for the two years' national service which all young men of eighteen years of age were required to complete.

3

Soldiering

Eventually, I received a letter ordering me to report to an address in Manchester for a medical examination and other tests. This was what I had been waiting for.

On arriving at the building where the tests were to be carried out I saw that there were quite a lot of other lads of about the same age as myself reporting for the same tests. Eventually we were all lined up and told to strip. Several doctors worked quickly along the rows. They prodded and looked at our bodies, ordering us to touch our toes, stand on one leg and balance with our eyes closed and all types of other tests. The only surprise for some of us was when the doctor put his hand under our testicles and told us to cough. I learned later that this was to see if any of us had ruptured our abdominal wall, leading to an inguinal hernia. We later had sight and hearing tests in another part of the building.

After the physical tests we went into a room with desks set out in rows. We were told to try to answer language questions and complete a basic maths section. The questions were written and the answers had to be written also. I was amazed at the simplicity of it all. I finished in about ten minutes and handed in my paper. I could see that many others had not even started. I came to learn later that an amazing number of the soldiers with whom I would eventually serve could neither read nor write.

After the written test, I was told to report to a room in which I found an officer and a clerk sitting at a table.

'You achieved full marks, McCue,' the officer said. 'You are intelligent enough to serve as a medical orderly or as a clerk in the Pay Corps. Would you like to apply for one of these positions?'

I told him that I would not and asked to join my local battalion, the First Battalion, South Lancashire Regiment, whose home base was in Warrington. I had found out earlier that the regiment had just moved to Khartoum and I really fancied going there.

However, before joining a regiment, it was necessary to undergo about eight or nine weeks of basic training, which would take place at Saighton Camp to the south of Chester. Little did we know what a life-changing experience that would be.

On arriving at the training camp I quickly realised that most of the other recruits were just as nervous as I was. However, among our number there were several "hard men" who took little notice of instructions given to them, and pushed some of the smaller or more nervous recruits around. I was given a hut number and realised that virtually all of the lads I had seen on the trucks which had picked us up at the station were in the same hut as I was.

As soon as we had selected our beds and placed our belongings on them, we were ordered out of the hut and marched to the stores where we were issued with our army kit. We each were roughly fitted with a best uniform. We were then issued with boots, socks, denim trousers and jackets for everyday work, and underwear. A pouch described as a "housewife" was also handed to us. We placed everything on our beds and were then ordered to march to the medical centre.

Many of our platoon, as we learned to call it, could not march in step. Some were swinging the right arm as they stepped forward with the right foot etc. The corporals in charge were shouting at us as if we were all idiots. There was some quiet muttering from several of the lads, and this was heard by the Non-Commisioned Officers. We then witnessed our first example of what would happen to us if any more insubordination took place. The miscreants were instructed to report for toilet-cleaning duties when the rest of us were finally dismissed to our hut later in the day.

When we arrived at the medical building we were lined up and told to strip to the waist and place our hands on our hips. We were then given several very painful injections in both arms. We were told that these were to protect us when we went abroad.

From the medical centre we were taken to the armoury, where we were each issued with a rifle. Then, with throbbing arms, we started to learn rifle drill, which, we were informed, would be needed for parades etc. This made our arms burn, as the effect of the injections on our working muscles increased the pain.

After we left the parade ground we were taught the correct way of cleaning a rifle, and were then told to open our "housewives". Inside these small canvas pouches we found needles, thread, cleaning cloths and a small brush. We were told to buy our own polish at the NAAFI (Navy, Army and Air Force Institute), which was an on-camp facility where odds and ends could be bought, as well as cheap meals.

I don't intend to spend too much time on our basic training except to say that, as a group, we quickly bonded and helped each other to overcome difficulties. During our training we developed a proficiency which earlier we could not have imagined. We came to like our trainers and their sick humour.

We became proficient in the use of the rifle, Bren gun and Sten gun. We also gained some basic knowledge of self-defence. In bayonet practice we enjoyed screaming loudly as we drove our bayonets into sand-filled sacks, which swung from trees or lay in various half-hidden positions in the practice area.

I can't leave basic training without mentioning a few examples of things which stand out in my memory even to this day. Very shortly after arriving at the camp I had to report to the sickbay with my first and only attack of boils. They appeared on the back of my neck and head. The doctor said that it was the worst case he had ever seen. He lanced each boil and squeezed out the pus from inside it. I was in such a mess that I was bandaged from the top of my head to the lower part of my neck. Only my eyes, nostrils and mouth were visible Rumours rapidly circulated that I had been shot on the firing range and these reached my parents, some thirty miles away, faster than the letter that I posted that same evening.

We had in our platoon a lad called Cornelius Herbert Thrush-Bush Kerfoot. The "Thrush-Bush" part of his name related to the place where he had been conceived. He had belonged to a travellers' community and had worked on the fairgrounds. He had slept rough before being drafted into the army and had had no fixed home. He was a very unhappy recruit. Unused to being ordered about, he suffered more than most. Everyone helped him as best they could but he became more and more unhappy.

There were, however, several skills, prized highly by the army, which he possessed. He was a brilliant shot with a rifle and he knew more about concealment and camouflage than any of the instructors. He was also a superb tracker and could follow a trail that none of us could even see. Unfortunately, he could not adjust to the discipline and after he had run away for the third time and been returned by the police, he was released from army service on the grounds that he was not trainable.

Finally the time came for our platoon to "pass out". We had successfully completed our basic training and it was time to join our battalion as trained, if not experienced, soldiers. At the end of our training we were allowed a weekend pass and went home to say goodbye to our families and friends. We were all bound for Khartoum, and were looking forward to visiting a warmer and drier country.

On the following Monday we were transported to Formby on the coast, a few miles north of Liverpool. Here we were to stay at a Royal Artillery training base as we waited to board the ship which would take us to Egypt. Eventually, we were taken into Liverpool to join our ship. The weather was atrocious, with storm-force winds and driving rain. I doubted that we would sail in such weather, but what did I know?

We took a pilot on board to guide us out into Liverpool Bay, from where he would disembark and return to Liverpool in the following pilot's boat. As it turned out, the weather, which was rapidly deteriorating, prevented him from leaving our vessel that evening and we had to transfer him to a pick-up boat near Bristol the following morning.

The accommodation on the troop ship was atrocious. We were expected to sleep where we ate. There were hammocks for about half of us, which were taken out and strung above the tables off which we were supposed to eat. The ones without hammocks had to sleep on the tables or on the floor.

We were all violently sick for the first two days. The galley could not produce any meals due to the conditions, and anyway, the kitchen staff were also sick, so we did without. We managed to get a supply of water, which one or two of the hardier souls obtained for us. When we were well into the Bay of Biscay the storm became so fierce that we stopped moving for most of one day. We were told that a sea anchor had been put out and that the ship was now facing into the storm, and we would ride it out until conditions improved.

The following day the storm abated a little and we started to make progress again. Members of the crew told us that the waves had been over sixty feet high and that the ship had sustained quite a lot of damage. Now our time was spent in washing and scrubbing our quarters, and washing ourselves. We arranged a rota system for the use of the hammocks and then discovered that there were pillows and blankets stored away, which we could use.

After two days of misery we began to feel human again. We even enjoyed being called up on deck for PE sessions. What we did not enjoy was being called out for inspection when there was little or no chance of appearing neat and tidy due to the cramped conditions under which we were living.

Finally, we passed through the Straits of Gibraltar and into the Mediterranean. We didn't stop anywhere but headed straight on towards Egypt and the Suez Canal. Again we were unfortunate to run into stormy weather, which abated as we approached our destination. I could now see Port Said faintly in the distance.

The day had become gloomier and as we approached the port the temperature dropped noticeably. I noticed small particles of sand in the air, which increased in number as we approached the port. Visibility dropped to the point where it was difficult to see clearly. The wind, blowing from the land, was increasing in strength.

'A sandstorm,' I said to a crew member who was leaning on the rail next to me. He started to laugh and told me that this was just a bit of dust.

'Wait until you are in a real sandstorm, lad. You won't be able to see your hand in front of your face.'

4

Egypt to Khartoum

We eventually docked on the eastern side of the canal and started the business of disembarking. When at last we climbed into trucks with our gear, we set off on a journey through a built-up area.

The main things that struck me were the smell, the unceasing noise made by traffic, and the shouts of traders, who appeared to be everywhere. I saw no friendly faces among the people in the streets, just sullen looks. The streets were filthy and scattered piles of rubbish lay everywhere. Many of the people wore little more than dirty rags.

Eventually the buildings started to thin out and we came into what appeared to be a residential area. The buildings here were larger, but the smell was still heavy in the air. I tried to think of a description for it, but all I could think of was that it reminded me of untreated sewage. I was, of course, new to Africa, and in due course such smells quickly became a normal and accepted part of living on the continent.

It was in this urban area that we found the transit camp where we were to stay. We would eventually travel by road, heading south for the whole length of the canal before joining the ship which would carry us down the Red Sea as far as Port Sudan, as it was then called.

Before any of this happened we had to get used to life in an army transit camp. We stayed at the camp for some time, doing our share of guard duty around the camp perimeter and carrying out various duties required to keep the camp in good order. Life was boring and tiring. On guard duty we started at sunset and worked until breakfast. We patrolled round the camp perimeter for two hours and then were relieved and had four hours' rest. This was then repeated.

Rest consisted of stretching out on beds which had no blankets, no mattresses and no pillows, just the bare springs. We were expected to remain fully dressed, in uniform and able to turn out for inspection within twenty seconds when the duty officer turned up to inspect us. This could be at any time during the night and could occur on several occasions. Duty officers had the habit of creeping up on the patrolling guards, and woe betide any guard who failed to challenge them correctly and demand the password for the night. It was unlikely that we would ever find an intruder inside the barbed wire which surrounded the camp, but we lived in hope that one would come our way.

At last, Christmas Day 1951 arrived and we were introduced to an old army custom. Christmas lunch comprised turkey and all the trimmings, and Christmas pudding of course. It was served by the commissioned officers and senior non-commissioned officers. There was much joking, which was taken with good humour by those serving, and everyone had a good time. As soon as dinner was over, however, everything reverted to normal as it was bound to do.

Eventually the day of departure arrived and we loaded our kit into the trucks and headed south along the canal road towards Suez. We saw numerous ships of all types and sizes, and noticed that they were all pointing north towards the Mediterranean. At a rest point where we stopped for a short break, it was explained to us that in parts of the canal there was insufficient room for two large vessels travelling in opposite directions to safely pass each other.

As we drove south we eventually came to the town of Asmara. This was situated on the west side of a large lake, upon which ships of all sizes were anchored or manoeuvring into position to take their turn to progress north to the Mediterranean or south to the Red Sea. I noticed that there were many British troops moving about the area and was told that the town was heavily garrisoned.

As we proceeded on the final half of our journey to Suez we eventually came to a huge expanse of water. Due to the haze it was impossible to see the far side of this lake, and neither, when I looked towards the south, could I see any end to it. There were uncountable numbers of ships, mainly anchored, but some were moving their positions, and there must have been many more lost in the haze. We had come to the Great Bitter Lake, so called because of the high level of salt the water contains. It took us some time driving southwards to come to the southern end of the lake, but eventually we had a clear, high-speed run to Suez at the southern end of the canal.

On arrival we were driven directly into the docks area and quickly started to board the ship which would take us south, firstly through the Gulf of Suez and then into the Red Sea. We would eventually pass the border between Egypt and Anglo-Egyptian Sudan. Directly across the canal from the border lay the historic town of Jeddah, and then later, further south, the holy city of Mecca, neither of which we could see with the naked eye. We would continue south until we came to Port Sudan. Here we would disembark; then continue our journey to Khartoum by rail.

We were, as a group, allocated a large area to use as a sleeping and hanging-out place. Here we each had a bunk bed equipped with a pillow, an under-sheet and a sheet for cover should the weather turn cold. We were all, by this time, unaffected by seasickness, and with light winds to accompany us down the Red Sea we were a happy bunch of novice soldiers.

We spent each day carrying out various chores, and had regular fitness training from PE instructors. We all aimed to develop a tan before arriving at Khartoum, but heeded the warning that sunburn would be treated as a self-inflicted injury, which would be followed by punishment. With this happy thought in mind we proceeded southwards with the temperature rising steadily each day and the dolphins, now accompanied by flying fish, providing entertainment of which we never tired.

We eventually arrived at Port Sudan, a noisy, bustling place with a busy docks area, and from what I could see, a thriving town. We were given a meal and then driven to the railway station where our train, powered by steam of course, was waiting to depart. When I say "our" train, I am exaggerating. The train was as full as any train could be. We were allocated one carriage in which to fit ourselves and all our kit. The rest of the train was overcrowded, with standing room only for many of the African passengers.

We set off to a hooting from the engine and a roar of approval from the passengers and the people left on the platform. Within minutes we could see African people further down the train climbing out of windows and on to the carriage roofs. I decided that there must be no low bridges on the journey, and so it proved.

Very soon we pulled into a village station where there was an exchange of passengers. A number of people got off and slightly more got on. All of this was accompanied by shouts and cheers. Our journey continued in this manner and day turned quickly into night. I was getting used to how little time there was between sunset and the total darkness of the tropics.

As the journey continued our thoughts turned to our sleeping arrangements. Even without the luggage, which took up two sections of our part of the train, we were still six men to each compartment. It was suggested that two could sleep on the floor, two could stretch out on the seats and the remaining two could each have a luggage rack. We all looked dubiously at the luggage racks. I wondered if they would bear the weight of the larger members of our group. I also felt that the contortions required to negotiate the metal support holding up the middle of each rack would be hazardous, even for a contortionist.

It was finally decided that the luggage racks would not be used. If we used the seats and the floor we could work out a system whereby one pair remained awake for an hour and a half; then wakened the others. The two on the floor would move to the seats, the two on the seats would take over staying awake, sitting one at the very end of each seat, and the two who had done the shift would lie on the floor. In this way, with much good humour and much farting and objections, we got through the night.

The next day was a repeat of the first. We had now left the Nubian Desert behind us, but the scenery was much the same. I found that I was developing a sore throat, and as the journey continued, the pain increased. We gazed out at a flat wilderness gleaming in the relentless rays of a sun that ruled a cloudless sky. Talk soon died as weariness overtook us.

Eventually we stopped at a place much like all the others, but we were informed that we would be there for about half an hour as the engine took on water. Leaving one of the lads to keep watch over our carriage, we wandered into the small market nearby to buy fruit and bottled water, which we were told would be safe to drink. I bought some bananas and a large bottle of what I thought to be orange juice. We settled down and the train moved on. I opened my bottle of juice and took a long drink. There was an explosion of pain as the grapefruit juice burned my already ulcerated throat. The pain was almost unbearable. I screwed the top back on to the bottle and gave it to the other lads to share. They did so, slapping their lips and saying how good it was.

5

Khartoum

Eventually we arrived at Khartoum late in the day, and were picked up by several army trucks, which conveyed us to the regimental barracks. We were told that reveille would sound at five o'clock each morning and that washing, shaving, bed-making and room-tidying for inspection etc. must be completed by six o'clock, when breakfast would be served. Room inspections would take place after breakfast before the day's duties were allocated.

The sergeant giving us this information paused and looked at our faces; then smiled and told us that we would be excused room inspection the following day and would not be allocated duties. We were to use the day to find our way around the barracks and familiarise ourselves with the layout of our surroundings. He then led us to the building that was to become our home for the next year.

As we approached them, the barracks became more impressive. A large two-storey building of a very imposing height stood before us. We clattered up a long flight of stairs and out on to a wide, railed veranda. We were led to a long, wide room with beds lining each wall. There were no bunk beds, thank goodness. Each bed had a mattress, and sheets and a pillow were neatly stacked at the top of each. Many of us had made friends already, and chose beds next to them. The floor was highly polished and was already showing boot marks. My attention was taken not only by the height of the ceiling, but more so by a number of huge, slowly turning fans suspended from it. It was something that became very familiar to me later on as I moved around other parts of Central Africa. Having put away our belongings, we made our beds and sat about, chatting. Most of us were tired and soon the room became quiet as lights were turned out.

Reveille came as an unpleasant shock for most of us. It was still pitch-black and the sky was filled with bright stars. We made our way to the washrooms, which were unlit, and so shaving was done by touch and was hazardous. There was no such thing as hot water in the washrooms and people sharing a washbasin constantly bumped into each other. I found it uncomfortable and unpleasant. Most of us returned to our room with blood oozing from our faces and necks.

As we had no room inspection to contend with, we made our way to the dining hall, which was large and filled with noise and the clattering of cutlery on plates and dishes.

A great deal of banter was directed towards us, and shouts of, 'Get your knees brown!' echoed through the room.

For breakfast we were served bacon and eggs, liberally seasoned with a strong curry powder. I felt really sick from the smell of the curry powder, but I was hungry and so I ate it. There was toast and marmalade, but no butter or margarine. When I enquired about the curry powder on bacon and eggs I was told that it was used on any food which could go bad in the heat.

There wasn't any refrigeration as we would have today, but each day an "ice team" was sent to a local refrigeration plant. From there, large blocks of ice, each weighing about a hundred pounds, were collected and brought back to the kitchen. Here the ice was used to keep those things that were likely to go bad quickly in the heat usable for a few days more. The only drink served at mealtimes was lemonade made from powder and served from large silver containers. We served ourselves and filled our mugs.

Before going back to our tables after getting our food, we had to pass a sergeant, who handed us each a salt tablet and watched as we swallowed it, swilling it down with our lemonade. If at any time a soldier collapsed with heat exhaustion and it could be proved that he had not taken his salt tablets, he would be charged with having a self-inflicted medical condition and would be punished accordingly.

As I walked around the camp that first day in search of the cricket ground, I could see that most of the soldiers who worked in the various areas of the camp were stripped to the waist and wore denim trousers. These were held up by belts that had been scrubbed with soap and water, but had not had blanco applied to them. This was to keep the belts clean rather than looking smart. A daily scrub kept a belt in good condition and went some way in the fight against prickly heat. From about ten o'clock each morning, denim tops would be put on as a protection against sunburn.

Eventually I found the cricket field. It was a large piece of ground covered by short tufts of grass. The wicket, I learned, would be covered by matting. Such grass as did exist was kept alive by means of flooding the ground each morning. This was done by using water pumped from the nearby River Nile. In one corner of the ground was a large hut, which contained games equipment, mainly for cricket.

As I gradually got my bearings I saw that there were more buildings in the camp than I had initially realised. There was an administration block, a medical centre, a NAAFI, officers' quarters and another accommodation building much like ours. There were also maintenance buildings for the many different types of vehicles, and an armoury for weapons and ammunition.

On our second day in Khartoum we were inspected and issued with new kit. We were each given two sets of denim overalls, each set to be washed once a week whilst the other was worn. New water bottles, new webbing and a few odds and ends were added. We were then individually allocated to various duties, but most of us were placed in Support Company. We would, together with other members already in the company, become specialists in the use of Bren gun carriers, Bren guns, Vickers machine guns and mortars.

To my surprise, I was told to report to the intelligence section, where I found one other member of Support Company. He welcomed me and showed me what we were to work on. He took me into a room which contained a large table and a few chairs. On the table lay stacks of photographs taken from the air. The photographs were old and were in no way numbered or labelled. They were shots of the desert area surrounding Khartoum. There were thousands of them, and most of them looked the same as each other. We had been given the job of putting them together in such a way as to produce a map of the area surrounding the city on our side of the River Nile.

We spent the first day extracting those shots which showed features such as dried riverbeds and raised ground, especially rocky ground. Our main problem was that we didn't know where this high ground was. It could have been anywhere.

On the second day we explained the problem to the battalion intelligence officer and asked permission to take a vehicle out into the desert to map the area extending to a distance of about five miles from the city. To my surprise he agreed and arranged for a vehicle and driver to take us to wherever we needed to go. On the bonnet of the truck I was amazed to see a sundial. I was told that all the vehicles in the battalion were equipped in the same way, and that all drivers, and people liable to drive vehicles, had to know how to use the dials. By using a watch for the time of day and the shadow cast by sundial, we were able calculate our direction.

We also carried a compass with us to plot our way from feature to feature. By noting our distance and direction from our setting-off point and measuring the distance and direction from one feature to the next, we were able, over a number of days, to put together a pretty accurate map of the desert around Khartoum on our side of the river. We took great pains in exact measurement of distance and showed how all the features were linked to one another. We did this, as a final part of the exercise, by numbering and linking all features by distance and compass reading from one to another, and by giving names to and describing each feature on the map. We backed up the map by taking photographs of all the main points of interest and linking them to their numbered features.

When we were finished we handed in the map and photographs for inspection. The intelligence officer was delighted with the finished product and took it to the commanding officer of the battalion, who commended us on our work.

6

Death of the King

The following day, sad news arrived from England and was conveyed to the whole battalion by the officers in charge of each company. We were told that King George VI had died the previous night, and that the battalion would march through Khartoum to the cathedral on the day of his funeral. We would cover the final quarter of a mile at the slow march, and would need to follow the beat of the battalion band. There would be a practice held every morning at sunrise, firstly by companies and, nearer the time of the funeral, by the whole battalion as a unit.

In the days that followed we spent hours perfecting our march, both at normal speed and at slow-march speed. We did this in the early hours of the day from just before sunrise. Of course, as we found to our cost when the day of the funeral came, marching at daybreak was easier and more pleasant than marching under the midday sun.

When the day of the funeral was over we all felt that we had acquitted ourselves well. The local press certainly seemed to think so. The service was long but very moving. On arrival back at the barracks we were told to take things easy and were excused inspection the following morning.

The following few weeks passed quickly as we worked on driving skills with the carriers and firing our rifles and the Bren guns until the sun rose higher and mirages made it impossible to fire accurately. It was a different matter with the Vickers machine guns. By using a special sight called a lensatic sight, we were able to return the gun to points which we had marked earlier with the gun site and hit the targets even though we now couldn't see them. I enjoyed firing on the range and became quite proficient.

Driving the carriers was also fun once you got used to the steering. There was no steering wheel. Instead there were two push-pull levers, one for each hand. By pushing and pulling the levers, the carrier could be turned in any required direction. By pulling just one lever, the carrier could be made to spin.

We had a great amount of fun driving them, particularly through the main streets of Khartoum. However, to the rage of the CO, one of the drivers, while returning from the range one morning, lost control of his carrier and almost demolished the famous statue of General Gordon, the British general who had been killed on the 26th January 1865 defending Khartoum from the forces of the Mahdi, the Muslim religious leader.

After a few weeks in Khartoum I was surprised, one morning, to be called to the office of the CO, who told me that he was pleased with my work and that I was being promoted to the rank of lance corporal. He held out his hand and told me to keep up the good work. I was now put in command of a section of two carriers, their crews and their machine guns. I would be responsible for the placing of the guns, after receiving general guidelines from the sergeant who was in charge of the three sections of guns. Manoeuvres now became more interesting to me, and I began to enjoy battalion life even more.

7

Big Brother

Another part of army life that I had not anticipated was my developing role in the barrack room. Gradually I seemed to become the big brother to a number of the lads in the same room as myself. At first it was just one of them who came to me for help with reading a letter he had received and didn't understand. As time went by, a number of others in our room and also from other rooms came by and asked for help, sometimes with reading but more often with writing letters.

I decided that it would be better to carry out this help on the veranda rather than in the room where all the others were enjoying their time off in the afternoons. The main reason for maintaining privacy arose from an incident where I had to tell one of the occupants of my room that the girl he thought he was going to marry had found someone else. He broke down and cried, and a number of the less sensitive lads started laughing at him and mocking him. I had taken him outside and talked with him, and on a nod from me a couple of his friends had come out and talked with him as well.

One afternoon, during our free time, I was on the veranda when one of our company sergeants came by and asked me what I was doing. I explained that I was helping with the reading and writing of letters for those who needed help. He just nodded and walked away. I realised that he had spoken about this when, a few weeks later, the officer in charge of firing practice on the range asked me about it.

8

Abandon Ship

One morning when we were assembled to receive our orders for the day, we were told that in a few days' time we were going to carry out swimming activities in the middle of the Nile.

There was a stunned silence until one brave soul asked, 'But what about the crocodiles, sir? The river's full of them.'

There was much nodding in agreement, and noisy discussion filled the room.

The sergeant quickly silenced us and said, ominously, 'Don't worry, lads, the army allows for a certain number of accidents and deaths when training is considered hazardous.'

This really cheered us up.

When the day came for the exercise, none of us was in a cheerful mood. Even the hard men in our company were pale and quiet.

Just before dawn we marched down to the Nile. Here we saw several strange craft moored at the edge of the water. Each had the appearance of a large skip of the sort people throw rubbish into these days, but was about six or seven times longer and much wider. Each vessel was fitted with a motor, but this would be turned off when we were jumping into the water and would only be used again by the people in charge of the vessels once we had jumped.

Before boarding our "skips", we were each given a life jacket and shown how to fit it. I noticed that Danny, one of my room-mates, was crying and had not fitted his jacket. Two of us went over to him and helped him to put it on. He told us that he was terrified of water and hadn't slept since he had heard about the exercise. We told him that we would be with him in the water and would get him to the bank safely. We shielded him from the others by pushing him into a corner of our skip and standing between him and the rest of the lads.

As we reached the middle of the river, we slowed down and the dreaded order to abandon ship was given. With much trepidation, we jumped into the water. One thing was in our favour: the water was warm. We struggled to get Danny to climb over the side and into the water. Eventually we had to take an arm each and jump. Having surfaced, we saw Danny floating in his life jacket, but in his terror he was trying to force his head under the water. With some difficulty I grabbed his hair and hauled his head back, whilst my friend put his arm round Danny's back. We turned to face the bank, about four hundred yards away, turned Danny on to his back and each took an arm. As we started to kick our way towards the bank, Danny began to scream and kept trying to put his head under the water. I slapped him hard across his face but it made no difference. We decided to ignore him and then concentrated on getting him to the shore.

I suddenly realised that the place to which the boats had returned was no longer in sight, but I could still see the odd swimmer far away in the distance. We were being carried away from the landing area by a strong current. Eventually we felt ground under our feet and staggered up a sandy piece of the shore which stuck out into the water. Danny continued to make terrified sounds and was shaking violently.

As we were wondering what we should do, a launch appeared round a corner of the river, and sighting us, came swiftly towards us. It was our company commander, looking rather anxious. Danny was still making no sense and lay there on his side where we had placed him. As the launch pulled in I explained what had happened and we got Danny on to the deck. He was taken to the sickbay and we were left to tell the rest of the lads in our room that Danny had suffered some sort of seizure and had nearly drowned. The story soon spread through the barracks and he was treated with sympathy when he came out of sickbay.

9

Desert Exercise

As life in Khartoum proceeded, a number of notable events spiced the slow-moving and boring days. We were confined to camp except for duties such as weapon practice, collecting the ice on a daily basis and providing an armed guard for the weekly collection of money for our wages. In the late afternoons we could play cricket or kick a ball around, but most of the time it was too hot to exert ourselves too much. Fortunately, there were events and occasions which made it all seemed worthwhile.

On one occasion the battalion embarked upon desert exercises, leaving enough troops behind to look after the barracks. We moved at first light each day and made our way towards our objective, stopping in the late morning as the heat became too much to bear. When the temperature reached a certain level we had to stop as our carriers were not covering miles to the gallon of fuel, but using gallons to cover the mile.

After three days we were all suffering from sunburn and our facial skin was impregnated with sand and took on a leathery appearance and feel. This condition was known as "sand grouse". On the third day we bunkered down along a wide, dry riverbed. As usual we dug defensive positions and guard points. Suddenly we heard orders being shouted that we were to get ourselves immediately out of the riverbed, and move to higher ground. Amid cursing the CO and bemoaning our fate, we carried out the instructions and went through the whole business of moving the vehicles, digging in again and arranging new gun positions etc.

As we sat there frying in the sun we heard a distant noise. It sounded like explosions. We saw the officers standing together and looking through binoculars across the desert towards the area from which we had come earlier that morning. The sound of what seemed to be heavy vehicles was now accompanying that of the explosions. We ran to our posts and checked our weapons and ammunition. We could see the mortar sections doing the same. The infantry companies were by now all at battle stations and were checking their weapons. I saw the CO and other officers looking at us through their binoculars and then back towards the approaching sound, which was getting closer and louder by the minute. We saw dust clouds moving towards us at high speed, and waited expectantly for the order to load our weapons and for targets to be called.

Suddenly our enemy appeared from round a bend in the riverbed. A wall of water was roaring and smashing its way towards us, deep and strong enough to have carried vehicles and men along with it. It was ripping and demolishing the old riverbanks, which had dried out over many years without rain. We were high enough up the slope for it not to reach us, but we were affected by the speed and power of the water as it raced past us. We heard later that a message had been received warning the CO that the water was coming. Evidently it had taken almost two days to travel from the high mountains of Abyssinia before reaching us.

There was great excitement in the ranks, and we were allowed to move closer to the rushing water. It was a once-in-a-lifetime experience and it made clear to us how, in the past, the dried-up riverbeds had been flowing with the water that had created them.

Later that autumn we enjoyed the heaviest and most prolonged rainfall to be experienced in Khartoum for as long as people could remember. It only lasted for a period of three days, but it had an amazing effect. Suddenly, almost over-night, the desert turned into a sea of beautiful colours for as far as one could see. We went out in the carriers on a short exercise and drove to one of the high points we had noted on our map. Using field glasses and able to see as far as the distant horizon, I could see no break in the coverage of flowers. I noted four or five different-coloured varieties near to where we had stopped, but looking further afield I could see a number of other colours.

We gathered several large bunches of flowers, which we handed out around the rooms adjoining ours, and sent some to the officers' and sergeants' messes. Over the next few days other groups who happened to find themselves carrying out exercises in the desert would also bring back flowers. After about a week the flowers gradually died away, after producing more seed to be scattered by the desert winds.

Another once-in-a-lifetime experience occurred near to the end of our stay in the Sudan. We witnessed a total eclipse of the sun. We were well prepared for the event and had pieces of dark glass to look through. There were scientists from all over the world who had come to view the eclipse, and we were all excused duties for a couple of hours to witness the event. I noted the temperature in the shade just before the eclipse started. Another lad in our room had a thermometer in the sun on the veranda.

As the time approached, we waited expectantly until we saw the first signs of the shadow on the edges of the sun. As the shadow grew, the power of the sun began to fade. Suddenly the constant sound of birdsong and chatter stopped. It didn't happen gradually, but suddenly. It was as though a conductor had waved his baton to signal for the birds to stop. As the shadow advanced to darken the sun, a perceptible drop in temperature could be felt. Finally the eclipse was complete and a sort of darkness prevailed. It was not a complete darkness, but more of a half-light. Around the black disc in front of the sun there was a thin rim of soft light.

Before the sun's light began to return, I took a reading from my thermometer. I found that the shade temperature had, in that short time, fallen by just under eleven degrees centigrade. The other thermometer outside had registered a higher difference. As the sun returned, life and movement, with their accompanying sounds, returned as though nothing had happened.

It was about this time that I received a second promotion, this time to full corporal, so now I had two stripes. I was surprised when it happened, but I was told by the section sergeant that the CO had again been informed of my part-time work with illiterate members of the platoon during rest periods, and the effect this was having on morale. I had never thought of it in those terms but I wasn't going to argue. I had noticed, however, that when giving commands to my machine gun section, I always got an instant response and willing work out of the men. I suppose that some of this was payback for the time I spent helping them with letters and teaching them basic words, which they could use to construct simple sentences. Whatever the reason, I had established a good relationship with the majority of the men in my platoon and felt that I would always be able to rely upon them.

Towards the end of our stay in Khartoum a number of soldiers from the battalion, including myself, were selected to form a platoon to go to a training camp in the mountains near to Kassala on the Eritrean border. I think that the object of the exercise was to expose us to mountain conditions and to the effects of altitude.

After a long journey by train and truck we arrived at the training camp and were shown to two huts, in which we would store our gear and eat and sleep. There were no other facilities apart from a washroom with toilets, a small hut for our officer and a cookhouse from which we collected our meals before eating them in our quarters. This was easier said than done. The stretch of land between the cookhouse and our huts was patrolled by a flight of hawks, who knew exactly when meals were being served and would swoop and remove food from a plate with great expertise. The hawks were clever and always swooped from behind the victim. Many plates were stripped before we got used to protecting our meals.

One afternoon, two of us set out to walk to a gully which we could see from the camp. It split the nearest large mountain into two main parts. It was further away than it had appeared to be when viewed from the camp, and it took us some time to reach it. It was also very steep and showed evidence of once having had a watercourse running down the side nearest to us. We began to climb, but hearing the noise of baboons close by, discretion became the order of the day and we returned to camp.

The following morning we were told that we would no longer be required to wash and shave ourselves. Water was precious and we should learn to conserve it. There would be limited water for bathing. That morning, and on all subsequent mornings, we had to run round a difficult hill course that was plentifully littered with boulders and smaller rocks and stones. We struggled to attain the daily improvement required of us, but managed to do so as we became fitter and smellier. Eventually we were told to pack our kit. We were about to cross the border into Eritrea.

10

Eritrea

We set off in two trucks upon what would turn out to be a memorable journey. As we approached the border, the ground gradually became steeper and rougher. The act of passing across the border was an anticlimax. There was a hut, but it was unmanned and there was no barrier across the road to hinder our progress.

The next seven or eight hours were spent driving up and down mountain passes on twisting and often dangerous roads. The river valleys were mostly dry, or contained so little water that you could not say that they were rivers. Vegetation was largely poor or absent altogether, and the whole journey was completed with little sign of human life. We did encounter the occasional small group of men who, upon seeing army vehicles, stood with their hands in the air, holding up any guns they were carrying so that we could see them. As we had nobody who could communicate with them, we didn't stop. Eventually, we came to the village where we were to camp for the night.

That the village, named Adi K'eyih, was obviously used by the army became apparent when we found some basic buildings further up the hill in which to sleep and store our kit. The village was further down the mountainside but a crowd had gathered to greet us. Obviously it was a fairly regular experience for the villagers to see soldiers passing through their area.

Their friendliness towards us was explained to us by a local man whom we learned was to be our guide. It was largely British troops who had freed the area from Mussolini's army during the Second World War. The villagers' hatred of the Italians was obvious and intense. We discovered, however, an interesting anomaly in their hatred. Shortly after we arrived, a white man, probably about forty years old, came over from a brick-built house to talk to us. He was greeted by the locals with fondness. When he opened his mouth to speak, it was with an unmistakable, strong Italian accent.

He explained to us that he had been conscripted during the war into the Italian Army in Africa. Interestingly, he had ended up as a machine-gunner as I had, but had been so sickened by the army's treatment of the indigenous populations that he had deserted and had found refuge among the village people. On several occasions he had saved the villagers from the attentions of Italian soldiers by keeping a lookout and instructing them when and where to move to safety.

As we settled in, we were told to rest up as we were awaiting news of the whereabouts of a heavily armed gang of Eritreans and Abyssinians. The local men in the two countries had been armed by the British during the war to fight against the Italians. At the end of the war many had absconded with their weapons and ammunition. They now roamed over a wide area of Eritrea and Abyssinia, demanding women and food from villagers and killing anyone who opposed them. The collective name by which they were known was *shifta*. We now understood why we were there, and excitedly talked about what might be coming our way.

Two mornings later we heard the sound of a large number of horses' hooves clattering over the rocky ground. From the side of the mountain below us appeared a line of mounted horses. The riders were wearing light, sand-coloured uniforms and carried rifles and various pouches and packs filled with unseen equipment and ammunition. They introduced themselves as a mounted police unit working for the Eritrean government. As far as I could make out, there was only one Eritrean horseman. Most of the group were British, although I think I detected a South African accent amongst them. They told us that their latest information indicated that a group of *shifta* was heading towards the mountains, which lay to the east of us and formed a high and rugged barrier between us and the Red Sea. The mountains lay on a north-south axis, which stopped any direct approach to the village from the direction of the sea.

It was planned that we would travel by truck as far as possible towards the nearest pass, which would give us an entry into the mountains. We would then proceed on foot into the heart of the region to where the peak of the 9,806-foot Mount Soira stood above the surrounding peaks. There were several other mountains in the same range reaching a height of over nine thousand feet, and the whole area was wild and rugged, with many dead ends and unscalable cliffs.

The mounted police planned to investigate the various accessible valleys and ignore those which led to dead ends. Our task would be to climb into the highest area of the mountain range, eventually arriving at the summit of Mount Soira. We were to check accessible passes on our way. If we were lucky enough to locate the gang, it would be unlikely that they would hand over their weapons and they would probably open fire. In this event we were to reply to their fire with the intention of killing or wounding as many as possible. It was more likely that the gang would attempt to escape upon seeing us, or that we would never even contact them, but we lived in hope.

Our sergeant was left at camp with a stomach complaint so I automatically assumed the position of second in command. I asked our officer how we were supposed to carry a Bren gun with the many heavy belts of ammunition as well as blankets and our food and water supplies. Each of us was already carrying two pints of water and extra ammunition for our rifles, plus everything we needed in our packs. He told me that the guide would already be waiting for us at the point where we would leave the trucks, and that he would have two mules which would carry all the extra things that I had mentioned.

We mounted the vehicles and set off towards the nearby mountain range. After about an hour we entered a narrow mountain pass, which eventually led to the village where the guide and the two mules stood waiting for us. We spent the next hour rearranging our loads and loading the mules. The guide now impressed upon us that in many places we would be moving along narrow tracks, with vertical drops of over a thousand feet if we were to lose our footing. He warned us to be wary of passing the mules if they were ahead of us at any time, and never to try and pass a mule on the side of the drop. Some fool asked why.

'Can you fly?' the guide asked with serious look.

No more was said.

We finally set off and entered a narrow canyon. The going was rough, with numerous boulders and smaller rocks littering our way. We soon noticed the gradient beginning to increase, and despite our physical conditioning and general fitness we began to feel the effects of climbing in bright, burning sunshine. The first canyon soon divided into two new ones. The guide led us into the left one. Again we climbed, but after about half a mile the path started to descend and twisted through piles of shattered rock.

On that first day we covered about three miles, but it felt more like ten. As we made camp that late afternoon the temperature gradually dropped until we were glad we each had a blanket. We ate cold rations from packs, but were able to make a fire and boil kettles for tea. A guard duty list was prepared and I was given the task of sharing with our officer the checking of the guards during the coming night.

The following day almost destroyed us. We climbed and we descended, but we continued to gain height, burned by a blazing sun in a cloudless sky. The air was still and suffocating, and the need for water was extreme. We were told not to drink until ordered to. Water was rationed and each man had only the water in his water bottle. There would be no refills that day.

In one valley we came across several piles of stones, all of a fairly similar height. Flying above them were ragged pieces of different coloured materials attached to poles. We were told that the stones were graves and would contain the remains of human beings, and here I must introduce McCarthy, a man four or five years older than our platoon's average age of nineteen.

McCarthy had been released from prison in Manchester in time to join our squad in training camp. We never found out his first name. There was nobody foolish enough to ask him. Everyone in the platoon had one thing in common, and that was a deep fear of him. He was not your normal bully. He was sadistic and reckless, fearing nobody, whatever their rank or size. He was known to be very dangerous and so had no friends. He was also completely unpredictable. You never knew what he would do next. I think that he had been selected to be with us on this trip to give those remaining in Khartoum a few weeks' rest. It might also have been a sadistic way of breaking in our officer, who had been newly commissioned prior to joining the battalion.

Hearing that the stones were graves and very sacred to the people who had interred the bodies, McCarthy gave a shriek of delight and began removing the top stones from one of the graves. We all stood well away, not wanting to be connected with this sacrilege. Our officer said nothing. I think that he also was afraid. The guide just stood impassively, which surprised me, although he too may have been afraid to speak. McCarthy never paused, until finally he had cleared enough of the stones to expose the skull belonging to the body, which had been interred in a standing position. The guide moved nearer to McCarthy and spoke loudly to him.

'I don't think that you should touch the body.'

McCarthy turned and looked at him and snarled, 'Fuck off, you black bastard.'

With that he seized the skull and wrenched it from the body. He screamed in delight and held up his trophy triumphantly. Nobody joined in with his celebrations.

The guide suddenly shouted, 'If you put the skull back carefully now, and rebuild the grave, you may be safe.'

McCarthy glared at him. 'What did you fucking say?'

'I said that if you put the skull back and restore the grave, you might be alright. You see, these poor people were buried here, away from their village, because they died of the plague. You know, the Black Death.'

With a scream, McCarthy hurled the skull away from him and started scrubbing his hands with sand. We left the head where it was and the grave as it was and continued on our journey. We heard no more from McCarthy that day, and he was very subdued for the following couple of days. I did notice the guide having a quiet smile to himself when he thought nobody would notice, and raised my eyebrows to him. He just grinned.

As the day progressed, the slopes and exposure increased. By now we were moving along a steep, narrow path with a sheer drop of many hundreds of feet on our right, and an almost vertical cliff towering above us on the left. Welcome to a real mountain range, I thought.

As we came round a corner our guide pointed upwards, and there, towering about two thousand feet above us, was the peak of Mount Soira. As far as we could see there were other huge mountain peaks, but none quite as fearsome as our mountain. We continued well into the afternoon until we were instructed to stop and make tea, which we did with great alacrity.

We camped where we had stopped and spent a very uncomfortable night there. I was very cold despite my blanket, but the discomfort was worth it. About fifteen hundred feet below us, clouds obscured any view of the ground. Some miles to the east of us, and towards the Red Sea, we watched huge electric storms lighting up the sky and listened to the distant thunder.

When morning dawned we made tea, ate our cold rations and prepared to move on. Having checked the loading of the mules and looked at the level of our water containers, I felt that we would be fortunate not to run out of water even if we were to turn back immediately. I noticed another worrying thing. There was no sign of our guide. I asked if anyone had seen him, but nobody had. I talked with our officer and we decided that the sensible thing to do was to reverse our course and hope that we could remember our way back.

We were close to the summit of Mount Soira. It stood no more than about a half-hour's march from where we were, and I estimated that we were only about three hundred feet below the summit. Even so, because of our diminished water supply, it was decided that we should abandon the idea of completing the climb and head back the way we had come.

There was, however, a problem. How were we to turn the mules round on the narrow track without risking someone being knocked over the edge? I instructed two of the more reliable members of the party to scout ahead to see if the track was wider anywhere further along. Within a minute they reappeared, running towards us and shouting.

They reported baboons, 'Hundreds of the bastards, Corporal, coming towards us.'

I told the two of them to load their rifles, and I loaded mine at the same time. I quickly told our officer what had happened and said that I was taking the two men to investigate. I added that if necessary, we would try to halt the baboons with warning shots. He started to rouse the rest of the squad and bring them to readiness.

Creeping to the corner, I stopped, knelt down and peered round a large rock. There they were, not hundreds of baboons as reported, but about thirty at most. They ranged from juveniles to adults, with some of the females having babies on their backs. There were a number of males, mainly larger than the females, and one huge male who was obviously the pack leader. The baboons were in a line, except for the leader, who turned towards us and snarled. I watched in horror as the line of animals, one by one, jumped over the edge of the cliff and disappeared into the void. Their leader snarled, looked at us, and then followed them. We ran to the edge of the drop and, to our relief, saw that they were making their way down what to us was an invisible track on the almost vertical cliff face.

To cut a long story short, we managed to turn the mules with no loss of life and set off towards the point where we had left the trucks, only following a couple of false trails on the way. We made good time, moving downhill and no longer thinking about bandits, but about water. The mules had been given the last of our water, to some muttering in certain quarters, and everyone was suffering.

When, by my reckoning, we were about a mile away from the village and our transport, we heard the sound of approaching voices. Round a twist in the track came three riders from the group we had met before. To our great relief they were carrying water for us. This we quickly drank, leaving enough for a top-up for the mules. As it turned out, the village was just round a couple of corners and we were only about half a mile away from it.

We slept well that evening after a hot meal and a good wash and a shave. The following morning we said goodbye to the people of the village and set off on our drive back to the training camp on the border.

A couple of days later we boarded a train which was to take us back to Khartoum. As we chugged along the endless track, I found myself wondering. Had there even been any bandits close by, or had it just been another army training exercise? It didn't really matter. It had been a good experience and had shown us how dangerous McCarthy was. We would have to keep an eye on him.

Our arrival in Khartoum was marked by the revelation that, whilst we had been away, the battalion had been instructed by the army authorities to supply men for transfer to Korea. They were needed to replace men who had been killed or badly wounded in the bitter fighting there. Evidently the whole battalion had been paraded in our absence and asked if there were any volunteers. We were told that virtually every man in the regiment had stepped forward. I imagine that this was an exaggeration, but many of the men were sick of the burning heat and I'm sure the impending move to the Canal Zone didn't appeal. How they enjoyed the bitter Korean winter when they got there, I never found out.

The weeks leading to our departure for the Canal Zone passed quickly. We worked day after day to ensure that all equipment, vehicles, munitions etc. were in good order. At last, the handover being complete, we boarded a train which was reserved just for the battalion and set off on our journey to Port Sudan. There we would board a ship to take us to Suez, and to an Egypt that was even more restless than when our group had last been there.

11

Return to Egypt

Our return to Egypt was uneventful. We carried out our regular physical training on deck every day, company by company, but also enjoyed plenty of leisure time. The thing I enjoyed the most was the steady fall in temperature as we sailed northwards.

When we reached Port Suez we did not dock, but anchored some way out and came ashore on landing barges carrying our weapons. We made landfall away from the main docks and unloaded the equipment from the barges. The full battalion and its equipment having been brought ashore, we departed from Port Suez and headed north along the main Suez Canal road in a convoy of trucks. Eventually we arrived at Shandur, which was situated at the southern end of the Little Bitter Lake and was guarding the last point before the canal proper resumed its way southwards. This was to be our base in Egypt.

I saw a large tented area with a few buildings. It was surrounded by not just one high, barbed wire fence, but two. They ran parallel to each other and stood about thirty feet apart. Between the fences was an area of soft sand, which was graded each day until it was completely smooth. Along the length of the inner fence were placed powerful lights pointing at and beyond the sand. Guards patrolled the fence day and night. Someone remarked how like a prison camp it was. I had to agree.

We were allotted large tents in which we were destined to live for the rest of our time in the Canal Zone. Each tent held six soldiers. The accommodation was reasonably roomy, with space for our kit and personal belongings. There were proper beds and there was also electricity for lighting, so we would be reasonably comfortable. Nearby there were wash buildings with showers and washbasins. Everything seemed to have been well set out. I noticed that there was a NAAFI from which we could buy cheap meals and drinks.

The canal was within sight of the camp. Far away to the north were the large garrison towns such as Ismailia, containing the main body of the army. It appeared that our job was to guard our part of the canal at the point where it became a straight section of water again as it flowed out of the Little Bitter Lake. This part of the canal would obviously be ideal to use as a choke point by anyone with a mind to block canal traffic. From here the canal continued in a straight southward line until it reached Suez. Away to the west was the city of Cairo and also the pyramids, but they were well out of sight and we were destined never to set eyes upon them. The Nile, of course, was out there too, but we were never close enough to see it. Life in Egypt, it seemed, was going to be boring.

Shortly after our arrival the battalion was assembled and our situation and the reasons for it were explained to us. We were told that a treaty had been signed between Great Britain and Egypt in 1936. It allowed Britain to remain in the Canal Zone until July 1956, but it had been torn up by the Egyptian government in late 1951. With encouragement from the Egyptian government, atrocities against British forces started almost immediately. There were attacks in all areas carried out by many different people and in many different ways.

The British government responded with a lightning increase in troop numbers, which raised our total Canal Zone forces from about twenty thousand to eighty thousand in just ten days. British forces were put on "active service" footing from October 1951 to October 1954. This meant that we were considered to be almost on a war footing. The good part of this was that our pay was increased slightly to reflect the increased dangers.

Those dangers were very real. All sorts of actions were being taken by armed gangs of thugs as well as individuals. In some areas the Egyptian police took part in the harassment as well. There were organised terrorist attacks on military camps and on vehicle convoys. Wires were stretched across roads with the intention and achievement of beheading dispatch riders, and all our vehicles were equipped with wire cutters attached to their bonnets. In the towns, sniping took place and the murder of British troops was the prime objective. The use of roadside bombs became commonplace.

In the period from late 1950 to late 1954 (the time of active service), a large number of military and civilian personnel lost their lives. Some of these casualties were the result of accidents or health problems, but the majority were due to vicious attacks by gangs of thugs using the situation to feed their own desire for blood. The actions of the IRA nearer to home in later years come to mind.

Most of the fighting units suffered losses. However, with a few exceptions, losses were relatively light. Of the units losing five or more men, the Parachute Regiment and the Grenadier Guards lost eleven and twenty-three men respectively. The Lancashire Fusiliers lost seven and the Coldstream Guards six. The Cheshire Regiment and 45 Commando both lost five men, while five other units lost four men each. Of the non-infantry units, the Royal Engineers lost forty-four men and the Royal Army Service Corps forty-three. The Royal Artillery lost thirty-eight men and the Royal Corps of Signals and the Royal Electrical and Mechanical Engineers each lost thirty-two men. The Royal Army Medical Corps lost eight members.

The Royal Air Force lost a total of eighty-six personnel. Of Commonwealth troops serving in this period, the East African Pioneers lost forty-four men, and forty-one Mauritians were also lost. This period was known by many as "the Forgotten War fought by the Forgotten Army".

12

Recreation

Life at Shandur consisted of training, guard duties, sport and patrolling the wider area of the district around but away from the camp. While doing my share of training and other duties, I engaged in as many sports as I could fit in. I had a trial for the battalion seven-a-side rugby team and was invited to join. This was my first experience of rugby union and I took to it very quickly. Most of the squaddies in the battalion were soccer players or supporters and were not interested.

We didn't have enough players to form a full fifteen, plus reserves, but we did have sufficient to put out a good seven-a-side squad. Officers formed the majority of the team but a sergeant and I were picked as well. We trained as a group without reference to rank and hit each other hard in practice sessions. We drove back to camp from the training facility nearby as a happy, joking group, but rank and respect returned as we entered the base. We eventually took part in the Canal Zone sevens but lost our second match narrowly and were knocked out.

Another sport for which I enrolled was boxing. I had always been a peaceful sort of person but the idea of learning the technique of boxing appealed, and anyway, it was a good way of passing time and keeping fit. The rugby was coming to the end of its season as the temperature steadily rose and the ground became rock-hard, so why not replace one sport with another? Bad decision!

It all started well enough in the training. The instructors were good and blows didn't hurt that much when you were using soft training gloves. I discovered that I was able to learn quickly and I adapted rapidly to incoming blows by the use of footwork and body movement to avoid them. After about four weeks, with several sessions of training a week, we were told that some of us were going to represent the battalion in the Middle East Army Boxing Championships. Names were read out and I was surprised to hear my name called out.

The training continued but I noticed that we trained for longer and that the emphasis was upon stamina. We were also placed on special rations. When we reported for meals the would-be boxers were given more and better food than the rest of the battalion. I began to feel like a chicken must feel when being fattened up for Christmas dinner.

At long last it was announced that to entertain the troops, the first round of the boxing that would decide who represented the battalion would take place in our camp. When I heard that the draw had been made I went to the nearest noticeboard to see who I had drawn. As I approached the board I became aware that the people standing looking at the details of the draw were giving me curious looks. As I got nearer they all fell silent. I glanced at the board and found my name in the lightweight section. I looked again. I couldn't believe my eyes. Opposite my name was my opponent's name – McCarthy.

I had not seen him at training or anywhere about the camp for some time. Someone said that he had been doing several weeks' punishment duties and had been confined to the cells. He had evidently been on the beer one night and had been collapsing tents around the camp. He had also been emptying his bladder on the sleeping occupants of other tents and had been arrested and then detained.

He had been so drunk that he wasn't in a fit state to do any damage to the people who had arrested him. He had evidently let it be known that he had taken part in illegal bare-knuckle fights for money in Manchester in the past and would like to fight in the Middle East competition for the title. And now I had to face him. I felt sick.

Fight night eventually arrived. The ring was a full-sized professional one and the lighting was similarly professional. The seconds were the PE instructors who had been coaching us. There was no referee in the ring but an officer sitting in the front row had a microphone with which to conduct the fight, and the timekeeper sat next to him. The crowd was well over a thousand, swelled by members of the nearby air force base. I hoped that they could not see my knees knocking.

My second, who had spent a lot of time with me in training, said, 'This bastard is dangerous. If he starts to really hurt you, go down.'

'Don't worry, Sarge, I will,' I replied.

Instructions were given to us from the outside of the ropes and we went to our corners. I had noticed that my opponent's second had not spoken to McCarthy. I found out later that McCarthy had told him to "fuck off" when he had tried to talk to him.

The bell sounded. There was not a sound from the crowd. There were no shouts of encouragement as there had been in previous matches. It was as though they had come to watch an execution. As I stood up from my stool McCarthy was already halfway across the ring. He was coming at me in a crouch; both hands low and with his jaw tucked into his neck. I had a good view of the top of his head. I didn't think. I just swung a hopeful uppercut with all my force into his face. He stopped his rush, stood back and looked at me appraisingly. I saw blood, a lot of blood, running from his nose. For the first time I suddenly became aware of a roar from the crowd.

McCarthy smiled and suddenly leaped at me, pinning my arms and shoving his head against mine.

'Right, yer bastard, I'm goin' ter alter yer fuckin' face, and don't think yer can lie down, 'cause if yer do I'll come and find yer after th' match.'

That was it, really. I lasted until a good way through the second of the three rounds, having been knocked down twice and got up. I had tried to cover myself from the attacks. The blows that I did manage to land seemed to have little effect. My opponent knew all the tricks. When he got close in he used his knees, stood on my toes, and headbutted at every opportunity. He was warned on several occasions but ignored the warnings and carried on. He could have been disqualified several times but was revealing himself as a potential champion for the battalion in the Canal Zone Championships. In subsequent fights he adjusted his fouling to what he could get away with but was still able to progress.

After the fight I went to the medical centre and they patched me up. My right eye was closed, my lips were swollen and I found a number of red patches, already turning black, on various parts of my body. I also had some nasty bruising on my insteps where he had stamped on me. When I came into the centre, the duty nurse looked at my face and my vest and shorts and asked me where all the blood had come from. When I told him that it wasn't mine he laughed. It took a couple of weeks before my body began to feel normal again.

McCarthy went on to represent the battalion all the way through to the finals of the championships, but couldn't quite manage to beat his final opponent, who was obviously an accomplished boxer. Although McCarthy was the aggressor he found it difficult to land any telling blows and lost on points. He was also handicapped by being unable to use the fouling tactics that he had used earlier in the competition, and it was a case of the experienced boxer beating a scrapper.

Time dragged on with little relief from the round of duties and practices. The battalion used a rota system to send a continuous flow of small groups of soldiers to a well-guarded place on the banks of the Little Bitter Lake a mile or two north of Shandur. Here it was safe to swim and relax in the sun, and there was a bar and meals were available.

Doug Watker, my Norfolk gamekeeper friend, was in the group with me and we decided it would be good to try to swim out into the lake and round a large tanker which was anchored about half a mile away. As the name of the lake suggested, the water was very salty and we found swimming to be easy. Unfortunately the water was also very cold and Doug got cramp, so we had to return to land and the hot sun.

I noticed a couple of girls sunbathing. They were surrounded by soldiers, all with their tongues hanging out, who were trying to chat them up. It occurred to me that I hadn't spoken to a member of the opposite sex for almost a year and a half.

Such breaks helped to pass the time away, but it still passed slowly. In the middle of May I was summoned to the company commander's office and asked if I would like to go to London as part of a small group to represent the battalion at the coronation of Queen Elizabeth. I declined the offer with thanks. In my mind was a picture of polishing and cleaning my kit and practising marching in a cold and probably soaking wet London. I preferred the warmth of Egypt. On the day of the coronation we listened to the commentary on the radio and sure enough, the weather was cold and wet in London.

13

Flight Home

Eventually, after what seemed to be an age of waiting for our return to England, the day arrived and we were driven out to the aircraft which was to take us home. I had never seen one like it before and nor had anyone else. It was an ugly brute of a plane with four engines, a large, squat body and triple tail fins. It looked all wrong and rather unbalanced.

We were lined up and entered the plane one by one. Inside we found a long aisle running down the centre of the plane with pairs of seats on each side. We seated ourselves and were ordered by an RAF steward to fasten our seat belts. None of us had flown before and there was a lot of fiddling with the seat belts. As the plane started to taxi along the runway its whole body began to rattle and the increasing noise killed any chance of talking. As we took off and started to gain height, however, we began to get used to the noise and the rattling.

The steward came round with a bowl of barley sugar sweets and told us to take one each and suck it. The plane had no pressurisation system as planes have today, and the sucking of sweets was aimed at equalising the air pressure within our ears to the pressure within the plane. I noticed very quickly that there were draughts of icy-cold air pouring into the plane. It was going to be a cold and noisy journey. We were told that no food could be served on the plane but that water was available.

As late afternoon arrived and the light started to fade, the steward told us that we would be making a stop at Malta, as the pilot wanted something checked in the plane. The landing was rough and shook everyone up but we were all in high spirits and made little of it. We realised that we had made an unscheduled landing when we were told to take our bags off the plane and settle down for the night on the grass next to it. There would be no food but we were shown a tap at the side of the runway from which we could get water. Engineers would work through the night on the plane and we should, with luck, leave for England early the following morning. Had I known then what I now know from my research, I would have been terrified about getting back into that aircraft.

I now know that the York aircraft was constructed from the wings, tail and undercarriage of the Lancaster bomber. These were joined to a new square section fuselage, and this gave the aircraft a much greater carrying capacity. Early tests showed that the aircraft needed an extra central tail fin to go with the twin fins and rudders of the Lancaster. This aided control and directional stability. Two hundred and fifty-nine Yorks were built, including prototypes. Production started in 1943 and ended in 1949, and the aircraft was in use until 1964.

Unfortunately the safety record of the York was not good. I found that there were eighty-six instances of Yorks crashing or being damaged beyond repair. Several of the crashes resulted in considerable loss of life. Many were inexplicable. Of the eighty-six crashes that I found listed, sixteen occurred on take-off and thirty-eight on landing. More than a few resulted in deaths and several resulted in the total loss of passengers and crew.

On the 2nd February 1953 a Skyways York crashed into the sea off Newfoundland after sending out an SOS. This resulted in the deaths of thirty-nine passengers and crew. The wreck of the aircraft has never been found. On the 18th February 1956 a York carrying over fifty RAF airmen from Egypt crashed shortly after take-off when it stalled. There were no survivors. There were other York crashes which resulted in deaths but luckily we were ignorant of all these facts.

After an uncomfortable night we did eventually take off quite early the next day. As we approached the French border the steward told us to strap in tightly. He handed out barley sugar again and told us that the pilot would attempt to climb over a storm area which was in our path. As we climbed, the plane started to pitch about and it became a very uncomfortable flight. Several of the platoon were sick. We still seemed to be in the middle of the clouds when the steward announced that the pilot had decided that as oxygen was not available for passengers and the plane was not pressurised, he was going to take the aircraft to a lower level and attempt to fly round the storm.

We arrived late at our destination outside London due to the diversion. We were met by a sergeant who led us to a nearby café, which provided us with a meal which we quickly devoured. We were then taken by coach to London, issued with train tickets and put on a train to Manchester where we were met by a sergeant and conveyed to Peninsula Barracks in Warrington.

The sergeant and other NCOs led us to rooms in one end of the barracks. We were told to unpack our kit and stay in our allotted area, and on no account to have any connection with new recruits who were training at the barracks. The attitude of these people was stiff and unfriendly. I asked about home leave, as we were due to be demobbed in a few days' time. We were told that we would be charged with being absent without leave if we left the barracks. We were instructed to parade for inspection the following morning.

We paraded the following day in our crumpled uniforms and listened impassively to the ranting of the sergeant. He told us we were a scruffy lot and on no account were we to approach or talk to any of the new recruits in the barracks as we would be a bad influence. We were informed that we would be given useful work to do until we were demobbed in a couple of days' time.

We were instructed to work on the gardens in the barracks. One group was given scissors and told to get down on their knees and cut the grass in front of the sergeants' mess. The rest of us were given spades and wheelbarrows and told to dig up a rough area of grass to prepare it for planting. I was taken to one side and told that, as a non-commissioned officer, I should supervise the work. I replied that I would work alongside my men. I also gave him a mouthful about the treatment we were receiving. He was very unhappy with the way I spoke to him.

As the day wore on and the work slowly progressed, one of the lads came over and told me that the ones who were digging had come across a large pipe. It lay about two feet beneath the surface of the soil.

'I almost put my pickaxe through it,' he said.

'Easily done,' I replied and winked.

A minute or so after I had walked away there was a sudden roar and a huge jet of water shot into the air, spraying all of us until we were wet through. The jet must have reached about forty feet. I sent one of the squad to walk slowly over to the administration block and report the event.

The sergeant, accompanied by an officer, hurried towards us, arriving breathing hard. Before either of them could speak I rounded on the sergeant and asked him why we had not been warned about pipes in the area. He was left speechless and his face became red. I reminded him that it was he who had issued the pickaxes.

'And while you are here, Sergeant, when are the men going to be paid? They are due their wages, and I also expect that you will need to issue travel warrants to their homes.'

The officer stepped in. He could see the sergeant's face. He instructed him to report the incident and to get immediate help from the water authority. He then took me aside and, without saying as much, let me know that he understood the situation. He cancelled all remaining work for us and said he would push along our release as quickly as he could. He also said that he would speak to the non-commissioned staff and give them advice about how to treat returning soldiers. As he turned to go I brought the squad to attention and gave the officer my smartest salute. He was a man who understood how to treat soldiers.

14

The In-between Years

I intend to deal briefly with the period that lay between my return from army service in Africa in 1953 and my return to Africa in 1958.

Within a couple of weeks of completing my army service I had returned to my old job at Crosfields. Very little had changed but my salary had now increased to almost double the amount I had received before doing my national service. I now represented Crosfields at football, as their goalkeeper in the Warrington Premier League. I also worked on my high jumping, long jumping, discus and javelin throwing and shot-putting and eventually became the field events captain at Warrington Athletics Club.

I did almost all of my own training on the firm's recreation ground and was practising one evening in 1956 when I noticed a young girl running alone around the sports ground. I asked what she was doing and she told me that she was keeping fit. She lived nearby and so used the field. Looking at her, I saw that she was on the small side but strongly built without being overweight, and she looked to be a good prospect for one or more of the field events. When I asked if she had tried any of the field throwing events she said that she had not.

I got hold of a ladies' shot, which weighs eight pounds eight ounces, and decided to see just how coordinated she was and what her natural strength was like. She proved to be very promising. She was determined to get things right and listened attentively to comments and instructions, progressing steadily. I began to meet and coach her on a couple of nights each week, but it started to get dark early as the nights closed in and winter quickly approached.

Ann invited me to train at her house. Her father had cleared out the garage and offered it to us to use for training. I concentrated upon a fitness programme using weight training and running as a basis for our winter training.

When winter turned to spring the following year we went back to training outside. By this time I was convinced that Ann could do really well on the athletic scene. As spring moved towards summer I entered her for the Lancashire

Athletics Championships in the shot-put. It was to be held north of Warrington, somewhere near to Bolton. Where the entry form required the name of the entrant's sports club I told her to write "unattached".

On arriving at the venue for the championships we found that a large crowd had gathered. We went to find the shot-putting area and Ann booked in. There must have been at least twenty or more competitors having practice puts (throws) when we arrived. Ann was keen to have a few practice puts herself but I told her to wait and watch the other competitors. I could see that most of them were nowhere near her standard. As we watched them practising their glides across the shot-putting circle before launching the shot as far as they could send it, I knew that Ann could beat all of them. It was time to demoralise them.

I told her to join the girls who were practising and wait for her turn to have a practice put, but to just do a standing put without moving across the putting circle. As she awaited her turn I noticed that the other girls were looking at her with interest. They seemed mostly to know each other, but Ann was a newcomer. When it was her turn Ann stood at the front of the circle to do a static put. She was the smallest athlete there. I saw smiles appear on the faces of some of the other competitors as they watched this schoolgirl. She was obviously just a novice who had no idea about the shot-putting technique. Their smiles quickly disappeared when with one easy, fluid movement of her body she sent the shot five or six feet further than the best attempts of the other competitors. They regarded her with astonishment and considerable dismay.

When the competition started Ann used the full glide across the circle and considerably increased the distance that she sent the shot. Her superiority was so great that the other competitors, all of them older, bigger and more experienced than she was, were competing for second and third places.

At the end of the competition I was standing talking with her when an official hurried towards us. He asked if Ann would be free to represent Lancashire in the forthcoming Northern Counties Championships. She said that she would be and was told that she would receive details in the post.

When Ann did represent Lancashire she again won quite easily to become the Northern Counties champion. She eventually went to university in 1959 to study to become a doctor. She was selected for the team which represented the London universities against the Paris universities, and won again. Her biggest success in shot-put competitions, however, came in a competition in which she beat Mary Peters, who went on to win the Olympic Games decathlon championship held in Munich in 1972. Mary, who was over a year older than Ann, also won the Commonwealth Games shot-put championships in 1966 in Kingston and again in 1970 in Edinburgh.

*

In the meantime I had decided to leave my job at Crosfields and had applied for a position as a clerical officer at the Atomic Energy Authority HQ at Risley, the other side of Warrington. Having been offered the position I bought a motorbike, resigned from Crosfields football team as I was no longer working there, and joined Warrington rugby union club.

I started my rugby career in the fourth team with my first match against Bury third team. We were beaten but I managed to score our only try and was promoted to the third team for the following week. After a few months I was placed in the second team and the distances we travelled to our matches increased, as did the standard of the rugby.

It was during a game against Shrewsbury that when diving on a ball which had been kicked over our full back's head, I was kicked in the side of my neck. I remember nothing further until the following day when I regained consciousness in Warrington General Hospital. I spent a week there and was X-rayed several times before being discharged.

Last year, 2015, I started writing this book. Just before Christmas I was at my daughter's house when I fell backwards down a full flight of stairs, somersaulting twice before smashing my head into the front door of the house. I had been trying to get hold of my daughter's little puppy, who could get up but not down stairs. I was taken to hospital by ambulance and had the usual checks and X-rays.

As I lay in bed awaiting the results, my doctor and six assistants rushed into the ward, told me not to move and carried me back to the X-ray department, the doctor holding my head. The X-rays showed that I had fractured my spine near the bottom of my neck. Eventually, when all the fuss was over, it was found to be an historical fracture, which must have occurred in the game against Shrewsbury all those years ago. I did, however, have a new compressed fracture of the T4 vertebra, which eventually mended itself.

In February 1958 I was looking out of the office windows at Risley. The day was dark and sleet was blowing against the glass. I was not looking forward to the ride home on my motorbike. In the late afternoon we heard that the plane carrying the Manchester United football team had crashed in Germany. Like many other United supporters, I was upset. I was also fed up with the winter weather and my thoughts turned back to Africa. I realised that I missed the African weather and the scenery. I began to search the newspapers for advertisements for jobs in the police forces in Africa.

A few days later I came across two adverts. One was for police officers to work in Nyasaland; the second for officers to work in the Northern Rhodesia Police. After some thought, I decided to apply for the position in the Northern

Rhodesia Police. I phoned a number in London, received an application form, filled it in and posted it.

About a week later I received an invitation to an interview to be held in London a couple of weeks later. I duly went down to London, was interviewed, had a medical and was offered the position of assistant inspector. I was told that my starting date would be later in the year, but that I would be notified in time for me to give notice to my current employers.

In July 1958 Ann and I travelled down to Cardiff for the British Empire and Commonwealth Games. We had an enjoyable time and were sorry when it ended. Ann, whose eighteenth birthday would be in the October of 1959, won a scholarship to study at St. Mary's Hospital in London. She was still aged just seventeen and was a young star doctor in the making.

I was duly notified that my date of departure to Northern Rhodesia would be the 24th October. I travelled by train to London where, before I departed by taxi to Heathrow, I said my goodbyes to Ann, who had slipped out of the hospital to see me off.

15

Return To Africa

I made my way to Heathrow to join a group of men who turned out to be mainly younger than myself. Some of them had made journeys from various parts of the British Isles but the majority were from southern England. We assembled in the waiting area, having passed through passport and customs controls. We were accompanied by a man who gave us our flight tickets and wished us good luck.

When the flight was called we walked out to board our aircraft, which turned out to be a Bristol Britannia. It was a large aircraft, having four turboprop engines. When we boarded I found that, like the York which had brought me back to England from Egypt some years earlier, it had rows of two seats down each side of the central aisle. I found myself seated next to a handsome young man, somewhat younger than myself, who introduced himself as Nick Harris.

Eventually we took off on what promised to be a long, tiring flight. It was mid-morning when we set out on the first leg of the journey. Soon we were over France and then flying over high mountains until we arrived at our first stop, which was Rome. I can't remember that there was any food served on the plane although I think that there were liquid refreshments from time to time. We had a stop for about an hour and bought our own lunches.

Whilst we were there, I went to the gents' to empty my bladder. As I stood there, I became aware of a cleaning lady mopping the floor of the urinals near to my feet.

She said something which sounded like, "*Scusata me prego*" and continued to mop around my feet before moving along to the next urinal. I felt quite embarrassed but was told later that it was quite common for this to happen in Italy.

The second leg of our trip was due south on a course to take us to Benghazi in Libya. This meant flying down the length of Italy and then crossing the Mediterranean Sea to our next stop. By the time we landed it was becoming darker as night approached. It was in the restaurant at this airport that

I consumed the bottle of orange juice which would land me in Lusaka Hospital two days later.

To cut a long story short, we flew through the night, stopping at Aswan in Egypt near to where the great Aswan Dam on the Nile would be built a few years later. From here we flew to Khartoum, which brought back army memories, and then on to Entebbe in Uganda, where we landed as dawn was breaking.

By this time we were all very tired and it was with some relief that we realised that our next stop would be at Ndola in Northern Rhodesia. We had become accustomed to the relative comfort and low noise level of the Britannia, but now were told that we would be transferring to a Northern Rhodesia Airways aircraft for the flight to Lusaka. This aircraft turned out to be a DC-3 Dakota. It was a twin-engined, noisy and uncomfortable aeroplane, and we filled it. When our baggage had been loaded we were told to strap in. The pilot told us that we would experience uncomfortable turbulence for most of the flight and that we should remain strapped in. He was not wrong. It was late October. The rains were about to start in earnest and the temperature was at its highest level.

Our flight was bumpy to say the least. We were pitched about, and I could see why seat belts were needed. We eventually landed at Ndola, a bustling town at the eastern end of the Northern Rhodesian Copperbelt. We did not get off the plane but took off again after taking on board some extra cargo. Our flight to Lusaka took about an hour, and on arrival we gratefully stepped on to Northern Rhodesian soil. I was feeling sick and weak, and several others admitted to similar feelings. Our baggage was loaded on to a truck and a coach took us south to Lilayi, the site of the police training school.

16

Training School

On arrival at the training school we parked in front of a long, neat building which looked out on to a large parade ground. A squad of African men, dressed in overalls, was being drilled as we arrived. Two uniformed white officers took us inside the building and led us into an assembly room where we were allocated rooms. Two men would share each room, and I found that my room-mate to be was a guy named David Lewis, who turned out to be five years younger than me.

We entered our room and I saw Dave looking at the ceiling with obvious interest. I wondered what he was looking at and followed his gaze. To my horror I saw, directly above the bed nearest to the window, the most gigantic spider I had ever seen. Across the far side of the room was another. They were both about the size of an adult hand with fingers spread. The officer with us laughed at our reactions. He told us that they were camel spiders and killed their prey by using speed and cunning.

'They don't spin webs and you are lucky to have them. They are great for keeping other spiders and mosquitoes down. On no account must they be killed. Look upon them as friends.'

He then pointed to mosquito nets on each bed and showed us how to use them.

After this brief introduction to our room we went downstairs to join the rest of the squad and were shown the recruits' lounge and bar. A quick walk around the building revealed several classrooms, a gymnasium, a shower block and a laundry area. Everywhere was neat and well thought out. By now I was feeling terrible. My head felt as though it could burst, and I was dizzy. I told Dave that I would miss dinner and went to bed.

Morning came, after what had been, for me, a night of tossing and turning. When I tried to get dressed I found that I couldn't keep my balance. I didn't go down to breakfast but waited until we were called out to the parade ground to be addressed by Chief Inspector Oliver (referred to as "Chiefy" from that day on, but not in his presence). I don't know how I managed to get down the stairs and line up with the others but I was aware of a number of questioning looks from members of the squad.

I was told later that I had turned white and that sweat was pouring from my face. My shirt was soaked and I was struggling to stand upright. I vaguely remember Chiefy telling one of the inspectors to get me to the hospital immediately. After that it all became blurred, and I have an imperfect memory of being stripped, put to bed and catheterised and having needles stuck into my arm.

On that first day I gradually became aware of where I was and what was happening to me. Several times I had blood taken for analysis, but the nurses just told me that they would soon find out what was wrong with me. I felt constantly thirsty and was drinking all the water they would allow me. They told me that I was also being infused with a saline solution.

On the day after I had been admitted I was told that I had a bad attack of paratyphoid fever. They wanted to know what I had been eating and drinking during the previous week, but in the end felt that it must have been the orange juice that I had drunk in Benghazi that had caused the problem. I stayed in hospital for a week and lost a stone in weight during that time.

I still felt groggy on my return to Lilayi, but had to forget about how I felt and work hard to catch up with the rest of the squad.

After I was discharged from hospital I found that whilst I had been away everyone else had hired servants to do their laundry, make beds, polish floors etc. I had no choice in the matter of whom I would employ. There was only one small, chubby young man whom nobody had selected, so I was stuck with him. His name was Crispin Sakala and he remained with me for the whole of my time in the police force in Africa. He was a good worker who stole my chocolates and the occasional pair of socks, but he was a loyal man upon whom I knew I could rely. I genuinely liked him.

We worked very hard during the time we were at training school. We studied law, which was virtually codified English law, police duties, first aid and Chinyanja, which was the country's second language after English.

The imposition of English as a first language, to be taught in all schools, was a master stroke. For a country which had a large number of different tribal languages, it was a unifying factor imposed by an earlier administration. The use of Chinyanja as the country's second language for all government services personnel was also a brilliant move by the administration. Chinyanja, the language of the people of the lake, had been imported from Nyasaland, a neighbouring country on our eastern border, and prevented trouble between

Northern Rhodesian tribes who would otherwise each have wanted their own language to have been made the official second language of the country.

As well as law, language studies, police duties and first aid, we had a number of other areas to cover. We had to be proficient in the use of the 303 Lee-Enfield rifle, the .38 Webley semi-automatic revolver, and the Stirling sub-machine gun. We also trained in basic unarmed combat and we did a lot of parade ground drill, taking turns to drill the squad.

One of Chiefy's tricks was to take the squad to the far side of the parade ground, which was huge, and make whoever was in temporary charge stand as far away as possible. The chosen one then had to drill the squad for several minutes from there. Sometimes another squad would be carrying out a similar exercise and hilarious mix-ups would occur. Chiefy would keep a straight face and blast the unfortunate person in temporary command with a voice which could be heard clearly over considerable distances. Time passed quickly and we soon became a unit rather than a collection of disparate individuals.

Sport took up most of our free time when we were not studying. We played mainly cricket and rugby. I remember going for our first cricket practice under the watchful eyes of Chiefy, who, as a Yorkshire man, had played cricket himself and loved the game. I had played cricket for Crosfields in the Manchester Association when I had left the army, and had been their regular wicketkeeper. I had also filled the position for my battalion in the army. Unfortunately, a wicketkeeper had already been selected so I didn't get a chance.

When it was my turn to bat I faced a fast bowler who had already taken four wickets. His first ball was aimed straight at me and I went down on one knee and hit it to the square leg boundary. The second ball was on exactly the same line but even faster, and again I used the same stroke with the same result. His third ball knocked two of my stumps out of the ground.

Some weeks later, I was in Chiefy's office for a short chat to discuss how things were going. As we were talking he received a call and had to go out for a moment. I took a quick look at my file, which was on his desk. Under "cricket" was written, "Plays with more enthusiasm than skill". This was a fair comment, I suppose, but I wished that I could have had a chance to show what I might have done as a wicketkeeper.

During our time at the police training school I got to know Dave Lewis quite well, although when we were not training he tended to disappear into the bush around the school. He invariably brought a specimen or two back with him, and always took photographs. His habit of going off by himself earned him the Chinyanja name of Chukta (wanderer). I had a lot of time for him but after we left Lilayi I never met up with him again.

Training school was not all about studying, learning how to be a police officer and sport. We had plenty of time in the evenings to lounge about and talk. In this way we came to know each other quite well. I found that I liked some of the lads very much, but others, some of them ex-police officers in Britain, seemed to think they knew it all. This got right up my nose. We had a couple of "remittance men" in the squad. These were men who came from families wealthy enough to supplement their police salaries by remittances from home. We also had three ex-public school chaps, one of whom thought he was God's gift to the squad and had great ideas of a life rising rapidly through the ranks to high command, which he was unable to do. The other two were good men.

A couple of weeks after a boozy Christmas, we completed our training, and in the third week of January 1959 our passing-out parade was held. After the parade ended we all gathered round the noticeboard in the entrance hall and looked for our names. Next to my name was the word "Choma". By scanning a map I was finally able to locate Choma. It was a small town lying on the main road between Lusaka and Livingstone in the Southern Province of the country.

Early the following morning we gathered our belongings, said our goodbyes, wished each other good luck and set off by various means towards our allotted posts. I was to travel to Choma in a Land Rover, which would then carry on to Livingstone. The driver was an African who, I gathered, worked for the PWD (Public Works Department). We headed south towards Kafue along the T2 road. Kafue was a small town, more of a village really, and just to the south of it the road divided. The left-hand branch went directly to the Southern Rhodesian (now Zimbabwe) border just thirty-six miles away. We took the right-hand branch, the T1, and turned west. Throughout the rest of that morning and into the afternoon we headed mainly south-west until, after having driven a total of 170 miles or so on dirt roads, we finally arrived at Choma.

Like most of the other small towns we had passed through, the dirt road changed to a tarred road about two or three hundred yards from the actual entry to the town. We came round a sharp bend and there was Choma.

17

Choma

Choma was really a street village, with nearly everything of commercial importance located along each side of the main road. I had noted a hotel on the west side of the road at the northern end as we entered. Beyond it and on the same side was the police station where we stopped and I got out of the vehicle with my luggage.

On the other side of the road was a garage, and further along, a bar. There was a doctor's surgery and, in the distance, the PWD, towards which my driver was now heading. The town looked dusty and sleepy and there was little sign of movement. I could see that a number of narrow side roads led to what was obviously European and Asian housing. I learned later that African housing and a large beer hall were situated some distance away to the west of the town.

I picked up my case and walked towards the police station. As I came nearer to it I saw that behind the main building there was quite an extensive area in which a number of police vehicles and an ambulance were standing. I entered the station through the front door and saw that a sergeant was at the desk. I identified myself and asked for the officer in charge. An inspector came into the office, greeted me and showed me to my accommodation. This was a small apartment in a row of similar apartments for single officers. Married officers lived in houses off-station.

My apartment was spacious and looked comfortable. It had a small lounge, a single bedroom and a room with a toilet and washbasin. There were no bathing facilities in the apartment. A large bathroom with bath and shower was shared by the single officers. There was a dining room with food storage facilities and the usual crockery and cutlery, but this was only used for breakfast and the making of sandwiches etc. Dinner was taken in the evening at the hotel that I had noticed on the way in. The police had arranged a good rate for the regular evening meal and each officer paid monthly for what turned out to be good but, of necessity, rather repetitive meals.

*

On the day following my arrival I was asked by the inspector who was in charge of transport, among other things, whether I had driver's licences for driving motor vehicles, including motorcycles. I said that I had, omitting to say that I had never owned a car but had taken the test in an instructor's car a few days before setting off for Africa.

'What type of motorbike did you have?' he asked.

'A Triumph Tiger Cub,' I replied.

'Well, here we use the Cub's big brother,' he said.

He led me to a large motorcycle standing near the foot of a sandy slope.

'You know that the roads are graded sand roads, don't you?' he said.

I nodded.

'Okay, let's go for a ride and see how you are on dirt.'

I noticed that a couple of officers were watching as I mounted the bike and eased it off its stand.

'We'll take it slowly until you get used to the heavier machine.'

With that he set off up the slope towards the main road. I gently engaged first gear, opened the throttle and let in the clutch. Everything happened in a flash. The bike took off vertically and I ended up flying off backwards and landing on my shoulder just as the machine crashed down beside me, missing my head by a few inches. My examiner left his bike and walked over to me.

'You alright?' he asked, looking down at me and picking up my machine. I assured him that I was.

'Not a Tiger Cub, is it?' he said. 'Get back on and feel the revs. Listen to the engine and don't give it so much throttle.'

I did as instructed and eased away without a problem this time. I followed him out on to the road and through the town until we came to the dirt road leading south. We covered about twenty miles, gradually increasing the speed until I was comfortable on the road surface and with the bends in the road. By the time we returned I felt quite at home on the bike and my examiner was happy to pass me and give me force authority to use motorbikes.

We later took out a Land Rover, which was fun to drive, and after that the ambulance, which was a bit unwieldy on the dirt but again I felt comfortable driving it. He instructed me to drive the Land Rover along a dirt road leading west off the Livingstone road. This was a poorer road than the main road south, and was rutted and not well graded. It was an uncomfortable ride, which became more uncomfortable as it started to pour with rain and the track became slippery and treacherous. We stopped at the first farm we came to after about fifteen miles' driving.

My examiner told me that this was one of the smaller farms of only about four thousand acres. I was introduced to the farmer, a South African of Dutch descent, as many of the farmers were. That evening, at dinner, I was the butt of some friendly teasing about my first attempt to ride the force motorbike when I joined the rest of the single men having dinner together at the hotel. I began to feel that I could fit in nicely with my compatriots.

18

Sudden Death

On the Sunday it was my turn to look after the police station. I was told to get to know the African staff on duty with me but not to be too familiar with them.

'Familiarity breeds contempt,' were the words used.

I duly took up my position in the enquiry office. I had just started to look at the occurrence book, in which all complaints, incidents and information were written as they occurred, when an African man came into the office and asked to speak to the officer in charge, which was myself. He had come from a farm about twenty miles away, having been given a lift. He reported that the owner of the farm, a widowed lady, had been found dead in her bed by a house servant.

My heart pounded. This was my first body. I realised that I should take advice before setting out, so called Detective Inspector Ray Pritchard, who was in charge of CID. He came across to the station and ran through the procedures with me. I then called a sergeant driver to drive me to the farm in a station Land Rover and we set off.

On arrival at the farm I went to the bedroom where the body lay. The bed was undisturbed and the old lady lay peacefully with no sign of any injury. I quickly checked that she was in fact dead and then, with the sergeant, made a tour of the house and checked for any sign of disturbance. All looked peaceful and as it should be. I talked with the female servant who had found the body, and also the senior African employee at the farm. I felt that as far as I could ascertain, there was nothing suspicious about the death. I saw that the house was well kept and there appeared to be some valuable paintings in several rooms, as well as valuable ornaments.

I pointed out what I wanted to take from the house and instructed the sergeant to move everything to the front door ready for loading. There was a car standing outside, and the servants confirmed that this was the deceased's car. I then went through all the drawers in a search for documents, letters and any other material that might be needed by the court, executors or members of the family, if any. I told the sergeant to load the Land Rover with everything that we had removed from the house and went to speak to the African man in charge of the people employed by the deceased. I informed him that the death would be dealt with by the magistrate in Choma and any wages owed to the employees would be paid by court order.

I locked up the house after removing all the food from the fridge and giving it to the staff to share out. The police Land Rover was full of stuff from the house, as were the boot and back seats of the deceased's car. There was only one thing to do, and that was to sit the body in the passenger seat next to me. I went back into the house and found several pairs of stockings with which I secured her to the front passenger seat, and so we returned to Choma.

On our return I had to drive up the main street to get to the mortuary and several people walking along the pavement obviously saw the body, and word soon spread. At the rear of the surgery I found the mortuary and rounded up the man who worked for the doctor. Together we unloaded the body and placed it in the mortuary fridge.

I attended the autopsy the following afternoon and had my first meeting with the doctor. As he handed me a tube of wintergreen ointment and told me to put some up each nostril he asked if I had ever attended a post-mortem before. I admitted that I hadn't, and prepared to watch. At first I kept a respectful distance from the now-naked body but George, as I shall call the doctor, beckoned me forward and started to explain each step he was taking in the procedure.

Firstly he examined the body for external evidence of a suspicious death. Satisfied that all was perfectly normal, he took a scalpel and to my amazement, easily made a cut from each shoulder, slicing through the ribcage and meeting at the sternum. This formed a V-shape and, from the point where the two cuts met, he continued to cut down until he came to the pubic bone. The cutting was now Y-shaped. The front of the ribcage was then removed to expose the neck and chest organs.

I had long lost the slight queasiness that I had felt when the knife cut the first part of the V-shaped incision when George turned to me and said, 'I don't need to explore too deeply in this post-mortem. There are no suspicious circumstances from what you have told me and I already think I have the answer you are seeking.'

He reached into the chest cavity and took out the heart. He then proceeded to cut into it and handed me a cross section. He pointed out to me the large amount of fat present.

'She died from fatty degeneration of the heart. You can see blockages here and here.'

And so I could.

He turned to me and continued, 'I will put her back together later and stitch her up so that she will look as good as new, and I'll inform the coroner and provide him with the results. I believe there is a brother coming up from Southern Rhodesia and he will arrange the funeral. He may want to speak to you about how you found her etc. Time for a beer, do you reckon?'

We put the old lady back into the fridge, and having signed off for the afternoon, I joined him in the pub. We talked about our careers and about life in general, and found that we shared a lot of views about a wide range of things. This was to be the beginning of a friendship during which George taught me a huge amount about forensic science and greatly improved my knowledge of medical jurisprudence, which meant "the study and application of scientific and medical knowledge to legal problems such as inquests, and in the field of Law". There would be many more autopsies to attend before I left Choma and I decided to write up each one, taking notes during the procedure and revising them afterwards.

19

Tough Guy

A couple of weeks or so later I was on duty, again on a weekend, when a white man ran into the station. He told me that there was trouble in the bar down the road. From now on I shall refer to all white people as Europeans even though many might have been South Africans and white people from other countries. I told the sergeant to take over the station, checked my handcuffs were ready for use and walked slowly towards the disturbance.

As I entered the bar the noise abated and gradually the room became silent. I was aware that every person in the bar was looking at me with interest and anticipation. There was a large weekend clientele there and many were obviously looking forward to some entertainment. The crowd was assembled around the walls of the room, leaving the area around the bar free for the man who stood there.

My heart rate started to increase rapidly as I saw who it was. He stood, leaning against the bar and surveying the crowd with disdain. On the floor I noticed two smashed chairs and several broken glasses. When he saw me he smiled, as though I was the next part of his game. He had obviously had more than enough to drink, and he looked dangerous. I recognised him as one of the farmers who had been pointed out to me. He stood a good six and a half feet tall and had a huge, powerful physique. He had been described to me as a man renowned in South Africa for his strength when playing state rugby.

I walked towards him and there was a low murmur from the watchers. I stood in front of him and said, 'Don't you think you've had enough? Come out with me now and we can arrange with the owner to send you a bill for the damage.'

He grinned at me. 'Make me,' he said.

'Well, if that's the way you want it, but you'll end up in court.'

I walked to the side of him and quickly grabbed his wrist, twisting it so that the palm of his hand was facing upwards and his arm was straightened, putting pressure on the shoulder. Well, that was the theory. He hadn't moved, and I started to reach for my handcuffs. As I did so I felt his arm slowly begin to move. I applied force to my hold. I might just as well have not been there. Without showing the slightest sign of strain, and keeping his arm straight, he pulled me round to his side. He was not finished. Still keeping his arm straight, he rotated it and slowly raised me until my feet left the ground and his straight arm was level with his shoulder. I don't know why, probably the thought of my ridiculous position, but I started to laugh and released my grip on his wrist, returning my feet to the floor.

'Okay,' I said, 'you've proved you're the strongest man I've ever come across and this lot have had their entertainment for the weekend. Would you like to come with me to the station where you can have a bed in one of the cells until you sleep the booze off? I'll leave the door open for you and one of your friends can take you home when you're ready, but you must leave your vehicle here and collect it on Monday.'

He looked at me appraisingly; then started to laugh.

'Okay,' he said, 'let's go.'

As we walked out, him towering above me and with his hand on my shoulder for balance, there was a ripple of applause from some of the bystanders. We had just started to cross the road when I saw three off-duty officers walking quickly towards us.

'Everything alright, Dave?' one of them asked.

'We're fine, thanks,' I said, and carried on to the station.

It was at dinner that evening that I learned that a constable had been sent across to the mess to tell any off-duty officers he could find that I might be in trouble. It transpired that one of the tough guy's party tricks was to lift a two hundred-pound sack of cornmeal in each hand to shoulder height without bending his arms. I also learned that he was one of our civilian police reserve officers, and over the time that I was at Choma we became good friends.

20

Malaria

It was not long after the tussle in the bar that I had my first bout of malaria. The indigenous people of Northern Rhodesia, like those of many countries in Africa, suffered greatly from this terrible disease. Even today it accounts for more deaths throughout the world than any other single disease. The police personnel all slept under mosquito nets. I was no exception, but when you were out on patrol, as I was at that time, you did get bitten fairly often. We all took our anti-malarial tablets regularly but even this did not guarantee immunity.

One hot, rainy afternoon I began to feel very weak and started to shake. The spasms of uncontrollable shaking came and went at random and left me feeling very unwell. I was told to sign off duty and to go and lie down. By dinner time one of the lads came to see if I was coming for dinner. By this time, evidently, I was barely conscious and had, they discovered, a dangerously high temperature. I was almost incoherent and was covered in sweat, and my bed was wet through. They sent for my friend, the doctor, who confirmed that I had malaria. He gave me an injection as there was no way I could have swallowed tablets. He then told the officer in charge to ensure that somebody checked on me at regular intervals.

I was largely unaware of the comings and goings in my bedroom during the following few days but I found out later that there had been a steady stream of visitors concerned about my health. What I also learned was that Crispin, my servant, had been present most of the time, wiping the sweat from my body and bringing an endless supply of cold towels which, I learned, he had kept in the fridge. He had stayed with me until the fever broke.

After about three days I became able to recognise what was happening to me and began to think and talk rationally. I felt weak and helpless and suffered from disabling headaches and a rise and fall in my body temperature, but gradually I began to move about and take small amounts of food. I was not capable of continuing with my duties for almost two weeks, but then took up my farm patrol visits again. The driving of a Land Rover over rutted tracks for long distances took its toll and on several occasions I just stopped at the side of the track and went to sleep. I began to appreciate just how dangerous the disease must be for the average African villager who would often have no recourse to a local doctor.

Eventually I recovered sufficiently to carry out my work efficiently, but in the coming months and years I was to suffer from a number of incapacitating attacks requiring hospitalisation. In each case I could count upon Crispin being at the foot of the bed when I regained my senses.

21

General Duties

It was approaching lunch hour and I was in the station, filing farm patrol reports, when the building was rocked by a huge explosion. I rushed outside into the main street and saw smoke and a large cloud of dust rising from the direction of the garage down the road. I ran towards the scene of what I could now see, by the debris littering the road, to be a large explosion.

A crowd was beginning to gather so I used several constables, who had followed me, to keep everyone clear. I needed to establish the cause of the explosion and determine whether there was any danger of further ones, so I entered the garage. I also had to see if anyone had been injured. As the dust began to clear I could make out the shape of what had once been a car but was now a total wreck. The garage appeared to have been badly damaged, and as I looked around I saw, hanging from what was left of one of the windows, a pair of legs. I quickly went over and peered through the shattered window frame and saw, to my horror, that the legs were still attached to what was left of the torso of an African man whose overalls were shredded and badly burnt.

More officers had arrived by now and I reported, as first officer to arrive at the scene, what I had found. There was nothing more for me, as a junior officer, to do except to go back to the duty office and write my report on what I had done as first officer on scene. I left the more experienced officers examining and photographing the scene. Eventually, it turned out that the African employee who had been killed in the explosion had shown so much promise in his general duties that the garage owner had begun to train him in the skill of welding. He had been carefully brought along in simple welding work, but on that day had taken it upon himself, in the lunchtime break when the garage was unmanned, to weld the damage in a car's petrol tank.

He was not, of course, qualified to do such work and did not realise how dangerous the work could be if carried out by an untrained person. At the inquest, expert evidence showed that there must have been some fuel left in the tank. The garage owner agreed and said that he was going to purge the tank of any remaining fuel that afternoon before carrying out the welding the next day. He had brought along the deceased steadily and had several times warned the lad to learn the trade as instructed and never to attempt anything new until shown how to do it. When he left the garage to go for his lunch it had been empty and he thought that the deceased had gone for his own lunch as usual.

At the inquest the verdict given was death by misadventure, with no blame attached to the owner of the garage. As first on the scene, I had to attend court to give evidence. It was my second time in court, the first being to give evidence in the case of my first sudden death, and again it was Mr Hanna, the Southern Province senior resident magistrate, on duty. He was a slightly built gentleman whom I assumed from his accent to be British.

He was always accompanied into court by two large Irish Wolfhounds. To me, they appeared to be identical in height, colouring and looks. As he sat down behind his desk, the animals took up position, sitting one each side of the desk, and stared steadily at whoever was giving evidence. They never moved their positions until their master rose to leave the court. When standing, the dogs were about three feet tall, and even when sitting their heads were level with the magistrate's desktop. These dogs are taller than Great Danes but are built like Greyhounds. There is a saying that they are "Gentle when stroked, but fierce when provoked". Crispin told me, one day, that the Africans believed that the animals could tell if someone was lying and that it was always better to tell the truth in Mr Hanna's court.

I now found myself on general duties and call-outs, which I enjoyed as I could be instructed to deal with any situation that arose. During the next month or so I dealt with many different types of incident. These ranged from domestic quarrels ending in violence, violent arguments in the local bar, drunk and disorderly behaviour, theft, threats of violence and disputes between neighbours concerning all sorts of issues. My interest in autopsies had, however, been noticed and I found that I was assigned to deal with much of this work. Road accidents provided a number of bodies but many came from African villages and beer halls and were usually the result of drunken brawls or accidents.

George took me under his wing and set about acquainting me with the legal as well as the practical side of conducting an autopsy. Over time, I learned enough to hand him instruments before he had to look for them and to question him about areas for which I needed answers. He always accompanied his dissection of a body with a running commentary and, as I developed my own knowledge, would ask me questions designed to test my understanding.

Eventually I graduated to the position of emergency assistant to George on a number of occasions when he had to perform emergency surgery to save a life. One such occasion involved an emergency amputation of an African fisherman's leg following an attack by a hippopotamus in the Zambezi. Without the amputation the man had no hope of surviving a transfer to Livingstone.

One day George told me that he had a present for me and handed me a book titled *Medical Jurisprudence and Toxicology*. This book became very important to me, and at some point in most days I made time to read or reread a chapter.

This reading period also included study for the law exams, which had to be passed before one could be promoted to the rank of inspector. I had set my mind to achieving this rank by the end of my three years' mandatory period as an assistant inspector.

We had now reached June, which together with July heralded midwinter. They were the most pleasant months of the year in regards to climate in the Choma area. The nights could be quite cold and on a number of occasions there was evidence of frost when I got up in the morning. The days, however, were warm and sunny, with an average temperature of about seventy-two degrees Fahrenheit, and everyone seemed to have more of a spring in their step.

22

Transfer to CID

A few days after the headless body affair (see Prologue), I was called to the office of the CO. On entering I saw that Detective Inspector Ray Pritchard was already seated in front of the commanding officer's desk. I was informed that it had been decided to transfer me from general duties and appoint me as an aid to CID to work under the supervision of DI Pritchard. I couldn't believe my ears. I was delighted and had never even considered that a transfer would be possible this early in my career. As Ray and I walked out of the office I asked about uniform.

'Just dress smart casual and come over to the CID office when you've changed,' he replied.

From that day onwards I applied all my energy to learning new techniques and methods. I had to be proficient in the lifting of fingerprints and other marks left at crime scenes. I became quite skilled in taking plaster casts of tyre tracks and footprints. I learned how to preserve and examine crime scenes, take detailed statements and question witnesses. Only the Copperbelt and Lusaka HQ had specialist fingerprint officers, and they were only available to other areas of the country to help in the most serious of cases.

When fingerprints had been lifted or taken anywhere in the country, they had to be sent to Force HQ in Lusaka. Here they were compared manually with possible matches. This was a long and arduous job. We had to do all our own scenes-of-crime work and ability in this field came only with experience. In Ray I had a fine teacher. He was a quiet and patient man, five years older than me, and I accompanied him to crime scenes and sat with him in interrogations of suspects and witnesses. I was enjoying the work and Ray gave me every chance to practise the skills. He was pleased that I had a keen interest in forensic work and that I attended the post-mortem examinations whenever possible.

Life was good. I felt that I was employed in the sort of work that I could happily spend the rest of my life doing. Then everything almost went wrong.

I had reached the stage where I was allowed to question persons accused of even the most serious crimes. Ray would sit next to me as I interrogated the accused and at the end of my questioning would ask supplementary questions on points that I had missed or areas of my questioning which could have been expanded. I learned very quickly to think on my feet and his supplementary questions gradually became fewer.

One morning an African prisoner was brought into the station in handcuffs. He had been arrested by two district messengers. These were African civil servants with powers of arrest in tribal areas, and who were responsible to the district commissioner. They saved the police a lot of time which might have been wasted on tribal disputes, and which the DC and his staff were far better equipped to sort out. If a case was too serious for the district commissioner to deal with he would transfer it to the police. This was such a case.

The accused was of the Tonga tribe and from the Zambezi Valley, slightly closer to the Choma area than to Livingstone, so he was ours to deal with. His offence was the systematic rape of his six-year-old daughter. A villager had reported what was happening, taking a considerable risk in doing so. The accused was known in the village to be a violent man. Now we had him sitting across the desk from us in the interview room. His wife was at the doctor's with the child and an initial medical inspection was taking place. A more detailed examination would occur when we transferred the wife and child to Livingstone and to the hospital there.

At a nod from Ray I administered the formal caution, which was translated for the accused by a Tonga-speaking constable. The accused, who was sitting directly opposite to me, sat glaring at me.

'Who are you to tell me what I can do with my own child?' he shouted, his voice rising until it was almost a scream.

As the constable was translating, the accused leapt to his feet and started to lean over to my side of the desk. I quickly stood up and the constable started to move towards the accused. Before he could give me the full translation of what had been said, the accused leaned closer but then drew back his head. I acted instinctively, expecting a headbutt, and moved my head to the left. At the same time I swung my right fist in a curve and struck him just under his left ear, partly on the jaw and partly on the neck. The constable reached him just as I connected and caught him as he fell. All this took only about two seconds from start to finish and Ray hadn't moved. He quietly told the constable to get help to put the accused back in his cell, but to keep a close watch on him and report back when he had recovered consciousness and was acting normally.

'If he hasn't recovered in ten minutes you can go and get the doctor,' he said to me.

I then received a lecture, delivered in a quiet voice, which I would remember throughout my police career.

'There is no excuse for striking a prisoner, no matter what he is charged with,' Ray said.

'But he was about to butt me.'

'You could have got out of the way and then the three of us could have subdued him,' he replied.

'I'm sorry but I acted instinctively. I saw him pull his head back but he maintained his body position. To me that signalled that he was going to butt me.'

Ray smiled. 'It could also have meant that he was about to spit at you.'

I paused to think, and I realised that he was right.

'You have to understand, David, that we have a long-standing reputation for dealing justly with the indigenous people of this country. This is why they always want to speak with a white officer when they come into the station. They don't want to speak to an African officer because he might be of a different tribe and could be biased. They might not like us running the country but they prefer it to another tribe running it. Look, you have the makings of a good investigating officer and I shall give you another chance, but if you were to repeat what happened today, then your CID career would be over and possibly it could be the end of your police career as well.'

From that day forward I never raised my hand to anyone whom I was in the process of questioning, and I made sure that the CID staff under my command, later in my career, followed the same code. I like to think that my time under the guidance of Ray Pritchard formed the basis of a successful career in CID.

Life went on just as before and the incident was never mentioned again. The accused, who never denied the charge and never accepted that he had committed a crime, could have been sentenced to death but was sentenced to a long term of imprisonment and banned from ever going anywhere near his village again. I never saw the child in the case again but I heard that she and her mother had been returned to the village where the abuse had occurred, but where the mother had many friends.

Over time I dealt with many rapes and accusations of rape. It was often very difficult to get to the truth of the matter. Sometimes it was as simple as the accused defaulting on payment for services rendered. Our African police quite often had a better idea about what might have happened than a European officer had. We listened to their views carefully. We took each case seriously and usually, I like to think, arrived at a fair conclusion.

23

Learning the Law

Time passed and I worked hard at my law studies. I found it interesting and because of this was able to retain much of what I read. Local and applied laws varied from place to place, but an overall view was all that was required, along with a modicum of common sense.

Criminal law was codified, each offence being broken down into what constituted the offence and therefore what had to be proved. The more common offences I committed to memory, and can still to this day remember these points.

The Witchcraft Ordinance covered, if I remember correctly, about forty plus pages of interesting law that was so novel that it was easily learned. See Tim Wright's excellent book *The History of the Northern Rhodesia Police* for details of the very successful drive against witchcraft in 1956. That was the real start of the battle to wipe it out.

On top of all this we had to understand how courts worked. We had to have a have a good knowledge of the law relating to evidence, for example hearsay evidence and the law regarding dying declarations and so on. It was all fascinating, and I loved it.

As time passed and we moved towards autumn the temperature began its inevitable rise, and the humidity rose with it. By October the daily temperature often averaged eighty-six degrees Fahrenheit and would at times move above a hundred degrees in the heat of the day. The heavy rainfall increased steadily. Much of the rain fell in the afternoons and at night. Early mornings were often bright and fresh. Humidity rose steadily throughout the morning and clouds gathered into the afternoon. Heavy rain was often accompanied by thunder and lightning strikes, which were beautiful to watch but not good to be out in. As the humidity increased one's sweating increased in line with it, and a cold shower was the first thing you thought about after work. Most of us slept naked on top of the covers but under our nets. Lightning took its toll of the population but we were rarely informed of the deaths. They were acts of God or nature and the deaths were mourned but accepted. There was, in the mind of the simple villager, no need to inform the police.

Christmas 1960 arrived and, as was traditional, the single officers took up all the station duties to allow married officers and their families to enjoy a traditional Christmas. As each of us finished our duties we would go to the married officer's house to which we had been invited and join in the festivities. It was lovely to see the children with their presents and join in playing games with them, but to a certain extent it brought a deep feeling of homesickness with it.

New Year's Eve followed and required a total turnout of all members of staff throughout the force. We carried out vehicle patrols throughout the area and paid regular, good-tempered visits to the local pub and the hotel. It turned out to be the most trouble-free New Year's Eve and Day that anyone in Choma could remember.

24

Livingstone

One morning towards the end of January I was told that the CO wanted to see me. When I arrived he told me that I was to be transferred to Livingstone. I asked in what capacity I was being transferred. I desperately wanted to continue in CID.

'I'm afraid there are no vacancies for another aid to CID,' he replied, and my hopes of a career in CID plunged.

'Then, sir, I would rather stay here if that is at all possible,' I replied.

'I'm afraid that is out of the question,' he answered. 'In this force we go where we are instructed to go. You will go to join CID in Livingstone as a detective assistant inspector. The work that you have done here since joining CID has been noticed. Go and pack your belongings and be ready to leave in the morning. I dare say that you will want to buy your friends a drink this evening.'

The following morning I found that a lift to Livingstone had been arranged for me with one of the locals who was driving down there on business. About seven or so miles from Livingstone I caught sight of the huge cloud of spray rising hundreds of feet above the Victoria Falls as thousands of tons of water from a Zambezi River swollen by the rains plunged every minute over the four hundred-foot drop into the river below. I could not see the falls themselves, of course.

Choma, situated on the plateau, was 4,308 feet above sea level. Livingstone, at 1,479 feet above sea level, was therefore 2,829 feet lower than Choma and very much hotter. As we started to descend into the Zambezi Valley, I noticed that the temperature was beginning to rise and the humidity was rising with it. I was soon soaked with sweat. When I had visited Livingstone the previous year it had been in the dry season and I had thought it pretty hot then. This, however, was something entirely different.

My driver drove me to the police station and helped me unload my luggage, and I thanked him. I then turned to walk into the enquiry office.

The office was manned by two African officers, a sergeant and a constable, but as I entered a European uniformed assistant inspector came in through a door at the back. I told him who I was and he answered that they had been expecting me.

'You're the bodies man, aren't you?' he said.

I was surprised. I had never imagined that my Choma nickname would be known anywhere else in the province.

'Some of my friends in Choma called me that,' I replied.

'Oh, we've heard stories about you,' he replied. 'Would you like to see your quarters? I'll take you over and then you can unpack and settle in. I'll tell the duty officer that you have arrived. The CO will probably see you in the morning. I think he's out at the moment. When you've unpacked come back to the station and I'll introduce you to some of the crew.'

My room, compared to the one I had occupied in Choma, was huge. It was a bedsit with the bed at one end, next to the bathroom. There were two enormous fans, one almost above the bed and the other at the opposite end of the room. I switched them on and they began to turn lazily. I found that I could increase their speed by turning the switch and soon they were humming away. There was a large bookcase and a couple of easy chairs as well as a table with its own more upright chair.

The walls boasted three large, heavily framed paintings. On examination I found that they were original oil paintings, not prints. All of them were well painted and featured Scottish scenes with mountains and cattle. I didn't recognise the artist's name but whoever it was could certainly paint. They appeared to have been painted in the early 1900s.

I unpacked and began to hang my clothes in a large wardrobe. As I was doing so there was a knock on the door and there was Crispin, my faithful servant, who had come down the previous day and had already found accommodation in the servants' quarters. He greeted me, grabbed an armful of clothes from the wardrobe and walked out with them. I knew that before he finished work that afternoon they would all be back in the wardrobe, washed and pressed. I felt happy with the way things were turning out.

I wandered back to the station and met with another two European officers, and was introduced to an African sergeant and a couple of constables. I was then taken upstairs to the CID office. Here I was introduced to Detective Inspector Jack Gowland and Daphne, a woman assistant inspector and Jack's wife. We chatted for a while and Jack gave me a rundown on the area and the workload.

'You'll meet Assistant Superintendent Don Bruce in the morning. He's in charge of Livingstone CID. This will be after you have seen the divisional chief investigations officer for the Southern Division, Assistant Superintendent Blackwell.'

By the time we had finished talking it was late afternoon and I wandered over to the single officers' mess. Here I met other officers and joined them in a drink from the bar. After this we had dinner in the single officers' dining room. I was pleased to find that the food was at least as good as, and probably better than, that which I had eaten in Choma.

The following morning I met with Assistant Superintendent Blackwell. I liked him immediately and we had an interesting discussion. He asked me about my nickname "Bodies" and how I had come by it, and we had a good laugh about it. He explained that a good proportion of the sudden and unnatural death cases would be directed my way, and hoped that I would form good relationships with the pathologists in Livingstone. He went on to say that I would also be expected to carry out the full range of CID work to get a good grounding in all aspects.

'You will not be short of work in Livingstone,' he said.

Following my meeting with Mr Blackwell I went to the office of Mr Bruce. He was a large man and looked as though he could handle himself. In an easily recognisable Scottish accent he greeted me and told me to sit down. He questioned me about my career so far and about my ambitions. He too was interested in my experience with sudden or unnatural deaths but emphasised that my task was to gain experience in all aspects of CID work. He said that there were a number of young officers and several cadets on the staff, and as a more mature member of staff he felt that I could set an example to these officers. I said that I would do my best. And so my work began.

25

Lightning Strike

Most of the work was routine at first. There were the mainly petty thefts to deal with, and of course the assaults and affrays, but on the third week I was sent out as part of a team to investigate a report that two little African girls, both about nine years of age, had been struck by lightning. I jumped into a Land Rover driven by a uniformed officer, and two African constables jumped into the back. We raced to the scene about a mile and a half away, driving through a torrential rainstorm with lightning flashes lighting up the almost black sky.

On arrival at the place of the lightning strike I saw a large crowd of Africans, most of them women, gathered around a small, wet bundle. We ran to the place where the child lay and the constables asked the crowd to move back to allow us to examine the child. We could see that she was not breathing so we commenced CPR (cardiopulmonary resuscitation) on her after instructing the two African officers to take the second girl, who appeared to be suffering from shock, to the vehicle.

The child upon whom we were working appeared normal apart from a small burn mark on the top of her head and some singeing of the hair around it. We would later find, upon closer examination, that she also had a corresponding burn mark on one of her feet, which showed the exit point of the strike. We continued with the CPR for several minutes but there was no evidence of a heartbeat or breathing being restored, and we decided to stop.

I suddenly felt totally drained and leaned forwards to close her eyes. As I did so I felt tears well up and start to slide down my cheeks. I was astonished. I had not cried since I was a baby, and I quickly raised my head, opened my eyes to the rain and let it wash my face. I then stood and we turned to the crowd. The parents came forward and we explained to them that we would have to take their child to be examined by a doctor, but they would receive her back in the morning, shortly after the doctor had seen her. We said how sorry we were that we could not save her but that she must have died instantly. They stood quietly as we spoke; then watched as we carried the child to our vehicle and placed her gently in the back.

The other small girl was still obviously very shocked and we were worried about her. We took her to hospital where she was admitted. She eventually made a full recovery.

The following morning I attended the post-mortem examination. At Choma I had become used to the various post-mortem procedures and the dissections did not bother me, but watching a post-mortem taking place on such a young child was an upsetting experience. As the body was opened up I was unprepared for, and horrified at, the damage that was revealed. Most of the major organs had been badly affected. Some had been virtually destroyed. Our attempts to resuscitate this child had always been doomed to failure. The fact that she had been killed instantly had been a blessing. I left the hospital in a sombre mood, which was noticed on my return to the station. The boss, as I shall call Assistant Superintendent Bruce from now onwards, came over and looked at me.

'Not good, a post-mortem on a little child, is it, David? I take it that this was your first PM on a young child. I've only ever done one lightning-strike PM myself and that was on an adult. There's nothing to be done about it. Just add it to your experience. You all did everything that could have been done at the scene, even if it was doomed from the start.'

I felt better for his words and got down to writing my report of the case, which would be heard by the coroner the next day.

The following morning the coroner heard the evidence in a quick, private meeting and gave permission for the release of the body to the waiting parents. A date was set for the official public hearing.

26

A Curious Affair

A couple of days after the lightning strike I was sent to investigate a possible suspicious death in a village about twenty miles west of Livingstone. By this time I had been given a detective constable, Musa, to work alongside me on sudden or suspicious death cases. I also had first call on a Land Rover and driver for this type of work. Musa was from the northern part of the province and I quickly found him to be intelligent and a quick thinker. Perhaps more importantly, he had a wicked sense of humour, which on several future occasions was to prove useful.

Not only had I acquired the use of a vehicle and the help of a good constable, but I had started to build up a box of kit based upon what I had learned I might need when working at Choma. I asked for and received a first-class camera as well as a full set of everything a scene-of-crime officer might need. This I kept in my room for instant use at night on callouts. I also wanted to keep it out of the reach of the other officers, who were notorious for "borrowing" things and not replacing them. And so we set out.

'Each new task an adventure, don't you think, Constable?'

'Indeed, *bwana*,' he replied with a half-smile.

As we reached a point about three quarters of a mile short of the village, we found that we could take the vehicle no further as a stream with steep banks barred our way. We continued on foot, leaving the driver to bring along my scene-of-crime box. We eventually came to the village where we found a large crowd of villagers assembled to meet us. A spokesman told us that a respected elder of the village had been acting strangely for some days and had not appeared from his hut that morning. He pointed and I saw that the hut in question was large and well built.

'Has nobody been into the hut to check on him?' I asked.

The man spoke rapidly in Tonga, a language in which Musa was fluent. When he had finished Musa turned to me and said that everyone in the village was too frightened to enter the hut.

'It is a special hut, *bwana*. It is black inside and no light can enter. No villager has ever entered this hut.'

I walked over towards the hut with Musa following. I could hear the rising voices of the villagers behind me, but I noticed that nobody was accompanying us. I decided to take a look inside the hut for myself. I told Musa to wait outside.

'Gladly, *bwana*,' he said with a grin.

I entered the hut and immediately was faced with a wall. I could make out a narrow passage to the right and turned into it. As I did so I realised that the light was almost gone and I paused to allow my eyes to further adjust. Feeling my way along the wall, I found that it turned to the left and I moved into pitch-darkness. Not the smallest glimmer of light existed. I may not have had light but I could detect the smell of death, and I knew that there was a body in the room. There is no other smell quite like that of a body that has started to decompose. The smell was everywhere as I circled the walls, banging into objects propped against them. I needed light and my torch was in my bag, which should be arriving shortly, carried by the driver. Moving more quickly now, I walked confidently but slowly towards the entrance, or at least towards where I estimated it should be. As I eased my way forward my knee came into contact with something hard, sharp and painful. What the hell was it, and where was I?

Reaching out ahead, I leaned to feel for whatever it was that I had bumped into. The object extended out to either side of where I stood, so I leaned past it to feel for anything beyond. I found what felt like a mattress, and then a leg. I moved my hands along it until I found a foot; then reversed and worked my way towards the head. I felt my way from shoulder to neck and there I found a noose. It was tight and had cut into the throat. This was not good. I shouted for Musa, hoping that my voice was loud enough to reach him through the twisting passageway.

Eventually he came. The torch had just arrived. I glanced around the room. There were not four walls but six, and this accounted for my disorientation. The old man lay on his back, almost lying at attention. The rope which ended in the noose was tied to the head of the bed. After photographing the scene I eventually cut the rope between the noose and where it was secured to the head of the bed, leaving the noose with its slipknot where it was, around the neck.

I walked with Musa out of the hut and was blinded by the light. The villagers were instructed to find something upon which to carry the deceased and put together some planks to form a stretcher. Musa and I then carried him with great difficulty out of the hut. I instructed the headman of the village to secure the hut and not to let anyone enter. I told him that I had set traps which would show if anyone had disobeyed my instructions. We then set off in procession, male villagers carrying the body and the women wailing as they walked behind.

On our return to Livingstone I took the body to the mortuary and the post-mortem was arranged for the following morning. I then returned to the station and had a good wash. I reported what I had found and had lunch. That afternoon, now equipped with a powerful lighting unit, Musa and I returned to the village. This time we were able to complete a search for any evidence to suggest foul play. We found none. The room contained only the bare essentials for a person living a frugal life. Nothing had been disturbed and there were no signs of a struggle or of any form of violent activity.

The following morning I asked the doctor carrying out the PM to search for any signs of violence to the body. I described the conditions in which we had found the deceased and showed him photographs of the body as we had found it. He was intrigued and took great care to cover all the points that I had raised.

At last, the PM completed, he turned to me and said, 'I have found nothing to suggest that this is anything but a suicide. I have dealt with many, many deaths by hanging but this is the first where it took place on a bed. In fact I don't think we should call it a hanging. I think we must say that it is death caused by self-inflicted strangulation. If you could let me have a copy of your photographs of the deceased in bed, before and after you cut the rope and moved him, I should be very grateful.'

I said that I would. We shook hands and I went back to the station to write up my notes and prepare the case for the coroner.

27

New Friends

As February moved into March, my experience in all types of policing grew and widened. My trips to see the coroner continued. Although I wasn't given every sudden and suspicious death case to deal with, I was given most of them.

On my visits to the court I had noticed a very attractive woman who worked as a stenographer for the court. On one visit I said hello and she asked me where I had come from before arriving in Livingstone. We talked and I learned that she was a Londoner and was married to Roy, another Londoner. He worked for the post office as an engineer dealing with telephonic communications.

She asked if I had made any friends in Livingstone. I replied that my friends were all police officers.

'Do you ride?' she asked.

'Only motorbikes,' I replied.

She laughed. 'I mean horses. Would you like to have a go?'

It sounded like a good idea, and I said that I would but didn't know if I would be any good at it.

'Come and have a try at the weekend. Do you have a car?'

I confessed that I didn't.

'Okay. Roy and I will pick you up at the police station after lunch on Saturday if you are off duty.'

I said that I was and we parted.

As arranged, Roy and Anita Jacomelli arrived to pick me up at the station just after lunch on the Saturday. As we drove south towards the Zambezi I learned that Anita's family name was Trincairo, and that her father was of Italian origin and was a well-known and respected chief chef in a large restaurant in London. Roy's name also sounded Italian but he said that he had no Italian origins that he knew of. I confessed to my father's father being Irish, from the south in Eire somewhere, but that my dad didn't talk about his family.

Eventually we arrived at the Livingstone Equitation and Saddle Club, reached by a long dirt track.

Anita pointed towards the south and said, 'The Zambezi is through those trees, about three quarters of a mile away.'

She then got out of the car and opened a heavy wooden gate, which guarded a large grassed area with stables along its far side.

'Come and meet the horses and their owners. There are some owners here now and others will probably turn up later.'

The afternoon passed quickly. Anita introduced me to her mare, mainly grey in colour and called Greyling. She told me that she was a kind animal with a happy disposition.

'Now make friends with her,' she said.

I did as instructed, talking quietly to the animal as I stroked her coat gently. I called her by her name and whispered in her ear, telling her what a beautiful animal she was. I had a treat which I placed on the palm of my hand and offered to her. She took it gently, played with it in her mouth and then swallowed it. She moved closer, gazing questioningly at me.

'Sorry, sweetheart, but I don't have any more,' I said, and she seemed to nod acceptance.

That afternoon I learned to ride Greyling at walking pace and to turn her using the pressure of my knees or a touch of the reins. From walking we eventually progressed to trotting, which I found most uncomfortable until I learned to move my body to match the rhythm of the horse. After about an hour Anita called a halt.

'We'll stop now, Dave, or you will hardly be able to walk tomorrow,' she said.

The rest of the afternoon I spent talking to the members of the club and helped with mucking out the stables and doing odd jobs. I also studied keenly how other people exercised and trained their horses. In the late afternoon Anita found me in a stable talking to one of the horse owners.

'Well, have you had a good time with us, Dave?'

I said that I had enjoyed myself very much.

'Would you like to join the club? The other members seem to like you.'

I said that I would be delighted to join, and looked up to hear Roy, who had just walked up say, 'We had better take him back for tea and sign him up before he starts to feel the pain of this afternoon's lesson.'

Everyone started laughing, and later that evening, in some discomfort, I realised why.

This was the start of a lasting friendship with two lovely people, and it made some of the more stressful periods of my job much more bearable.

28

VIP Protection

One afternoon I was sitting writing up an account of an arrest that I had made. I would eventually be summoned to give the evidence in court. As I looked over what I had written I was touched on the shoulder by one of the team, who told me that the boss wanted to see me. I left my desk, walked over to the boss' office and was invited in.

'How would you fancy a spell on the VIP protection team? It will just be occasional work when protection is needed. I see that your experience extends to a number of different army weapons including the .38 Webley revolver. It appears that you are a good shot and your national service experiences all indicate that you should be good at protection work.'

I wondered how he had got access to my army files, but I didn't ask.

'The weapon that we use in protection is the Smith & Wesson .45 Chief Special. You'll receive a short course on its use and on VIP protection. Basically it's about putting your body on the line for whoever you are protecting. You will work with me as a close protection officer. We will usually work in conjunction with the client's own close protection officer. Further away from the client there will be a mix of uniformed officers and officers in plain clothes, and then beyond them, if needed, the crowd control uniformed officers. Right then, I'll arrange an induction course for you. By the way, you'll still be expected to keep up with all your CID work.'

The training turned out to be very brief and was followed by some familiarisation training with the Chief Special, a weapon I found rather cumbersome.

I did not have long to wait before being called upon to provide protection for my first VIP. It was not an exciting job. It involved a lot of waiting about until the person being guarded came out of meetings, and then escorting them to their next local destination. Fortunately, at night they were under protection of their own personal bodyguards.

Protection work was not glamorous. It was tiring work which required a constant state of alertness and an ability to assess possible dangers, but we protected some interesting people. Many of these people were just spending a brief period in Livingstone and were often on the way to somewhere else. One such was Harold Wilson who, a few months later, would become leader of the British Labour Party and subsequently Prime Minister of Great Britain.

One of my last protection duties in Livingston involved an important high-ranking official from the Congo. Unfortunately I cannot recall his name. He was a pleasant gentleman and spoke perfect English. He was, unfortunately, accompanied by a gang of undesirables who, until we disarmed them, flourished their guns in public and generally behaved like thugs. They also appeared to be affected by drugs. We took over close protection duties, having ensured that the bodyguards had lodged their weapons in our armoury despite their protests.

One evening, in a bar in the town, the so-called bodyguards were getting drunk. One of them had concealed a pistol down his sock and decided to show off by drawing it in front of other drinkers in the bar. In pulling the gun out of his sock he discharged it and shot himself in the leg. His gun was confiscated and he was taken to hospital for treatment.

The man we had guarded left the following day, closely guarded by the thugs, and was never seen alive again after being driven away in a car from the airport at which he had landed in the Congo. There were rumours that he had been tortured and then killed, but we heard no more. I can't say that I enjoyed the protection work, but it was interesting.

29

Alcohol

In April 1960 a number of things of note happened. As instructed upon arrival in Livingstone, I had spent a couple of nights each week going for a drink in one bar or another in Livingstone. I gradually got to know a number of people who became friends. I made no effort to disguise the fact that I was a CID officer or that I would appreciate any help they may be able to give me in preventing or solving crime. I gave them limited details about cases we were working on where help would be appreciated. I bought more than my share of drinks.

Talking of drinks and drinking, I had found out very quickly that drinking alcohol did not agree with me. I would often return to my room after an evening drinking session with my contacts and spend half an hour or so being violently sick in my bathroom. After about a month of this I decided to give up drinking alcohol, which obviously did not agree with me and provided me with no pleasure. I invented a stomach ulcer and turned to soft drinks and to a better life. No more being called out at night with a hangover or going into the office in a morning with a headache. I haven't drunk alcohol since that time, except perhaps for a toast at a wedding or at someone's birthday party.

From early in my time in Livingstone I had developed a friendship with a CID officer of the BSAP (British South Africa Police) on the Southern Rhodesia side of the Victoria Falls. I also got to know the customs people on both sides of the river. It became easy to informally meet each other and chat about police matters. We passed each other names and descriptions of people we wanted to arrest or question and talked about the political situation in each country.

We usually had a drink in the Victoria Falls Hotel on his side of the river, and he learned of my aversion to alcohol and was happy to buy me a soft drink. I kept the boss informed of my visits and he approved. Occasionally useful pieces of information came my way and I was also able to help my friend at various times. We sometimes treated each other to dinner to celebrate.

The distance between Livingstone and the Victoria Falls is just over six miles and the single main north-south road joined the two. Partway down the road, nearer to Livingstone than to the falls, was a restaurant called The Falls Tea Rooms. This was a favourite place for a night out for many people in Livingstone, and we in the police were no exceptions.

Every two or three weeks a group of us would drive down there and spend the evening having pre-dinner drinks while watching the spectacular sunsets from the veranda. I was a popular driver as I didn't drink alcohol and always took four passengers.

The food served at the tea rooms was excellent, as was the service. Trout grilled in butter was my favourite meal, although I varied it from time to time. I tried the crab that they served but wasn't keen on the process involved in killing it by dropping it into boiling water. The desserts that were served were to die for. In those days I could eat anything and not put on an ounce of weight, so I indulged myself. The visits to the tea rooms formed an enjoyable part of life in Livingstone.

Drivers travelling along the road down to the Victoria Falls at night had to be wary. The road lay between the river and prime grazing land, which was often frequented by hippopotami. To reach the grazing area the animals had to cross this busy road. There were many near misses and an occasional accident, which usually involved a car swerving off the road and into the bush to miss an animal. Once the hippos reached the grazing area they tended to stay there during part of the night, returning to the river in the early hours of the following morning. These animals were very dangerous to approach, especially if they had young with them. Fortunately most people knew this and kept their distance.

30

Tip-off

The drinking friendships I have mentioned provided fairly useful information in several cases that year, but our relationships really bore fruit the following year when one of my "friends" came to find me in the cinema one evening. He told me that he had heard that a gang of African youths who had been raiding stores and committing housebreaking offences were meeting that evening to share out some of their ill-gotten gains. He knew where they would be meeting. I didn't ask where the information came from.

We left the cinema and returned to the station where a team of uniformed and CID officers was assembled from those on duty. Several of the off-duty officers were invited to come as well. Everyone who worked at the station had been frustrated by the break-ins, which had been going on for many months but had been investigated without success. Extra patrols had also had no effect. We set off in three vehicles and, guided by my friend, stopped a hundred yards or so short of the house where the criminals were supposed to be meeting. It was a house on the edge of the European area of Livingstone, and of the type which would most likely be occupied by an African or Asian civil servant. My friend then excused himself and quickly left us.

Officers were organised to block all exits from the house and I was given the honour of knocking on the door. To my great relief it was opened by an African lad aged about sixteen or seventeen.

I identified myself and said, 'Are you going to ask us in?'

He looked beyond me and his face fell as he saw the backup. He beckoned us to come in. Inside we found the rest of what turned out to be the gang. We also found huge amounts of all types of stolen property. The four lads were arrested and gave us no trouble. The parents were out and a note was left for them to contact the station.

The following day the station was alive with officers checking the goods we had recovered and calling people to come to the station to identify their property. As the goods had been taken and immediately hidden away, they were still in the same condition as they had been when they were stolen. The boys pleaded guilty and even confessed to several more burglaries that had not been reported. A good number of cases were cleared up and my friend received a substantial reward for his services sometime later.

31

Heatstroke

June and July were the most pleasant months of the year. The temperature began to fall in April and continued to fall until partway through July, when it began to rise again. There was little rainfall between April and September and the humidity fell steadily from March to September, after which it started to rise again with the onset of the rains.

On the 13th May we had a royal visit from the Queen Mother, who arrived from Kariba where she had that morning officially opened the Kariba Dam. She had several visits to pay in Livingstone and was heavily guarded by her royal protection team, who had accompanied her from London. Don Bruce joined them but I wasn't needed, so I was given the job of keeping watch on the airport, and on the royal plane, of course. I spent half a day under a blazing sun looking through powerful binoculars. I was positioned on top of the airport buildings and in the process of concentrating on the job in hand, managed to ignore the fact that I was developing a blinding headache.

By the time the Queen Mother and her entourage had taken off on their way home, I was having difficulty focusing my eyes and was on the point of collapse. Somebody was sent to look for me and found me in such a state that I was rushed to hospital, but I have no memory of this happening.

I am told that in hospital I became violent and floored one poor nurse with a blow to the jaw. I was held down and injected with a drug called paraldehyde, a central nervous system depressant. I then slept for two days, awaking to a vile smell. I quickly realised that the smell was emanating from my own body as the drug, or what it had turned into, oozed out through my skin.

I was told about what had happened and made a grovelling apology to the nurse I had knocked down. She was very good about it, and on my release I took her flowers and a very, very large box of chocolates.

I was amazed that when serving in the army I had been stationed and worked in far hotter places than Livingstone and had never suffered heatstroke. But then, of course, I hadn't been using high-powered binoculars for such a long, unbroken period. My lesson had been learned; especially when the boss, showing no sympathy at all, told me that I was a bloody idiot if I didn't I know that I should have taken frequent rests from using the binoculars.

32

Flight from the Belgian Congo

On the 4th July, shortly after the granting of independence to the Belgian Congo, the main body for ensuring stability in that country, the Force Publique, mutinied. In the riots and the general mayhem that followed, murder, rape, looting and destruction of property took place. People of European origin in various parts of the Congo were the main targets and victims, and fled the country in large numbers.

In Livingstone we had received advance warning that convoys of vehicles, carrying mainly white and Asian families, were fleeing south and that large numbers should be expected to pass through Livingstone. We were to help these people in every possible way.

As predicted, large numbers of cars and vans did arrive and we did what we could to help. People needed places in which to wash themselves and their children, and obviously toilets were much in demand. By the time the convoys arrived in Livingstone most of the vehicles were in good shape, having been serviced in the Copperbelt and Lusaka.

The people, on the other hand, were haggard and tired. All they wanted to do was to move as far south and away from the Congo as possible. Many had harrowing stories to tell. Some had seen friends or relatives murdered by rioting mobs. It made many local people wonder whether such events could ever happen in Northern Rhodesia. Fortunately, nothing like that ever did. The British administration, including the civil service and police, had established, over many years, a structure which had served the country well, unlike the Belgian administration, which had left the Congo in a mess.

33

Leisure Time

Being a police officer and on call several nights each week in addition to normal day shifts sounds hard, but I also had plenty of leisure time, especially at weekends. There were obviously exceptions where sporting and leisure activities took second place, but on the whole football, cricket and equestrian activities occupied my time at weekends.

My horse-riding was progressing steadily and I gradually got to know all the horses and their owners personally. I was now able to ride competently at the canter and gallop and was deemed a safe enough rider to accompany other riders on the road running alongside the Zambezi above the Victoria Falls.

However, just as I began to think that I had mastered the art of riding, I found that I was wrong. One Sunday afternoon I was offered a ride on Flash, the club's star jumper. This was indeed an honour, especially as we were going to ride down the road alongside the river. On a Sunday there were always cars driving slowly along it as well as walkers enjoying the views.

Flash was the club's only stallion and he had a mind of his own. He didn't want to go for a Sunday walk. He loved to gallop, and failing that he wanted to go back to the stables. I didn't know this, of course. On our way out towards the river Flash started to play up. I had to urge him on with my knees when he kept trying to turn back, and I began to ache with effort of pushing him on. Eventually we reached the Zambezi and continued our walk until we came to the point of turning back towards the club. I turned him round. Now he was happy and became a different horse, reacting to instructions and nudges from my legs.

I should have known that this was too good to last. Anita came up alongside on her horse and said quietly, 'Watch him, Dave. He's ready to take off.'

As she was speaking the horse leaped forwards. I almost lost my seat, but thanks to Anita's warning I had a tight hold on the reins and pulled him back under control. On the way back along Riverside Drive he tried three times to bolt. By now I was growing tired. My arms and legs ached and I felt that I was close to losing the battle.

I was just wondering whether it would be best to dismount and lead him the rest of the way to the stables when he took off at full speed and I was left hanging on for dear life. I leaned back in the saddle, and with all my strength pulled back on the reins. His head was forced round until he was almost looking back towards where other riders were watching in horror. It had no effect and I had to let him turn his head to the front again to avoid him crashing into cars or people, but considering the way he was galloping, I feared that he didn't care. Then, without warning, he swerved to the left, jumped the large ditch at the side of the road and galloped into the bush.

As we galloped I realised that he was heading directly towards the stables, which lay beyond the trees and about a mile away. There was only one problem. Immediately ahead of us, about a hundred yards away and lying directly across our path, was a huge concrete drainage channel. Such channels were used to carry floodwater into the Zambezi in the wet season. It was about eight feet deep and must have been all of sixteen to eighteen feet wide at the top. I had a sudden picture of Flash and myself lying dead at the bottom of the channel, and without further thought, kicked my feet out of the stirrups and rolled off the horse, landing about twenty feet short of the edge of the channel. I hit the ground on my left side and rolled on to my shoulder. I felt pain throughout my body and was bleeding from grazes in a number of places. My head was spinning and I couldn't hear properly. There was no sign of Flash.

With great trepidation I staggered towards the drain and peered over the edge. There was no body, no equine fatality. I sat down in relief, already feeling slightly better.

Sometime later I heard shouting in the distance and looked up to see an anxious line of people moving towards me. As they spotted me they began to run. I heard a voice say, 'Good grief, look at the state of him. He's covered in blood.'

And so I was, but it came from grazes and looked far worse than it really was.

'Come on, Dave,' Anita said. 'On your feet. Let's get you back to the stables. You need to get back up on Flash. Let him see that he hasn't won.'

She helped me up and I was helped back to the club. Once there, and with some misgiving, I got back up on Flash. He was a different animal. We trotted and galloped around the training area and he was as sweet as honey (the bastard). Everything I asked him to do, he did without hesitation, but he had a gleam in his eyes.

In July 1960 Mr Hanna the senior resident magistrate and coroner for the Southern Province, joined the club. In my dealings with him in court in Choma and in Livingstone I had always found him to be a very pleasant man and easy to talk to. Off duty he was just one of the club's members. He came to the club with his horse Manners and a reputation for success in jumping events. My friendship with Roy and Anita blossomed and I always had somewhere to go to relieve the stress of some of the more upsetting cases that I had to deal with.

34

Death by Lion

In late July I was called into the boss' office and instructed to go to Ngoma in the Kafue National Park to investigate the death of a child. The child, a little girl about six or seven years old, had been killed by a lion at Ngoma, the main administration site for the park. The park itself covered 8,600 square miles. Ngoma lay to the north of Livingstone and was a drive of 127 miles over poor dirt roads.

I reached my destination after about three hours of hard driving.

When I arrived at Norman Carr's headquarters I was greeted sadly by the great man. He was dressed in a loose, open-necked grey shirt and long grey trousers, and he looked strained and upset.

'If you would like to see them, I have put both lions in an enclosure, which they hate. They are used to complete freedom to come and go as they please,' he said.

'I think that I had better view the body first,' I replied.

'I'm afraid the parents have taken her to the village.'

'I have to see the body. Would you come with me to the village?'

'Of course,' he replied.

When we arrived at the village I spoke quietly with the mother and father of the little girl and explained that the body would have to go to Livingstone so that a doctor could see it. I also informed them that there would probably be a court case. Norman said that he would be willing to take the parents, relatives and the body to Livingstone and would drive back with me in convoy. I noticed that the parents did not seem to be blaming anyone for the death of their child. Norman Carr was well liked and respected by the African population everywhere he went.

I decided that it was time to interview witnesses. Before we left I briefly examined the dead child. There was not a mark on her body except for a faint reddening of the left side of her neck. I noted, however, that her head was at an angle to the rest of her body. As I examined it more closely it became obvious that the neck was broken. There was no evidence of claw or bite marks anywhere on her body, so it appeared that she had received a single slap from a closed paw.

On the return trip to the camp, Norman, who had rescued the two lion cubs when their mother had died and had subsequently brought them up, was very quiet. He was obviously upset. He was revered in Africa as the man who first introduced the idea of national parks and was instrumental in developing them. He had developed the Kafue National Park to the extent that it could be safely handed over to others to run. He was due, shortly, to go and take over and develop the South Luangwa National Park. He was famous for persuading Africans to protect the animals instead of shooting them, and in return receive money gained from the tourist trade. Villagers also benefited from the culling of animals to maintain the required balance of their populations. Money plus meat from culls was attractive to them, as was the possibility of employment by the national parks. He became very successful in his profession, and famous not only in Africa.

When we arrived back at his camp I asked him to bring me anyone who might have witnessed the death. He had not witnessed it himself but had run to the little girl upon hearing the other children screaming. I talked to several children who had witnessed what had happened. I asked Norman to put my questions to them in their own language, in the exact form in which I posed them, and to give me their replies in the exact words they used. This he did and we gradually formed a picture of what had happened.

Despite there being a rule that strangers were not allowed to visit the compound and surrounding area without permission, the local children had that morning invited the little girl into the camp. She was from another village and had been visiting the nearby village with her parents. The local children, whose parents worked at the camp doing various jobs, had the free run of the camp and had invited her to come with them to see the lions. Upon sighting Big Boy she had panicked and run away, screaming. Big Boy, sensing a game, had chased after her and tapped her on the head to stop her. The children said that he then lay alongside her purring, and seemed to be waiting for her to get up and continue the game.

I wrote my report for the coroner. The case never came to a trial. It was found to be death by misadventure. The coroner expressed his heartfelt condolences to the family who, after the post-mortem, took the body back for burial in her home village.

35

Livingstone Villa

Shortly after arriving in Livingstone I had asked for, and been given, a trial for the position of goalkeeper for Livingstone Villa, the top club in the Southern Province Football League. I was lucky in applying at the time that I did. At the end of the previous season the team's regular keeper had returned to South Africa. I was signed on and started training with the team. I soon got to know them all and found that, for an amateur team, they possessed a high standard of ability.

Our captain, Glen Doherty, played for the Northern Rhodesia national side and led our team by example. Because of Livingstone's geographical position in the far south of the country and its location in a province which had no large towns apart for Livingstone, our football league comprised only five teams. To add to this number we recruited two teams from a coal-mining town eighty miles away in Southern Rhodesia.

In 1960 football played by Africans took place largely on football pitches located in the African townships. There were no multiracial teams. Surprisingly for an all-white team, we commanded quite a crowd of African supporters each week. The football season was largely confined to the period of April to September. The ground was hard and parched for most of that period, and until the final month of the season, we rarely had rain. My knees rapidly became grazed, and as the scabs were just about healing towards the end of each week, they were opened up again the following Sunday. I soon settled in and played well enough to eventually be given a trial for the Northern Rhodesia national team.

In 1960, the team had an excellent season. We won all our games in the Southern Province League and gradually progressed in the Northern Rhodesia FA Cup. Having disposed of the local opposition we were drawn to play against our first team from the north, the much-fancied Lusaka Municipals, later to become City of Lusaka.

The newspapers concentrated upon a final, as they saw it, between Lusaka and Nchanga, the favourites from the Copperbelt who had won the cup in the previous two years. The people behind the Lusaka team had visions of making the capital's top team a presence in Central African football. We as a team were largely ignored by the national papers. The *Central African Post* and the *Northern News* had little to say in our favour. Playing in Livingstone, so far south, we were not known and were hardly considered. You could say we were off the radar. We had to make do with only hopeful support from our own weekly local newspaper, the *Livingstone Mail*.

The semi-finals and the final were scheduled to take place at Nchanga over the weekend of the 27th–28th August. Traditionally the previous year's winners hosted the following year's final and we had a journey of some 551 miles to make on the Friday in order to play on the Saturday.

Earlier in the year I had taken out a bank loan and had bought a 1956 model Morris Minor. We split the team members between the available cars and I was asked to take four of the team with me, which I did. It made for an uncomfortable journey for the three in the back and I was forced to arrange a rota system so that everyone had a turn in the front seat. When we finally arrived at Nchanga in the early evening, having set out shortly after midnight the previous night, we were, to put it mildly, knackered.

On arrival we were almost overwhelmed by the friendliness and the generosity of our hosts. Everything had been arranged for us. We were all to stay with families in the area. I found that I was to stay with the family of one of the Nchanga team. Nothing was too much trouble for our hosts. Before we split up to go to our various accommodations, Glen instructed us to meet before breakfast the following morning for a run and some loosening exercises. We were to play in the morning game against Lusaka, with Nchanga scheduled to play the Broken Hill Railway team in the afternoon. The local spectators could then enjoy the cup final on Sunday afternoon.

Our game against Lusaka surprised the press, the pundits, the spectators, but most of all the Lusaka team and their officials. We held the Lusaka team's attacks, which came often in the first twenty minutes, and then scored ourselves on the counter-attack. In the second half we scored our second goal after ten minutes and our third seven minutes later. We then eased back.

However, our long journey to Nchanga had taken its toll of the team's stamina. If there is one thing a defence hates, it is to have its forwards falling back and crowding it, which gives the opponents a chance to take over the attacking initiative. The Lusaka team, with the freedom to press, did so and scored their first goal with ten minutes of the game left. They scored again five minutes later and our tired players, realising that extra time, if Lusaka scored again, would finish us off, pulled themselves together and saw out the remaining few minutes of the game.

Nchanga easily won the other semi-final that afternoon, beating the Broken Hill Railway team nine-nil. Most of us didn't watch this game. We went back to our rooms and went to bed.

On Sunday, acting on instructions from our trainer and Glen, we stayed in bed until about eleven o'clock and then reported for a loosening set of exercises. There were groans as painful limbs were forced to operate, and generally the players were lethargic. I felt that I would be in for a busy afternoon, and so it was.

Nchanga had six players on their team who played for the national team, and the other five were very useful. Our captain also played for the country, but none of the rest of us did. We were massive underdogs and I reckoned that we would do well to keep the score down to single figures. You only had to look at our team to see how tired and lacklustre we were.

In the end we lost the game by six goals to one. We had at least scored against them. I felt that if we had not had such a long journey getting to Nchanga we might have at least kept the score down to a more respectable level. It turned out to be the one game in my life when I was involved in defending my goal for the whole of the match. There were no peaceful periods when our team were on the attack.

The Copperbelt newspapers were very kind to me.

The *Northern News* of the 29th August said, and I quote:

By the end of the game, McCue, having been continually tested, came off the field as one of the most tired footballers of the game.

The *Nchanga News* of the 2nd September said:

Goalkeeper McCue's performance must surely rank him as one of Northern Rhodesia's best.

I must admit that my spirits were lifted by these remarks. After thanking our hosts and arranging a visit by Nchanga to Livingstone for Easter 1961, we set off on the journey home. The journey was horrendous and I had to stop several times for us all to have a rest. We arrived back in Livingstone on Monday afternoon and I went straight to bed. I needed to be fit for duty the following day.

36

Railway Accident

Some days later, just as I arrived in the CID office to start work for the day, I was instructed to get down to the Livingstone railway goods yard to investigate a report of a fatality.

Taking a uniformed officer with me, I drove down to the station, parked the vehicle and walked into the goods yard. A crowd had gathered and were looking in horror at the remains of a body lying partly under the wheels of one of a line of goods wagons, which I learned had been in the process of being shunted to a far part of the goods yard when the accident had happened.

I viewed the body. It lay on its back, the right leg vertical to where the foot was wrapped round a horizontal structure above the wheel. The left leg and arm were missing, as was the head. It was time to take photographs. As I did so I instructed the constable, who was looking rather queasy, to find witnesses to the accident and to get their names and addresses.

Having taken photographs I pulled on my overalls and set off to find the missing body parts. I didn't have far to look for the arm and the leg, but the head proved rather more difficult to find. It had rolled for some distance. It was discovered by one of the searchers, who declined my suggestion that he might like to crawl under the wagon and retrieve it for me.

Having photographed the head and other body parts in situ, and having personally retrieved them, I got help to load them on to our truck to take them to the mortuary. The four most reliable witnesses were rounded up and told to report to the police station. They all worked for the railway and would still get paid for helping us in working hours. On my return to the station I went to find the boss.

'Have you finished with the rail accident yet?' he asked.

'Yes, I've handed it over to uniform. Why did we take it? It was always going to be their case.'

He started to laugh. 'Well, after all the charging about on horseback and playing football on the Copperbelt, I thought that you might appreciate a nice juicy body to add to your portfolio.'

37

Identification

In early September I was sent upriver from Livingstone to recover a body from the Zambezi. By now I had a team of African police officers including Sergeant Musa who, when I made a request, were attached to me. I took an open-backed truck and we set off. The location of the body was not far from the town, and was upriver from the falls. It was in a quiet stretch of the river where the flow of the water was relatively slow.

When we arrived at the scene I was pleased to see that the body had already been removed from the water by the local villagers.

I first examined the dead man without touching him. He was a well-nourished black African and I estimated his age to be between thirty-five and forty-five. He was dressed in a well-cut suit and was wearing an expensive shirt, compared to the normal cheap African clothing. He was also wearing good shoes and socks. I then searched through his pockets for clues to establish his identity. There were none. His pockets were empty. I took photographs of the body and of the scene, using an African villager to stand and point to where the body had first been seen. Musa questioned the other possible witnesses to see if there were any clues which might aid us in establishing how the body came to be in the river. I was told that the deceased had not been there the previous evening. No sounds such as splashing or a scream or a cry for help had been heard. There was nothing else we could do at the scene. The officers whom I had sent to check the riverbank, both up- and downstream, had found nothing.

We loaded him up and took him to the mortuary. The post-mortem was arranged for the following morning.

On arrival for the PM the next day I was glad to see that John, my favourite Livingstone pathologist, would be conducting it. As the dead man's clothes were removed I went through them meticulously in an effort to find some form of identification. I found none. There was nothing in the pockets and the clothing bore no labels. We checked the body for any form of injury. We found none. I began to think that all forms of identification had been removed on purpose, either by the deceased or by a third party. The body had no identifying marks, which was unusual. Most people have some sort of identifying mark. We had a mystery. Maybe when he was opened up there would be some clue as to how he had died.

As the PM progressed I began to realise that this was going to be a difficult case. The lungs revealed that he had drowned. There were no injuries to the body, no other forms of trauma, no bruising. I asked the doctor if he would take samples to check for poisoning and alcohol and he agreed, adding that he would carry out a complete toxicological check. This would eliminate or reveal the possibility of poisoning, accidental or otherwise. I then took a number of photographs of the dead man's face for circulation in the local African township in case no relative or friend reported him missing in the next couple of days.

On leaving the mortuary I called in at the local chemist and asked the owner, who also ran a photograph developing and printing business, to urgently develop the photographs of the deceased's face that I had taken during the PM. He said that he would do them immediately. In 1960 we did not have the technical facilities that would be taken for granted today.

Later that day I took a copy of the best photograph to my friend, the editor of the *Livingstone Mail*, and asked her if she would publish it in the next edition of the paper, which was due out three days later. She said that she would be delighted to do this and would include details of the death and an appeal for anyone who knew the identity of the deceased to contact the police.

Time passed, and after a week we still had no idea of the deceased's identity. The post-mortem had revealed no suspicious details. It was, so far as the pathologist was concerned, a straightforward drowning, but I was uneasy. Normally, with a dead body I would take fingerprints and circulate them, but with this body that would be impossible due to the state of decomposition. I also knew that if nobody claimed the body within a few more days the coroner would have no option but to order Livingstone Council to bury it.

I decided to ask for the coroner's permission to try to remove the skin from the deceased's hands in an attempt to take fingerprints from it. I had thought of a way by which I might do this. Having received the go-ahead, I met with the pathologist again and asked if he would remove the skin of both hands, starting from the wrists. Having taken the body out of the cooler, he examined the hands. The low temperature had slowed down any further decomposition, but looking at the hands, I began to wonder if I was being overly optimistic about what I hoped to achieve.

My friend took out a scalpel and stood for some time looking at the body.

'I shall make an incision around the wrist, a few inches above the hand,' John said. 'We will soon find out if this is feasible. The skin is so sloppy that it may slide off, but then again it may stick and tear. If it does tear then I'm afraid that your idea will not work. By the way, you do realise that if I am able to remove them, the skins could be inside out and it will be up to you to puzzle out how to obtain prints?'

I said that I understood and thanked him for going along with me this far. As it happened, we were lucky. The skin of both hands did not slide off but rolled off, and no damage occurred. Now it was up to me.

I left the CID office directly after lunch, leaving a note to say where I would be. I took the skins to a sandy piece of ground halfway between the police station and our accommodation area. I spread a towel on the ground and placed the skins upon it. I had washed them in cold water by gently running the water over them, and had started to dry them in the sun. Meanwhile, placing a plastic glove that I had taken from the kitchen on my right hand, I rubbed a thin ointment that I had bought at the chemist's over my left hand and wrist. I then took the skin from the deceased's right hand, and with my right hand, now gloveless, tried to feed the inside-out skin on to the fingers of my left hand. I couldn't do it. The slippery and floppy skin kept sliding off. As I introduced one dead finger to my own finger, I lost control of the other "inside-out fingers". (If you are having difficulty visualising this, don't worry. My right hand was the controlling hand and my left hand was the receiving hand for both skins. For one skin my left palm was face down and for the other face up.)

I pondered upon what to do. Then I had an idea. I needed something upon which to rest my receiving hand and arm, and also the dead skin. Then I could work one finger at a time and slowly introduce the skin to my fingers, with the support taking care of any slipping off. Placing the skin carefully on the towel, I went to my room, took the low table which I used for holding magazines and papers and returned to my "surgery". I bent down, folded the towel and placed it on the table. I then knelt down and laid my arm on it. I carefully put the skin in position, middle fingertip touching middle fingertip, thumb opposite thumb but not yet touching. It seemed obvious that I should start with the longer middle finger. If I could establish a gentle penetration of the dead skin by my middle finger, the fingers either side would follow, and so on.

Gently, I eased the dead skin towards and then over the nail of my middle finger.

It works, I thought, it bloody well works.

'Good grief. What the hell are you doing?' demanded a loud voice in my ear. I was so startled that my body made an involuntary jump and I almost lost control of the hand.

'Don't ever creep up on me like that again, you idiot. You almost wrecked what I'm trying to do,' I shouted.

It was one of the European uniformed staff, and he was looking queasy. I explained what I was trying to do but he walked away, shaking his head.

By the time I had managed to insert my hand halfway into the dead skin I was able, very slowly and very carefully, to pull the rest of it over my own hand. By now there were a small number of both on-duty and off-duty officers standing in a silent group, watching. The second hand was easier, as I had learned from the first attempt, and finally I held two hands with fingers waiting to be printed, except they were not ready.

What I possessed were two sloppy hand skins, which needed to be treated before they would be of any use. The afternoon was hot, and the sand where I was working was hot. It gave me an idea. I asked a junior member of the watching group to get me a medium-sized spoon from the kitchen, and with this I began to gently ladle small amounts of hot sand into one of the skins. As more sand dribbled in and started to fill the fingers, I balanced the skin, now about a third full, on the palm of my hand.

By doing everything so slowly, I believed that a drying process had already started. Giving the first hand a rest, I followed the same procedure with the other hand. Eventually both of the hands were packed with sand and, by having worked so slowly and carefully, I had succeeded in maintaining the shape of each of them almost perfectly.

I now selected the hottest part of the area and dug two shallow holes. Into each hole I placed, very carefully, a packed skin. I next removed hot top sand from a nearby area. I used this to pack gently under and around each hand until both were buried. I marked the spot carefully and told the assembled officers to tell those who had not been there to keep clear of the area.

I went back to the office and told Assistant Superintendent Bruce what I had done. He asked me to come and get him when I was ready to take the hands out of the sand. I left them for another two and a half hours and then, together with the boss, most of the CID team and a group of uniformed officers, went to the burial site. I carefully removed the sand from around each hand and lifted them out. Both hands were hard and solid with the sand inside them. I carefully turned the left hand so that the sand trickled out of it and was thrilled to feel the toughness of it. I then emptied the sand out of the other hand. I felt that if I were to give them a good tap against the table, which still stood in place, they would not break, but I had no intention of chancing it. I allowed the hands to be passed around, keeping a sharp watch in case someone decided to mess about, but nobody did. They were all very quiet.

'What would you suggest doing now?' the boss asked.

'I'd send the hands to HQ in Lusaka for checking by the fingerprint department to see if they have a record of him in this country. If they don't I would ask them to circulate the photos with copies of the prints to all the neighbouring countries, and to South Africa. I would also check with customs to see if there were any details of the deceased in their records. It might also be worth checking hospital records in this and the other countries we are contacting.'

'I agree with you,' he replied, 'but don't worry about doing all this yourself. We'll get a team working on it. I'll put some of the people who came to watch today on to it and I think the cadets could be part of it. There's nothing like a real case to boost their morale and sense of worth.'

'Would you also ask Force Headquarters what they are going to do with the hands when they've finished with them?' I asked.

'Will do, but I bet that they will be put in the police museum at HQ.'

And so they were. The boss received a congratulatory call from Lusaka, which he passed on to me. The team worked hard during the following weeks, even extending the areas covered, but to no avail. The case remained unsolved and the man was buried in a pauper's grave, but at least I felt that we had done our best for him.

38

Samene William Mwape

In late October 1960 I happened to be in the station reception area near to the holding cells when two African male prisoners who were handcuffed together were brought in. One of them, a well-built man, was obviously drunk and was resisting being put into a holding cell.

I told the African officers to get a grip of the situation and turned to face the booking-in desk with my back to the struggling prisoner. The next thing I knew I was lying face down, in pain from a blow to the right side of my head. I managed to roll into a sitting position, facing the handcuffed prisoners. As I did so the prisoner, whom I later found was named Samene William Mwape, drove his foot into my stomach. I could not breathe, but saw that every officer within sight or sound of the attack had converged on Mwape and thrown him to the ground, taking the man handcuffed to him down with them. I found myself being attended by two anxious African officers, who were asking if I was alright. I was far from being alright.

Eventually I managed to get my breath back and, with help, got to my feet. I was in severe pain. I felt that some real damage had been done to my stomach and I was dizzy from the blow to my head.

I was taken to hospital for an examination. Nothing sinister appeared on the X-ray but my head still troubled me. I found that my hearing was affected by buzzing noises and my balance was shaky. I was told to take a couple of days off work, but to report back to the hospital if the stomach pain did not ease or the trouble with my hearing and balance did not clear itself.

Needless to say, things did correct themselves in time. Mwape was eventually sentenced to six months' imprisonment with hard labour.

I mention the case because, several years later, Samene William entered my life again.

39

Evacuation by Air

Everything settled down as the work of identifying the "hands" body finally came to a halt. We retained, of course, all the evidence, photographic, medical etc., in case we had, some day in the future, to reopen the case.

Later in the month I was called into the office. The boss was seated at his desk, looking sombre.

'Come in, David,' he said. 'We have an emergency at Mulobezi. A constable, not one of ours but from further north, was brought in by villagers this morning. He has been stabbed and they don't think that he will last much longer. We have hired a plane and pilot to try to bring him to Livingstone in the hope of saving him. I want you to go in the plane and bring him back. Do you know what a dying declaration is?'

'Of course I do, sir,' I replied, 'but a dying declaration has to sworn in front of a magistrate or other high official.'

'That's correct, but there is nothing to stop you taking a dying declaration down in writing in the hope that he survives long enough to affirm to the magistrate that what he has said to you *is* his dying declaration. You know the format, I assume?'

'Yes, of course I do, sir,' I answered.

'Please say it for me.'

I gave him a reproachful look, but commenced to say as follows:

'"I [name of dying person], believing myself to be dying and having no hope of recovery, state as follows..." And then you take the statement and ask any necessary questions.'

He smiled at me. 'The plane is waiting at the airport and will take off as soon as you board. Conditions will be rough, I've been told. Have you had a good breakfast?'

'My usual: a large bowl of cornflakes with three quarters of a pint of milk,' I answered.

'Oh dear,' he said, and smiled at me again.

I asked one of the uniformed guys to drive me to the airport and he did so, enjoying using his flashing lights and siren.

'I don't often get the chance to use these,' he said.

He took great delight in racing down the runway to where the plane waited, its engines already turning over. I thanked him for the ride and boarded the plane, which I saw was large enough to take a stretcher.

'You'd better strap in tightly. We are in for a rough trip,' the pilot said.

As I strapped in I looked at the sky, which was covered by a dark layer of low, heavy cloud. The rains had started a few weeks earlier and the humidity was approaching its ceiling. There had been a couple of thundery afternoons the previous week and the temperature was almost at its maximum for the year.

Marvellous – that reduces our chances of getting our injured constable back alive, I thought.

The first part of the flight was not too bad. The pilot and I got talking and I discovered that he was one of the pilots who had attacked the German battleship *Bismarck* in 1941 when flying a torpedo carrying Fairey Swordfish of the Fleet Air Arm. It was this air attack which crippled the *Bismarck* by smashing its steering, and allowed the navy to sink it. I was flying with a war hero, now long retired from the Fleet Air Arm. I felt much more confident with him as the weather steadily deteriorated.

He brought the plane down from under the clouds and we flew at about two to three hundred feet above the trees. Even at this height the visibility was poor. Eventually I saw the Saw Mills railway line, which we followed as it turned towards the north and we left the Zambezi behind us. After flying a further seventy miles we saw, though hardly visible through the driving rain, several flashing lights, and beyond them the lights of Mulobezi. I could see a cleared space in the bush and assumed this to be our landing strip. This was confirmed by the pilot.

'This isn't going to be easy,' he said.

'No, I don't fancy that runway,' I replied.

'No, the runway's okay. It's a bit bumpy and sometimes has holes in it where animals have burrowed, but our reception party will have filled any of those in as this is an emergency flight. No, the real trouble is the wind. It has veered since we set out, which means we have to approach from the west.'

'But doesn't that put the railway embankment between us and the runway?' I asked nervously.

'Yes, it does.'

By now I was feeling worried and the milk in my stomach was starting to make me feel sick.

'But if you fly in over the railway embankment, how do you stop the plane from running off the far end of the runway? Surely it isn't long enough for a plane coming in over the embankment?'

'Quite right it isn't, but a few pilots, including myself, know how to get round that.'

With that, he banked the plane and turned towards the west, leaving the airstrip to our rear and crossing the railway embankment, which disappeared into the rainy mist behind us. There were few trees in this area due to the logging process which had taken place over the years.

When we were a couple of miles or so from the airstrip he swung the plane round, dropped it down almost to ground level and increased our speed. I felt my stomach churn. I could see the embankment rapidly getting nearer and we were still below its level. I kept quiet. My stomach tightened, my fingers dug into the arms of my seat and suddenly the engine seemed to cut out. We were now gliding straight towards what I felt was certain death. The embankment rushed towards us, or so it seemed, but just as we were about to crash into it he blipped the engine, which had been idling. The plane rose like a bird, glided over the top with inches to spare and dropped almost immediately on to the runway at the far side. He was even able to stop us next to the waiting vehicles.

With shaking legs I climbed out of the plane and into the pouring rain. As I did so my stomach decided to rid itself of my breakfast. It came out of my mouth in one huge lump, which splattered as it hit the ground. Fortunately the aircraft was between me and the group of people awaiting us. The breakfast soon disappeared as the driving rain broke it up. We walked over to where the assembled figures stood. I was now feeling much better.

The patient was in the back of a truck, well covered and protected from the rain. There was a doctor present and I talked with him outside the truck.

'I doubt that he will last the flight,' he said. 'He is weakening by the minute. His lungs are filling and he needs emergency surgery. We've done our best but I think that he's beyond saving. Let's get him into the plane.'

As we were preparing to move the patient I could hear my pilot talking to one of the welcoming committee just outside the van.

'There would normally have been no way that I'd have flown in this weather,' he was saying. 'It is almost impossible for a plane of this size. I thought that we'd had it when I jumped the embankment. I must have missed it by inches.'

'We all thought that you were goners,' said the guy he was talking to.

Eventually, we were able to load the patient into the plane and did our best to make him comfortable, but it seemed to me that he was fading. By now I was heartened to see that the clouds were breaking up and the rain had eased. I began to feel more optimistic about the take-off but I was increasingly pessimistic about our patient's chances of surviving until we could get him to hospital.

By the time the plane took off, he had lost consciousness. I never did get a chance to record the dying declaration. He died just before we reached Livingstone. I told the pilot that he had died and he, like me I suspect, seemed very down about the way things had turned out.

'Well, we did the best that we could to give him a chance,' he said. 'You know that we risked our lives for him, don't you?'

'Yes, I heard you talking, when I was in the van with the patient.'

We shook hands in the plane and I got out to supervise the unloading of the body.

I briefed the boss when I arrived back at the station, having deposited the body at the mortuary. He was no longer in his earlier jocular mood.

'I hear that you had a hell of a trip,' he said.

'You could say that, sir.'

'And all in vain,' he said.

'Well, at least we gave it our best shot, and I got to experience a superb piece of flying. I think that a letter of thanks to our pilot from you, or from the divisional commander, would be appropriate, or maybe even a letter from the commissioner himself. After all, he was risking his life in an attempt to save one of our own.'

'Yes, we'll give that some thought. Why don't you take the rest of the day off to recuperate?'

I glanced at the clock on his wall. There were twenty-five minutes of my shift left. He saw me look at the clock and gave me a beaming smile. The person who stabbed the constable was never found.

40

Corporal Punishment

As the rains really set in, our uniformed officers finally caught the two European youths who had been causing trouble throughout the Livingstone area. For several months the town had been subjected to a spate of vehicle thefts. The stolen vehicles were being taken and then driven to destruction in the rural areas surrounding the town. Their driving of these vehicles was reckless and dangerous and the police were subjected to an ever-increasing number of complaints from the public.

The miscreants had been chased on many occasions by different officers in various vehicles, but no arrests had been made. The car thieves knew the district even better than our local patrol officers. Because they enjoyed wrecking the vehicles that they were driving, they could avoid police drivers, who were not prepared to wreck police vehicles pursuing them.

When the boys were finally arrested we all had a good look at them. Both of them were eighteen years old and they had been to school together. They were not related and neither had a job. They were insolent when questioned and remarked that they had only been caught because the engine of the stolen car they were driving had failed. They showed not the slightest sign of regret for what they had done.

When the case came before the court the prosecutor appealed to the magistrate to hand down a strict sentence to act as a deterrent to other young people in the Livingstone area. Police hopes died when the magistrate started to hand down his judgement.

'I could send you to prison for these offences,' he said, 'but I have decided to give you one last chance to change your ways.'

I could see smiles beginning to appear on the lads' faces.

'I sentence you to three stokes of the cane.'

They started to relax. They had got away with it. They had been caned at school on a number of occasions and it was no big deal.

Then I saw that a couple of the police officers in the court were also smiling. When I asked why they found it amusing, they replied, 'Come and watch the caning in the morning. We'll give you a lift down to the prison.'

The following morning we went down to the prison and entered a court-yard where the canings were to take place. In the middle of the yard stood a contraption the like of which I had never seen before. It was constructed of wood and fashioned in the shape of a letter Y. The downstroke of the Y, upon which the person to be caned would be secured face down, was padded. His hands would be handcuffed to the upper arms of the Y. In attendance for the canings were the prison governor, several prison officers and a doctor. I remember particularly how quiet the prison itself was.

Eventually, from a far door, there emerged two figures. One I recognised as one of the car wreckers and the other was a huge African prison officer carrying a cane. As they approached, I could see that the boy to be caned was absolutely naked. He walked with his hands behind him and as he stood before us I noticed that his testicles appeared to have almost retracted into his body. The penis itself looked much diminished for a young man of his age. The doctor whispered to me that the effects that I was noticing were caused by the body reacting to approaching danger or the threat of imminent physical harm.

The prisoner was told to lie face down on the padded bench and his hands were then secured to the wooden frame. It was a hot day but I noticed that he was shivering violently. His legs were then strapped to the bench so that he could not move and a long, thick, padded cushion was secured over his lower back until his lower spine was completely protected. Finally, a thin cloth soaked in disinfectant was placed over his buttocks and the prison governor nodded to the warder with the cane. It was a light cane and appeared to be very flexible. I could see that it had been selected to deliver the maximum pain without causing critical damage.

There was complete silence from the prison, although I could see faces at some of the windows. The officer with the cane flexed it a few times. I was astounded at the speed and force of the first blow. The prisoner's body contorted and then shock waves seemed to ripple through his body. He emitted a low, continuous moan and then began to cry quietly. The doctor quickly removed the cloth and checked his buttocks, nodded to the governor and replaced the cloth. The second stroke was delivered with the same force as the first, but landed slightly below where the first had been placed. This time the air was filled with the scream from the recipient, and a strange thing happened. A huge roar erupted from the prison. It was a roar of delight from a prison community, largely African, which had been waiting for the scream. The same routine as for the first two strokes was followed and the third stroke was delivered. The

131

screaming gradually turned into an almost infantile sobbing as the doctor disinfected and dressed the prisoner's buttocks.

The second young man, who had been standing in the doorway and had been made to watch the first caning, could hardly walk towards the caning area. He was the tough guy of the two but he broke down after the first stroke and begged them to stop, which, of course, they did not.

They both came to the police station the following day to collect property that we had been keeping since their arrest and both of them assured us that they would never touch another car again. They were still finding it difficult to walk. They never did come to our attention again during my time in Livingstone.

41

The Idiot's Lantern

As Christmas 1960 approached and the weather grew hotter and wetter, a new craze hit the country and especially Livingstone. The television era was approaching. Southern Rhodesia had television in 1960 and Northern Rhodesia in 1961. Television sets started to appear in the shops in Livingstone in November 1960. They sold like hot cakes. We were the furthest south of all the larger towns in the country and nearest to Southern Rhodesia, so we were within range of their broadcasts. The population embraced "the idiot's lantern" with enthusiasm. Watching TV became the new main sport of the mainly non-African population.

One Sunday afternoon I was on duty and was called to a pleasant-looking house on the edge of town. Many houses I had visited had doors only to bathrooms and bedrooms but nowhere else – apart, that is, from external doors. This allowed air to circulate around the house. This house was no exception. On arrival at the house I was met at the gate by the whole family. The wife and older children were tearful, the husband full of anger.

'We've been burgled,' he told me.

'When did this happen?' I asked.

He told me that the burglary had taken place that morning.

'Didn't you lock up when you went out?'

He stood without answering for a few seconds and then, in a quiet, embarrassed voice, said, 'We didn't go out. We were watching television.'

'So your doors were unlocked?'

He nodded and looked at the ground.

'We had left the doors open to let cooler air in.'

'Well, they can't have got away with much, then.'

'They've almost stripped the house,' he replied.

I asked him to show me. He led me into the house, followed by the family, and I entered the lounge where the television set proudly stood. By today's standards it was tiny, but in those days it was an object of wonder. It stood on a low table facing the entrance to the room. A semicircle of chairs, backs to the door space, showed where the family had sat engrossed in the wonders of the television whilst the theft of their goods was taking place.

The audacity of the thieves was brought home to me when I was shown the extent of the theft. It wasn't burglary, as had been reported, but entry and theft. The thieves had walked into the house through an open door without having had to break in. All the bedrooms had been ransacked. Wardrobes had almost been stripped and even small items of furniture had been removed. Jewellery had been taken, and pictures from the walls. It seemed that about the only removable item not to be taken was the family's cat. The removal of the family's belongings was even more amazing when you realised that to take what had been stolen to their van (established later) would have required the gang to walk past the opening to the lounge a considerable number of times.

I took statements, of course, and circulated the descriptions of all the identifiable stuff, but none of it ever surfaced. I came to the conclusion that the van was from Southern Rhodesia, and my thoughts were reinforced later when enquiries revealed that a number of daring raids similar to this one had been reported in Southern Rhodesia. The family had insurance, as it happened, but I'm sure the following year's premium hurt.

42

Christmas Eve 1960

To say that Christmas Eve 1960 would always stick in my mind, when subsequent Christmases arrived, would be a considerable understatement.

At about five o'clock on Christmas Eve, I was just about to go off duty when a car arrived outside the station and a man ran into the enquiry office. He said that he had heard the sound of a shot from the house next door to his and was sure something bad had happened. I informed the boss of what was happening and promised to phone the station when I reached the scene and had learned what had happened.

The house, like the majority of houses in Livingstone, was a single-storey building and stood close to the house of the man who had reported the incident. On arrival all seemed quiet, so, together with a uniformed assistant inspector and the two constables who had come with me, we slowly and very carefully circled the house. We looked in through each window until we arrived at one of the bedroom windows. The curtains were open and a light was on in the room. A body lay face down on the floor, and a shotgun lay nearby.

I went to the front door and found it unlocked. We entered very carefully and I used the house telephone to call the station and report the situation to the boss. Having promised to keep him informed, I made a search of the house without entering the room in which the body lay. I sent the driver back to the station to collect my scenes-of-crime kit and my overalls. I could see by looking into the room that the whole place was a mess, with blood and body pieces scattered around. We would have to be careful about how we entered it. The African officers were both looking very queasy and kept glancing into the room and then looking away again.

I realised that the body was that of a white man, so I informed the boss by phone. He said he would send a detective inspector to oversee the case. In a way I was relieved and when the inspector arrived I was happy to act as his assistant. Most of the sudden or unnatural deaths which we dealt with were African and were dealt with by any experienced European or African CID officer who was available. All complicated sudden deaths or violent deaths of white people were very rare apart for those caused in traffic accidents and were at that time mainly dealt with by teams lead by a qualified European officer. This all changed of course following Independence and the departure of most of the white officers.

As we worked I realised that I would have managed quite well on my own. The course followed by the inspector was exactly the one that I would have followed myself.

The deceased had removed his right shoe, placed the gun in his mouth and pulled the trigger with his toe. I won't sicken the reader with details of the case. Suffice to say that dealing with this particular death by suicide was extremely unpleasant, but straightforward.

My reward for the work that I had done at the scene was to be given the post-mortem to attend at eleven o'clock the following morning, which of course was Christmas morning. The detective inspector who had taken over the case was married and, as tradition dictated, the single men always took over all duties on Christmas Day to allow married officers to observe a family Christmas.

The doctor performing the post-mortem was not my usual friend and turned up over an hour late. By the time the post-mortem was completed it was 1.30pm. He had hardly spoken during the whole of the procedure and seemed to hold me responsible for spoiling his Christmas Day. When we had finished I returned to my room and showered and changed my clothes. I then went to the dining room and found it deserted. The table had been cleared except for my place, where I found a single cracker. I took my food out of the kitchen where it had been keeping warm.

'Happy Christmas, McCue,' I said aloud to the empty room. 'Happy bloody Christmas.'

43

Crocodiles

The heavy rains of November and December eased considerably in January, but as if to make up for this, the humidity was almost at its highest level. It was hot and sticky and families with a swimming pool in the garden were very popular.

Unfortunately, not everyone had access to a pool and it was quite common, mainly for younger people, to sunbathe and paddle at the edge of the Zambezi above the falls. Here the water flowed at a reasonable speed so the chance of contacting bilharzia was low.

At the side of the road, about three miles above the falls and near to where people parked their cars, was a large noticeboard which could easily be read by people in a passing vehicle.

BATHING IS SUICIDAL
BECAUSE OF CROCODILES

Strangers to the area were often attracted by the sign and would stop their cars to have a look. Sometimes they would be lucky and see one or more of these dangerous creatures. They obviously would not go close to the edge of the water. The local teenagers, however, used the area to hang out in when there was no school. Living near to the Zambezi they were well aware of the dangers. They might kick water at each other at the edge of the river but none of them would dream of swimming there, or even wading out.

The river was full and flowing quickly on this particular Sunday afternoon. A strong wind was blowing against the flow of the water, which made it choppy. Everyone was having a good time hanging out when one of the girls started asking people if they had seen her friend. The last person to have seen her was one of the boys. He said she had been paddling up to her knees in the water, and that he had shouted to her to come closer in to the sand. She had waved to him and turned back towards the edge of the sand. He said that he was then distracted by some of the other kids and never noticed her again.

I learned all of this when, a short time later, I was called to go down and see what was happening. We hadn't been called immediately as the kids had been searching and calling for her for some time before they started to panic. When I arrived on the scene I found shocked and crying youngsters and adults gathered together in groups. One father who had connections with the flying club had already contacted a friend who had an aeroplane, which was about to take off and do a search from the air.

What the search revealed was shocking in the extreme. From the air, the pilot and his observer had counted over twenty crocodiles in the immediate area of where the kids had been enjoying their day. None of these could be seen in the choppy water from our position on the bank. The pilot searched from a low level up and down the river for some time before giving up. Later a search was made in boats, but no body was ever recovered.

The number of youngsters using the riverbank dropped considerably during the rest of the time that I was at Livingstone. The ones brave enough to use the area stayed well away from the water.

Later in the year a young African woman was washing a batch of clothing in the Zambezi just to the north of Livingstone. Other women were washing their clothing nearby. When she had completed her laundering, the young woman in question laid her washing on the bank of the river to dry and found a place to lie down and relax about forty paces from the river's edge.

She was wakened by a severe pain in her right ankle and realised that she was being pulled towards the river by a crocodile. As the crocodile was backing towards the water she stopped screaming long enough to contort her body in such a way that she was able to sink her teeth into the beast's snout. She caused enough pain for it to release her, and she was pulled to safety by the other women, who had seen or heard what was happening. She was taken to hospital by the police and was found to have a broken ankle and severe lacerations to her leg.

44

Sports

At the start of the wet season in late October the previous year, I had deputised as navigator in a car rally run by the Livingstone Motorcycle and Light Car Club. The original navigator was not able to take part due to illness. Twenty-eight cars took part over a long and rough course. Each car had to carry at least two people, but more were allowed. The car in which I was navigator was a Volkswagen and we finished ninth, incurring a penalty of one hour, twelve minutes and twenty-six seconds. The last car to finish had a penalty of six hours, twenty-two minutes and thirteen seconds. A pigeon was supplied by the local pigeon club for every checkpoint in case of an emergency. There were, of course, no mobile phones in those days.

I had at this time become friendly with a new assistant inspector who had recently been posted to Livingstone. His name was Peter (Pete) Jameson and he came from Leigh in Lancashire. We were the only two northerners in the mess. Pete was a good cricketer and an excellent footballer. I had decided to enter my own car in the next rally and Pete was happy to act as navigator. This rally took place on the 23rd December (the day before the shotgun suicide), and this time I felt happier driving my own car and Pete and I finished sixth out of twenty-three finishers.

There was a police cricket team in Livingstone. There was no cricket league as such, but we played friendlies, mainly against Asian teams but also against European teams made up of administration guys and doctors etc.

On one Saturday afternoon we were playing the top Asian team in Livingstone and I was, as usual, keeping wicket. The opponents' top batsman was batting and knocking the ball all over the place. Pete was bowling at a medium fast pace and I was standing back from the wicket. At the end of one over he said to me that he would bowl the third ball of his next over much faster if I would stand up to the stumps for it. The batsman had started to move up the wicket and out of his crease to hit the slower balls. This way we might be able to stump him.

The third ball was delivered at a far greater speed than the previous balls. The batsman had moved out of his crease as anticipated and had swung at the ball, which caught the top edge of his bat. I found myself flat on my back with a crowd of players looking down at me. The ball had hit me on the cheekbone directly under my right eye. There was blood all over my face and shirt, and for a few moments I was stunned. One of the spectators offered to take me to the hospital, so off we went.

At the hospital a doctor put three stitches into the wound, gave me some painkillers and told me to go back to my quarters and rest. I went back, changed my shirt, got my car and drove back to the cricket ground to continue the game. When I arrived the teams were taking tea. Our captain took one look at me and told me to go back to the mess and get some rest. In a foul mood, I drove away from the ground and went to Anita and Roy Jacomelli's house looking for sympathy.

Anita opened the door to me. Roy had been called out on a job. Seeing my face, she asked what had happened. As I sat down ready to recount the events of the afternoon in detail, I noticed that she was getting out her paints and a piece of board.

'I feel in the mood to paint,' she said. 'Just sit as you are and try not to move.'

'Aren't you even going to offer me a coffee?' I asked.

'After I've finished the painting.'

'Good grief, I've just been hit in the face by a cricket ball and been stitched up at the hospital and you can't even give me a cup of coffee.'

'Don't worry, I won't paint the injury or the swelling round your eye. I'll paint your face injury-free, but scowling.'

She had already begun to paint.

Anita was without doubt one of the most talented people I have ever met, and I have met many bright, intelligent people. She was talented in many different ways. She spoke faultless French, Italian (with a slight London accent), and had started to learn Chinyanja just out of interest. Her horse-riding abilities I have already mentioned. She had a beautiful soprano voice and had, when younger, sung in an eisteddfod. In a semi-professional production of Dylan Thomas' *Under Milk Wood* she had played and sung the part of Polly Garter. Anita was also an accomplished writer, and when she and Roy left Northern Rhodesia before independence and moved to South Africa she found no difficulty in securing employment, writing articles for two separate South African newspapers.

It took her just an hour and a half to complete the painting. She declared herself satisfied and went to make the coffee. I got up to look at the end result and then looked at myself in a mirror. She had captured my likeness perfectly, right down to the sullen stare. I started to laugh as she came in.

'That's better. Save the scowl for the interrogation room,' she said.

When Anita died, after suffering a massive brain haemorrhage at her home in France a few years ago, Roy sent me the painting, which she had left to me in her will. It is something that I shall always treasure.

45

Serendipity

Early in 1961 a number of arsons and attempted arsons occurred in and around the Livingstone area. We had our fair share of hotheads who just couldn't wait for independence. One morning in late January I was sent to investigate an attempted bomb attack on an electricity substation just outside Livingstone. I was told that a senior official from the electricity authority had already gone to the scene and was waiting for me there.

On arrival at the scene I found the official sitting on a rock and writing notes in a notebook. I introduced myself and we examined the scene of the explosion together. The substation was housed in a small, strong building. It had no windows and could only be entered by way of a heavy, metal door. The remains of what appeared to have been a small explosive device were scattered around the area, with the majority lying close to the door. I took photographs of the scene, putting markers down to indicate the main bomb fragments.

The device had obviously been home-made and the explosive used had hardly marked the door, let alone damaged it. It had been a very amateurish attempt by someone who was probably in the very early stages of experimenting with explosives. I completed my photographing of the scene and the collecting and labelling of the fragments. Being satisfied that there was nothing else I needed to do, I completed my notes and then sat down to eat my packed lunch.

The electricity official sat next to me and we started chatting. He was quite a bit older than me and obviously very experienced. It transpired that he had worked in many different emerging countries as an adviser and was enjoying his time in Northern Rhodesia.

As we talked he kept looking at me as though he wanted to say something, but didn't. Eventually, after a pause in our conversation he looked at me and asked, 'What did you say your surname name was, Dave?'

'McCue,' I answered. 'Why?'

'Well, when I started in the electricity business I had a mentor. He was in charge of a section of the Warrington electrical power station before it was nationalised just after the war. He mentored all his staff and pushed those of us who were ambitious into going to night school and studying and all that sort of thing. The ones of us who really wanted to move up in the industry, especially when nationalisation came in, could always rely on him for advice and help. His name was McCue. I've never met another McCue since then, until now.'

'Do you know his Christian name?' I asked.

'Yes, as a matter of fact I do. His name was Richard, although we older members of the department called him Dick.'

I nodded. 'I think I know the man you are talking about.'

'Really?' he said, looking interested.

'Do you know the Warrington area?' I asked.

He nodded.

'Well, I was born and lived in Stockton Heath, about three miles away from the power station we are talking about. The man you described is my father.'

He jumped up and held out his hand, which I shook.

'I remember now how pleased he was when you passed your eleven-plus exams to go to the grammar school,' he said.

We spent some time talking and he told me that he had virtually finished his time in Livingstone and that his next job would be in Southern Rhodesia.

That night I wrote a letter home, and in it gave a full account of our meeting. When Mum wrote her next letter to me she said how pleased Dad had been to receive my news.

My father died in January 1968, riddled with cancer. I arrived home from Africa in the summer of 1967 and took over his nursing during his last few months. Our doctor produced an orange and a syringe and showed me how to inject morphine by inviting me to push the syringe into the orange. He then drew an imaginary cross on my dad's buttock and indicated the upper outer quadrant as the area in which to inject. This would ensure that I didn't hit the sciatic nerve. He handed me a prescription for the morphine and never appeared again.

It was a duty doctor who signed the death certificate. My father was so diminished by the time he died that I used to pick him up and carry him in my arms up- and downstairs with no effort.

On the day of his funeral the family fitted into one funeral car. A few friends made their own way to the crematorium. We had, if my memory serves me correctly, arranged a small buffet at Mum's chapel for after the cremation. The crematorium was having a busy time on that cold January day. When we arrived, there was a large crowd standing in the snow outside the door leading into the hall where the service would take place.

They must be from the last funeral, I thought.

The crowd parted as we followed the coffin into the hall. To my amazement we were then followed in by at least, I estimated, two hundred people. As I looked around the hall as they came in, I realised that they were all men. Then I saw a figure whom I recognised. It was Arthur Adey, a friend who had worked with Dad and whom I remembered from years before when I was a schoolboy. I beckoned him over to sit with the family and he came and sat next to me. He told me that every one of the men there had served under my father, and that they had come from all over the British Isles, and several from different parts of Europe. I began to panic. We could not cater for so many people. Arthur realised that I was upset.

'Don't worry, David. We are all going into Warrington later for a few drinks in memory of your dad. You couldn't have known so many would come.'

After the service I shook as many hands as I possibly could and thanked them for honouring my father as they had. I heard only kind words about Dad and realised, on that day, just how much he had been liked and respected by the men who had worked under him and had gone on to fashion their own careers.

46

Taking a Break

In early 1961 Roy and Anita Jacomelli and I decided that it would be a good idea to take leave owing to us and have a holiday in a game camp at Kasaba Bay on the southern shore of Lake Tanganyika. The southernmost tip of the lake lay in Northern Rhodesia and the camp had an excellent reputation for viewing wild-life and for fishing. We decided that May would be a good time for the holiday as it was the third coolest month of the year and had negligible rainfall. Partly because May was such a pleasant month, it had a lower suicide rate in Livingstone than any other month. Crime in general also tended to be lower, so it was easier to get permission to take leave then.

It was decided that we would travel in the Jacomellis' car, and when the due day finally arrived, we set off early in the morning a couple of hours before sunrise. We had 506 miles to travel to our destination. At least we should not have many traffic hold-ups to worry about.

The journey was largely as expected. We had a few short stops but the time taken by these was largely offset by driving at a higher speed than we had antici-pated. The roads were in good condition, having been graded following the rainy season. In the last twenty or so miles of the journey we saw a wide range of wild ani-mals near to the road or even crossing in front of us. It boded well for our holiday.

Everything about the camp proved to be well above our expectations. Roy and Anita had a hut next to mine. Their hut was larger than my single one but both huts were well built and fitted out. There would be no roughing it in this camp! We were too late for dinner but food had been saved for us and we had a delicious salad with fresh fruit to finish. The coffee was excellent and the bar was open for as long as guests required it to be. There were only a few people in the bar and they soon left. Early starts and long treks seemed to be the norm, but we decided to take it easy for our first day.

I awoke the following morning to the sound of birdsong and the muted sounds of movement around the camp. People were going to the dining room for breakfast and most of them appeared to be dressed for a trip out into the bush. Many of them carried cameras and all wore some sort of headwear.

I joined Anita and Roy and we went in for breakfast. There was a wide choice and the food was well cooked and presented. I enquired about the presence of crocodiles in the vicinity of the camp and whether it was safe to swim from the nearby shore. It appeared that crocodiles had never been seen in the area during the years that the camp had been in existence, but I was warned that the water deepened rapidly only a few yards from the shore.

When we asked about fishing, the owner of the camp became quite interested. He said that the other guests, most of whom we had seen, were not interested in fishing but we could hire a boat and fishing tackle whenever we felt like it. He would also provide a man to sail the boat to wherever we wanted to fish. He added that he would gladly buy any *kupi* (a fish good for eating, and generally weighing between one and four pounds) that we might catch. We arranged to fish the following day after an early breakfast.

We spent the rest of our first day finding our way around the area surrounding the camp and went along the shoreline, watching the bird life and coming across all sorts of small creatures in the bush. Feeling hot towards midday, I stripped off for a swim. I had my trunks on underneath my clothes and the water looked inviting. I got a shock when I jumped in. The water temperature was very low, probably due to the great depth of the lake. Once I recovered my breath I set off for a slow, leisurely swim.

My first, and as it happened, my last swim in the lake did not last long. The water was quite choppy due to an onshore breeze. I was swimming parallel to the shore and about thirty or so feet out from the bank when out of nowhere, I was suddenly confronted by a large snake. I think that we were both as surprised as each other. The snake was brown and about two feet of it was erect and above the water. I didn't see any markings, but when it opened its mouth to hiss at me and I saw the black inside of its mouth I knew it was a black mamba. I threw myself backwards away from it so that I was on my back with my feet towards the snake. It stared at me for a couple of seconds more and then slid beneath the water. I think that I possibly broke the world backstroke record for ten metres, and definitely the speed record for getting out of the water and on to dry land. Anita had seen what had happened but Roy was further along the shore and missed the excitement. The event took away any further desire I might have had to swim in the lake.

That evening as I got ready for dinner Anita knocked on my window as she and Roy walked past towards the dining room. It was only half past six and I knew that dinner was not served until seven o'clock, so I didn't hurry. A few minutes later, just when I was ready to go across to the dining room, my room suddenly darkened. The window on that side of the hut was fairly narrow but tall. Thinking that rain must be approaching, I walked over to look at the sky. The sky was blocked from my view by a large female elephant, who was rubbing her body against the wall of the hut and, from the look in her half-closed eyes, enjoying herself. I stood silently watching, and as I did so could make out the movement of other elephants passing beyond her on the way to the lake. I didn't think that she had noticed me, but she had. Slowly turning so that her back end was turned towards me, she suddenly let out the loudest, longest fart that I had ever heard. That was not all. A jet of semi-digested vegetation and liquid was projected towards me, much of it striking the window, which was slightly open. A strong smell accompanied it. She turned partly round towards me and I'm almost certain that there was amusement in her eyes as she sauntered off towards the lake.

Elephants were not the only animals to pass through the camp that evening. I counted at least seven different species of animal moving down to the lake. I had missed out on the briefing the previous day when it was explained that the camp had been built near to a well-trodden path used by the local animals on their way to the lake each evening. It had also been explained that all animals had the right of way when passing through the camp and were not to be disturbed.

When eventually the path was clear, I made my way to the dining room, arriving to a loud cheer and much laughter. When I told the owner of the camp about the elephant emptying her bowels against my window he laughed and told me it wasn't the first time she had done it.

The following morning we met up with our boatman and checked the fishing tackle we were to use. I had decided that it would be prudent to concentrate upon catching fish for the kitchen and for our boatman, and arranged the tackle for this purpose. Anita and Roy had never done any serious fishing but I had, and had fished in competitions at junior level back home.

We used relatively small hooks (size tens). These would have been looked upon as large back in England where I had fished before coming to Africa, but they seemed right to me for what we were aiming to do. Before we had set out I had filed the barbs off all the hooks that had been supplied to us. This would help us to unhook the fish without too much fuss.

We set off following the contours of the bank, but staying about fifty yards out from it. On our hooks we attached small pieces of leftover meat and fish, which I had asked the cook to save for us the previous day. This was raw and had not been used in the cooking of the previous day's dinner. Some of it he had diced, and I took a handful and threw it into the water. It took only about twenty seconds for the water to start swirling and for the occasional fish to break the surface.

The boatman had brought two large containers, both containing several lumps of ice from the kitchen. Anita sat next to him and was to cast back into the water behind the boat, and Roy sat halfway along the boat and cast out to the left. I sat in the bow and cast ahead of the boat, which was now drifting slowly. I instructed my friends to cast out a good way and then to reel in the line slowly, and so we started.

In all of my fishing in England I had always had to fish with patience, waiting until I could get the fish feeding. This fishing was, however, totally different. On my first cast a fish took my bait and my rod bent immediately. We were using heavy rods and strong line and it was really just a matter of casting and reeling in a fish, again and again until our containers were full. Being used to holding and unhooking fish I was catching three fish to every one caught by Anita and Roy. The boatman had brought his own container which, to his great delight, we filled.

Once we had as many fish as we could take we returned to camp and hauled our catch into the kitchen where we were greeted by the chef and his helpers. He was delighted with what we had brought him and started to transfer the catch into the fridges in the kitchen. The fish weighed from about a pound up to five pounds each.

That evening the owner came to see us and said how delighted he was with the catch. He said that he had room in his freezers for twice as many fish if we cared to fish for him again, and that he would deduct the cost of one day's stay at the camp for each of us if we could produce a catch of fish similar to the one we had already brought in. The use of the boat would not be charged.

During the holiday we fished on three occasions for the kitchen, but were beginning to tire of catching so easily. One morning I set up the tackle for catching large fish, for which the lake was famous. On this occasion we would not be baiting hooks but would be using artificial, articulating fish. These could be made to rise and fall as we reeled them in according to the speed we applied to the reels. My articulator was about nine inches long and comprised three separate parts loosely joined together. Each of the parts carried a large triple hook. As we sailed out into the lake I began to wonder whether I would catch anything on such a large, clumsy-looking lure. I dangled it in the water as the boat moved towards our fishing area and was relieved to see how realistically it moved.

We fished for over an hour without any sign of fish and I began to feel that maybe our tackle and set-up were too unrefined to tempt any thinking fish. We tried various parts of the area but without success. Eventually, as we sailed round a promontory and into a large bay we were suddenly startled to see that we were within about forty or fifty feet of a large group of hippopotami who were bathing in some shallower water. Some of the young hippos were playing around nearer to the shore.

We were delighted and Anita and Roy started to take photographs, but Simon, our boatman, had become alarmed and started to turn the boat away, increasing its speed as he did so. We only realised why he was doing so when, about ten yards away from where we had been a few seconds before, there was a large splash and a very angry hippo surfaced. Simon was visibly shaken and kept shaking his head and talking to himself. It was some minutes before he recovered his composure. To us it had been an adventure, but when he told us that hippos accounted for a number of deaths of fishermen each year we realised why he had been so frightened.

We decided to fish for another hour or so and to move from area to area, fishing as we did so. There appeared to be nothing taking an interest in our lures and we were just discussing the idea of making our way back towards the camp when my rod was almost ripped from my hands. I hung on as best I could and tightened the drag on my reel but the line continued to be stripped from it. Eventually the rate at which the line was being stripped slowed until I was able to lock the reel. The boat, however, was being towed along steadily by whatever was on the other end of the line. We were being slowly towed away from the shore and directly into the breeze. We were also moving directly towards the low sun and were pretty much blinded.

Simon kept shaking his head and muttering to himself in his own language. He was not happy. I, however, was very happy and was enjoying every minute despite the pain I was feeling in my tiring arms.

Just as I was about to admit that I could not hold on for much longer, the line went slack and I realised that whatever had been on the other end had gone. I felt a mixture of disappointment and relief and began to reel in the line. It took some time and I slowly began to realise just how much line had been taken. At last the articulator appeared on the surface of the water and I lifted it out. The two main body parts had been ripped away from the head of the articulator and the wire which had held them together was frayed and broken.

'Well, Simon, what do you think? Was it a catfish, do you reckon?'

'I don't think so, *bwana*. I am sure that you hooked a crocodile. I could not see clearly because of the sun and the waves but I think it was a crocodile.'

He shuddered and wrapped his arms around his knees. 'You are a dangerous man to take out on this lake, *bwana*. We have been twice in danger today.'

He suddenly began to laugh. I knew that the story, well embellished, would circulate around the camp.

We had been out with one safari group and had enjoyed the experience, seeing a fair number of different animals and getting close to some of them. We saw lions in the distance but they were resting up and would wait for evening to catch their supper if they were hungry enough. Elephants were also sheltering from the mid-morning sun and were largely obscured by trees and bush.

On our last day we were able to arrange a late afternoon and early evening walk through a heavily forested area. We were accompanied by one of the African ranger staff, who carried a loaded rifle. We obviously paid for the special arrangements but felt that it would be worth it if we were able to get closer to the less-approachable animals.

At first the walk went well and we were accompanied by monkeys, who swung along beside us for a way. Our first sight of a large animal was when we walked into a glade with few trees and found two rhinoceroses grazing about thirty yards away. We quietly photographed them and they slowly moved away.

The walk continued in the same way. We would come across animals unexpectedly. Some would be alarmed and would charge away, but others would just ignore us. We eventually came across a large herd of elephants and were able to take photographs until we were challenged by a large bull, who was obviously their leader. We quietly left the area and so our walk proceeded until we were startled by the sound of two shots.

Someone was obviously firing what sounded to me like a heavy rifle. Our guide stopped and signalled for us to keep silent. We stood and waited to see what he would do. As we stood, straining our ears for further noises, we became aware of a distant sound like a continuous rumble of thunder. Slowly it began to increase in volume and intensity and our guide became animated, shouting for each of us to find a large tree to hide behind.

'Push yourselves hard against the trunk and don't look round it to see what is coming,' he shouted.

We watched him find a tree and take up a position, and we followed his example.

Suddenly I felt a rise in the air pressure and the noise increased to a deafening level. All at once we were surrounded by hurtling shapes, all travelling in the same direction. Looking sideways at them as they passed it was almost impossible to identify individual animals although large groups of the same species came past together. Eventually, the number of animals lessened until everywhere went quiet again. Our guide was shaking. I suspected that it was from a mixture of anger and the realisation that he could have lost one of more valued guests and maybe his job.

'We must go quickly back to camp,' he said.

He set off at a very quick walk. We followed, almost trotting, until we came within sight of the camp and he left us, running at high speed.

By the time we reached the camp a manhunt for the poacher or poachers was being organised. Two vehicles carrying armed men from the camp set off, but by the time we left, early the following morning, they had not returned. We never found out the result of their manhunt.

47

A Double Murder

On the 5th June, shortly after my return from holiday, I was called into the office and instructed to pack my rucksack with everything I might need and to prepare for a long trip to investigate a double shooting which had reportedly taken place in a wild area of Barotseland in the Mankoya (now Kaoma) District, about fifty miles north of Kataba. One victim, Kakusha, had died instantly, having been shot from the side, the bullet striking him in the chest. The other man had received a severe injury from a second shot and had been taken to Mulobezi Hospital.

I was instructed to take with me Detective Sergeant Mulenga, who spoke the language of the area and would assist in the investigation. I was told that the accused in the case was an African male, well known to the deceased victims and other villagers. His name was Wankie Sikwali.

The news of the shooting had taken five days to reach us in Livingstone and there were few details available. I decided that I would take a Greener shotgun with me, and also my personal police revolver and ammunition for both. I also carried my hunting knife as I always did in the bush, not that I ever hunted.

We set off in the early afternoon, aiming to get to Mulobezi by nightfall. As it happened the road was in poor condition and it was about ten o'clock in the evening when we arrived. The news we received upon reaching Mulobezi was disappointing. The victim, Muntoya, whom I had hoped would be able to tell us what had happened, had died before reaching the hospital. I decided that we would have to press on northwards to Kataba, about sixty miles away along a poor dirt road. On arrival at Kataba we rested until dawn.

Early the following morning we set off along a road which gradually became more and more difficult to negotiate. It was now leading us in a north-westerly direction and angling away from the direction of our crime scene. I stopped the Land Rover and looked at the map.

'This road is going to take us many miles away from the village where the shooting took place,' I said.

'Indeed it is, *bwana*,' Sergeant Mulenga replied, 'and soon there will be rivers cutting us off from this village.'

I agreed with him and took the decision to leave the road and head directly north towards our objective, following tracks whenever we could find them and they were pointing in the direction in which we wished to travel. Where there were no tracks we would find our own way using my compass to check direction.

To begin with we made good progress. The countryside was fairly flat and open with few trees and little in the way of obstacles. The only problem was that I first had to drive due east to get round the only river which stood in our way. I had to locate its source and then navigate my way around it in order to then head north towards Shakalongo village where the crimes had taken place. This part of our journey took all morning but eventually we came to the source of the river, a large area of swamp around which I eventually managed to find my way. After a pause to eat some of our packed food and drink some water I started to head north. We passed a number of villages, but as we progressed they became fewer. As night arrived I parked the Land Rover and we settled down to rest until dawn.

The next day, our third on this case, we had barely covered the first five miles when we came across lying water. It stretched across our path and to left and right for as far as we could see. I looked at the map but there was no indication of water in the area. The land was low-lying and we had had a very wet rainy season, so I felt that the water could not be very deep. It was showing signs of drying out at the edges so I made a decision. I would drive slowly through the water, testing its depth against the wheels of the Land Rover. I could see, about two hundred yards away, a point where the track that we had been following reappeared from the water on the far bank, and I aimed the vehicle towards it. It was impossible to judge the depth of the water by looking down at it as it was very dirty, and I drove slowly. Everything was going well and the water was, as I had hoped, less than a foot deep.

We hit a few small, unseen obstacles, probably stones, and were about twenty yards from where we would reach the continuation of the track when the Land Rover suddenly plunged to the left and sank until water covered the bonnet almost to the windscreen. I immediately put the vehicle into reverse in an attempt to pull out of the unseen hole, but to no avail. By now water was entering through the front part of the vehicle and, to add to our troubles, the engine had died.

I told Mulenga to take his rucksack and anything else he might have brought with him and to make his way to the bank. I followed suit, removing the vehicle's ignition key before leaving and grabbing my compass from beneath the dashboard. We both waded carefully to the bank.

Now it was a case of continuing the rest of the way on foot. I worked out the distance remaining to Shakalongo village – about fifty miles in a direct line, but probably sixty miles in reality. I felt that we should be able to cover about twelve to fifteen miles before the light faded. We covered, in fact, about ten miles. That night we rationed our food and water, but chewed on hard dried meat called biltong, bits of which I cut from a large piece which I carried in my rucksack.

We agreed that if we were to sleep in the open we would need a large fire, which would serve to keep us warm and also discourage attacks by predators. I had picked our stopping place with care. It was near to a forested area, which gave us fuel for a fire, but I sited our camp on a slightly higher piece of grassland far enough away from the trees, which could have allowed predatory animals to approach us undetected. I worked out a rota system which involved one of us keeping watch as the other slept. I decided two-hour shifts were just about sustainable, basing my decision on my army experience.

I showed my sergeant how to dig a shallow hole to take pressure off his hip bone when he lay down to sleep and we used our rucksacks as pillows. I loaded the shotgun and showed Mulenga how to use it if needed. I checked my revolver and knife and gave him the first shift, which started at about eleven o'clock. I instructed him to waken me at one o'clock. I slept very little as I kept waking up to check that Mulenga was still awake.

I need not have worried. He had never slept in the wild before and was very nervous. He came and wakened me when it was my turn to stand watch and then settled down to sleep. The night passed slowly and uneventfully for both of us, but I was glad to see the dawn.

On our fourth day I calculated that we had covered twelve miles, but we were beginning to tire. Our food was running low and we rationed it and chewed on more biltong. We were also, more importantly, running low on water and had seen no streams or rivers. There had been no sign of human habitation. We had seen many wild animals in the distance, including elephants, but no lions. We were not disturbed that night, although we were entertained by what I estimated to be two separate prides of lions about a mile or so from us having a quarrel, probably about territory.

On our fifth day, the 9th June, we had been walking for four hours and had covered about ten miles when we came upon a village. As we were walking through a forested area we were alerted by the sound of children playing, and very soon were surrounded by them as they led us into their village. We were greeted there by the headman and other adults, who told us that they had been expecting us. They even knew about our Land Rover. They also knew about the murders and told us that the killer had not been found. They filled our water containers and prepared a meal for us, and I felt my energy returning. Knowing that we had to push on, I thanked them for their hospitality, and rejuvenated, we set off and managed to complete a further five miles before nightfall.

That night, just as I was settling down to sleep after my first shift, I was shaken by Mulenga's hand on my shoulder.

'*Bwana*,' he whispered, 'elephants.'

I instantly became fully awake. I could hear what sounded like a large number of them coming towards us from the north. Our fire was burning brightly and should have kept them at a distance, but they were steadily drawing nearer.

'Get your things together and let's go,' I whispered.

We crept away to the side of our camp and stopped about three hundred yards away. In the moonlight we could see the outlines of a large group of elephants as they passed on the near side of the fire. It was a fine sight, but rather unnerving.

The following day, our sixth, we pushed ourselves hard and covered an estimated seventeen miles. We had passed several villages and had been able to refill our water bottles at one of them, purifying the water after leaving the village. Late that afternoon we were invited to spend the night in the last of the villages we visited before darkness fell. We were given a good supper and offered the use of an empty hut in which to sleep, with no worries about guard duty! We were told that Shakalongo village, where the murders had taken place, was about three miles away and the inhabitants knew that we would want to talk to them in the morning.

An early morning start saw us arrive at Shakalongo at about nine o'clock. Our early arrival had been anticipated and a large crowd of at least two hundred people was awaiting us. They were mostly sitting in an orderly manner at the east side of the village and quietly watched as the headman and two *boma* messengers walked towards us.

We greeted each other in a quiet and serious manner, as befitted the occasion, and I began to feel that the whole scene, although fitting, almost bordered upon the theatrical. Everyone there seemed to be playing his or her part in a great drama, but then I suddenly realised that we *were*, in fact, part of a great drama which would be embellished many times in the discussions and storytelling in the area over the coming years.

Thankfully the village headman and the *boma* messengers all spoke English. I was able to give the necessary instructions for the exhumation of the body of Paul Kakusha, which had been buried in a grave close to the village on the day after the shooting. I suggested that his relatives might assist us in the exhumation, as they would give the body the love and care it deserved. The rising murmur of protest from the crowd died away as the messengers explained to the assembly that the exhumation was necessary and that it was good that members of the family were being given the care of the process.

Accompanied by the whole assembly, we went to the burial place and carefully recovered the body. The exhumation was easy as the soil was sandy. Removing the blanket in which the body was wrapped, I started to take photographs. When it was necessary to turn the body I asked male members of the family to do it. I explained every move I took in the examination of the body to the village headman, and he translated my words to the family. One of the messengers took it upon himself to repeat to the crowd everything as it was said, and there was much nodding and quiet discussion among those assembled.

After I had taken all the photographs I needed I asked for the body to be turned so that I could examine the entry point of the bullet. The bullet had entered the chest below the left armpit but I could find no exit wound. The deceased had probably instinctively raised his arm to protect his face, giving the bullet free access to his chest.

Now I was faced with a problem. Did I need to arrange the removal of the body to Livingstone so that a post-mortem could be carried out, or had I so many witnesses that this would be unnecessary? I had to make up my mind quickly before the crowd became restless. I knew that I already had a bullet from the gun which had fired the shot that had killed the man who had died on the way to Mulobezi Hospital, so I didn't need to probe the body for another bullet fired at almost the same time.

I called Mulenga over. He had been using the time to find reliable witnesses. I asked if he had found any.

'Too many, *bwana*,' he said. 'So many people saw this happen.'

I immediately made my decision and told the village headman that the body could now be reburied and I would not need to take it back to Livingstone. I could see his relief as he turned to the crowd and gave them the news. I told one of the *boma* messengers to say how grateful my sergeant and I were for the way everyone had helped us, and that my sergeant would take statements from the people whom we had selected.

I now turned to the problem of locating Sikwali. He had a gun, and probably still had ammunition. I examined the hut outside which the murders had taken place and took more photographs. Even eleven days after the shootings an examination of the hut showed very visible traces of dried blood, which

I indicated for the camera with small sticky markers. The murders had been committed by Sikwali firing from inside the hut at his victims, who were seated outside. He had then broken his way out of the rear of the hut by smashing a hole in the grass wall. As he was doing so a third shot had been heard. Examination showed bloodstains on the inside roof of the hut and on the wall around the area of the hole in the wall. It was obvious that the gun had either been discharged accidentally or that he had attempted to kill himself but had failed. Whatever had happened, I could be fairly sure that he was injured, and probably seriously.

For many days a large-scale manhunt led by district messengers and villagers had been taking place. It had covered a huge area but I was sure that we would find our man closer to the scene of the murders. I ordered the searchers from the local villages to search an area of almost impenetrable bush much closer to Shakalongo village. I was told that it had already been searched. I ordered the area to be searched again. There was much muttering from the villagers.

On the 13th June the remains of a body were found in thick bush only two and a half miles from the scene of the shootings. There was little flesh left on what remained of the skeleton and a few of the bones were missing, but the wound left by the bullet, which had blown half of Sikwali's face away and shattered his jaw, was easy to see. His gun lay beneath a tree. He had fashioned a rope from grasses and creepers and had used it to hang himself, but it had broken.

What was left of him, after animals, birds and insects had feasted on him, was lying beneath the tree next to the gun, near which a small bag containing several bullets lay. These items, together with the two pieces of the grass rope by which he had tried to hang himself, I took as evidence. There was no flesh left on the hands to enable fingerprints to be taken, but the scene spoke for itself. There was little smell from the remains, which were mainly clean and shining in the sunlight. I took photographs from all angles and then ordered that the remains of the body and the few fragments of his clothing which lay scattered around should be carried back to Shakalongo for burial in a marked place to be decided upon by elders from the surrounding villages.

On arrival at the village the remains were positively identified as being those of Sikwali. An old break of the left arm was recognised and all the villagers were certain that it was our man.

Mulenga and I were later driven to Livingstone in a vehicle supplied by the local district commissioner. This time we travelled the longer route by road. When we arrived in Livingstone I found that my Land Rover had already been recovered and returned. I expected a reprimand for losing it, but did not receive one. It appeared that the authorities were satisfied with the way things had been handled.

In Livingstone on the 15th September 1961, at the inquest into the three deaths, the coroner, Mr WH Hanna, recorded verdicts of murder in the cases of Kakusha and Mutoya, naming Wankie Sikwali as the person who had murdered them. He recorded that there was evidence to suggest that Sikwali had later hanged himself, causing his own death.

48

Football, 1961

When the Easter holidays arrived the local football league matches were already underway. Nchanga FC, who had destroyed us in the cup final the previous year, had come down to Livingstone to play two friendly games against us and to enjoy the sights and activities that the town had to offer.

On Good Friday we beat them four-three in a superb game before the largest crowd ever seen for a sporting event in the town. Nchanga were suffering the same weariness from their long journey from the Copperbelt that we had suffered in the reverse journey the previous year.

'Wait until Monday,' their captain said as we walked off the field.

Monday's match was attended by an even larger crowd. Again it was a superb game but this time we were very happy to draw one-one after a hard-fought battle.

The Nchanga players, talking to us at the party we had arranged for them after the game, told us that at least eight of the team had been offered positions as professional players with several South African teams. The wages offered were excellent and some of them were going to take up the offers.

On Sunday 21st May, City of Lusaka came down to Livingstone to play us. Since we had defeated them in the national championships semi-final the previous year their club had turned professional and now had a number of black African players playing regularly. They now played in the Rhodesia and Nyasaland Professional League. In other words, the Central Africa League had been born.

Leading their attack, Lusaka had Jackie Sewell, who had played six times for England and had scored three goals. He had played for Notts County, Sheffield Wednesday, Aston Villa and Hull City and now was captain of City of Lusaka. When he had been transferred to Sheffield Wednesday, a transfer fee of £34,000 had been paid, a British record at the time. We were well beaten by six goals to one, their new black striker scoring three. Professional, multiracial football had been born, made possible by a huge injection of money. We stared into the future.

*

On Friday 16th June, shortly after returning from Shakalongo, I, together with Glen Doherty, the Livingstone captain, his brother Patrick and Brian Howlet, set out to drive to Broken Hill where the trials for the Northern Rhodesia national team were to take place over the Saturday and Sunday. Four teams had been selected by the national committee from players selected from all over the country. Out of the forty-four players selected to take part in the trials, Nchanga had six players despite having lost some of their best players to South Africa. City of Lusaka had three but in actual fact six, three of their team being listed in the programme as representing Lusaka Police.

The team with the largest number of players taking part was Mufulira, now the dominant team playing on the Copperbelt. They were recent victors by seven goals to one over Nchanga, the national champions for the previous three years. Out of the forty-four players in the trials, ten were from Mufulira. Mindful of the possibility of players being injured during the games, several players from various positions who had just missed selection for the trials stood ready to be brought on as substitutes.

Each team would play one match on Saturday and one on Sunday. I was placed in the white team together with Brian Howlet at centre half and the team captain, Glen Doherty, at right half. Glen's brother Patrick was to play right wing for the red team alongside Jackie Sewell.

To sum up, our white team won one match and drew the other and I let no goals through. I'm fairly sure that I was the only keeper to keep a clean sheet. The goalkeeper selected for the national team, however, was Pickering of Mufulira, a giant of a man and an ex-professional player from Scotland. On a calm day he was reputed to be able to kick the ball out of his hands the full length of a football field. Jackie Sewell, who captained the red team, having had his football boots stolen from the dressing room before the matches started, played poorly in borrowed boots. He was not selected for the national team at that time, but later coached the national team and played ten times for the country in 1964 and 1965, scoring seven goals.

By the time August arrived, Livingstone Villa had reached the position it reached each year at this time in the season. We had won every game in the local league so far and were preparing to take on the big teams from the centre and north of the country in the national championships, but this year things would be different.

A meeting of the Livingstone Football League had decided that, as the team from the league was representing the southern area of the country, it should comprise the best players from the area and not just be composed of players from one club, no matter how dominant such a team might be. After a long discussion a team was selected to play against Mufulira, whom we had drawn in the quarter-finals. With the demise of Nchanga and the likelihood that our opponents would be crowned Copperbelt champions at the end of the season, most soccer pundits, led by one Paddy Cangley, the FBC Radio sports commentator, were busy discussing which team would face Mufulira in the final. Even our local papers gave us no chance against them.

I am happy to say that we crushed them. They played well and I had a lot to do in the Livingstone goal but in the end we beat them comfortably by four goals to nil, to the amazement of football followers in other parts of the country. There was much comment in newspapers and radio discussions and we felt very satisfied.

I never had the chance to take part in the semi-final as I was out of the area, engaged in several serious cases including a spate of arsons which were passed on to me and my African team. I can't even remember who knocked us out of the competition but I know we were missing several of our best players through illness or work demands.

One unexpected but very welcome event took place in late August in 1961. I had just finished my shift and was off duty when the word went round that the divisional commanding officer, Superintendent J Waller wanted to see all off-duty officers in the mess. As we arrived there was much speculation as to why we were wanted. We were able to relax when we saw that the DCO was holding a glass of beer and chatting to the nearest officers. All became quiet as we waited for him to speak.

I was amazed to hear him say, 'Detective Assistant Inspector McCue, please come to the front.' I had no idea why he wanted me to go out in front until I saw him smile and hold out a Northern Rhodesia Police sports tie. I recognised that it was a tie awarded for reaching a high level in sport.

'Congratulations, McCue. You have been awarded your force colours for your performance in football over these past two years. You may be interested to know that you are the first officer ever to receive his force colours for football while serving in Livingstone.'

There was a burst of applause that increased in intensity when I said, 'Well, I suppose that I had better buy everyone a drink to help me celebrate then, sir.'

49

A Case of Witchcraft

Stationed at Livingstone we had a number of excellent police officers, both African and European. I cannot, unfortunately, remember all their names. One such African member of the force was a sub-inspector. He was a man who was thought of very highly by members serving with him and was destined, in most people's opinions, for higher rank in due course.

In 1961 he returned to duty after a period of leave, which he had spent with his family in his home village. Upon his return it was very noticeable that he had lost a considerable amount of weight and he appeared weak and listless. He was sent to see a doctor who, upon examining him, could find nothing wrong with him. He returned to duty but continued to lose weight and was obviously very ill.

It gradually emerged that whilst on leave he had been "witched". An unknown enemy from the village or somewhere nearby had attached a dead and mutilated chicken to the door of his home as he had slept. He had found it the following morning. From the time of discovering the chicken his health had started to deteriorate. This was an intelligent man who was studying hard in order to pass examinations to further his education. He was a well-liked man and was the last person one would have thought of as being susceptible to being affected by witchcraft.

After several days of struggling to do his job he was again sent to the hospital and this time saw a specialist who gave him a thorough physical examination. Again nothing was found, but the doctor admitted him for further examinations and tests. Nothing could be found to explain his condition. By now he had stopped eating and was being sustained by drips. Nothing could be done for him. He stopped answering questions and then stopped talking altogether. Eventually, to everyone's great sadness, he died. How could a man of his intelligence have been affected like that?

In due course a post-mortem was held which found absolutely nothing to explain why or how he had died. The verdict had to be, and was, "death by natural causes".

During my time in Livingstone I had dealt with a number of offences under the Witchcraft Act and over time had been able to amass a large and comprehensive collection of witchcraft artefacts which were surplus to requirement by the court. When I left Livingstone at the end of my first three years in the force, I donated my collection to the Rhodes Livingstone Museum.

50

A Final Examination

Earlier in my final year in Livingstone I had taken my law exams and had found them to my liking. I actually enjoyed writing my answers as I had prepared thoroughly and found the questions easy to answer. The final examination, which I had to pass before I could be promoted to the rank of detective inspector, was the language examination, and I was very nervous.

Shortly before I was due to go on leave I received the call to report to the office of the district commissioner. For months I had been practising and had built up a reasonable vocabulary. My worry was that in the oral examination I might stumble when listening to an African firing off lots of joined sentences as one complete sentence. This was an African trait. In my Chinyanja dictionary I had yet to discover a word that did not end in a vowel. As many Chinyanja words start with a consonant and all end in a vowel, imagine how easy it is to run one word into the following word and so on with little pause for breath, especially if the speaker is excited. Thinking of the oral examination found me nervous and sweating.

On the day of the examination I duly presented myself at the *boma* and was taken out to the garden area in the rear. There I found a district officer sitting in the shade of a tree. Next to his chair stood a table upon which was placed a paper that he was to fill in as my examination took place. He also had a large glass jug filled with some sort of drink in which ice cubes floated. I noted that he was drinking from the only glass. Already I was sweating profusely. He wished me good morning and good luck and leaned back in his chair, crossing his legs.

Out of the corner of my eye I noticed a *boma* messenger approaching, leading a thin old man in tattered rags. The poor fellow appeared to be terrified and prostrated himself in front of me.

I quickly left my chair and raised him up, talking gently to him in Chinyanja. He seemed to be reassured that I meant him no harm and I continued to question him in a gentle voice. I addressed him as "father" and he looked me in the eye for the first time. I asked him in Chinyanja why he had come to the *boma* and what his complaint was. He didn't answer and looked confused. He started to become withdrawn again and appeared to be very frightened. I began to worry that he was frightened of me.

I saw my examiner was now leaning forward and looking puzzled, so fearing that I was about to fail the examination, I left my chair and sat down cross-legged in front of the old man and reached to take hold of his hand. He flinched for a moment but must have realised that I meant him no harm, so I also took hold of his other hand, smiling at him and nodding. He began to nod back, but when I started to talk to him again he just averted his eyes. Occasionally he would look up at something I had said, but that was all. I decided to try signing with my hands and fingers, talking as I did so. Suddenly I seemed to break through and he became animated. My signing was having an effect. I pointed to him and started to use two fingers to walk between us; using the Chinyanja for asking how far he had travelled to get to the *boma*. He signed that he had walked for more than a day, pointing to the sun and miming its track across the sky.

As we progressed, using a mixture of signing and words that he understood, I came to realise that he was reporting the theft of his cow. We were by now laughing and making mooing noises at each other, and he seemed to be no longer afraid of me. He was even signing back at me and we were laughing at each other when we didn't understand at first, but finally did as the signing became more theatrical.

The district officer had now left his table and had pulled his chair alongside us, and was alternately laughing or looking puzzled as we progressed. It turned out that the old man was complaining that his cow had been stolen by another villager, who had threatened him when he had tried to demand her back. The other villagers were afraid of the thief and had told the complainant to report the theft at the *boma*. By now we were good friends and I was enjoying myself, but we were interrupted by the arrival of a *boma* messenger, who whispered something to the district officer, who then burst out laughing.

'There's been a mix-up,' he said. 'They brought you the wrong complainant. This chap is a valley Tonga. He doesn't understand Chinyanja. Someone will get a rocket for putting you through this but I must say I enjoyed watching you work it all out.'

'Does that mean that I have to go through all this again with a Chinyanja speaker?'

'Good heavens, no, you pass with honours,' he replied.

51

Accidental Death and Dr Lepene

In the final couple of weeks of my service in Livingstone I was sent to a remote area on the border between Northern Rhodesia and Angola to investigate the death of a young white man by shooting.

After a drive of about five or six hours I arrived at the place to which the body had been taken. Much of the journey by Land Rover had been achieved by travelling along bush tracks. I was guided by an African constable who was familiar with the area and spoke the local language.

When we arrived I was astonished to see a huge crowd of African men, women and children of all ages sitting in groups or walking about. I also noted a number of well-constructed buildings, into and out of which people were moving. I estimated that there were at least several hundred people in the area and their numbers, during the time that I was there, steadily grew. I realised that we had arrived at the hospital of Dr Lepene.

I must confess that I have guessed at the spelling of the doctor's name. I never saw it in writing. Phonetically it sounded like *Le* (as in French) *pay-nay*. The good doctor was, I think, French. He had qualified as a doctor in Europe as a young man and had taken a journey by ship to the west coast of Africa.

After disembarking he had started to walk inland in a westerly direction. This must have been about fifty years earlier, in or around 1911, just before the First World War. In those days, as today, there was little in the way of border markings in the wild areas. I don't know how he picked the future site for his hospital and built it where he did. He had, however, over the years and obviously with help, developed a place of which he could be proud. He had also gradually assembled a group of intelligent local men and women whom he had trained to be his nurses and medical assistants. Some of these were taking clinics as I arrived.

We were greeted by a young woman, who took us to a room where the body was lying on a table. It had been taken out of a cold box on our arrival. Sitting on a chair at the far end of the room was the doctor, to whom I was introduced.

Even after taking into account his age I was shocked by his appearance. He had a large frame but his flesh seemed to have melted away to the point where he had become a living skeleton. He didn't get up, but smiled and held out his hand. I took it gently, but was then surprised at the power I felt in his grip.

'I haven't much time left and I'm afraid that I can't carry out the post-mortem,' he said. 'The other problem is that I can no longer keep the body in the fridge, which will be needed later today. Take the body with you. I'm sure that the relatives will soon be in Livingstone if they are not there already.'

'Could I ask you a question, sir?' I said.

He nodded.

'You don't look well, sir. Would you let me take you to Livingstone Hospital? I could make you comfortable in the Land Rover.'

He held up his hand. 'I am dying, young man. A day, or maybe two, and I'll be dead. I am happy to hand over my work to the men and women whom I have trained. I am glad to have met you. Give my regards to my friend Mr Hanna and tell him to keep up the good work. This country needs men like him. Now I must go and see my people. Oh, and by the way, my nurse will give you the registration number of the van in which the dead man was brought here, and a description of the man who drove it.'

As we transferred the body to our vehicle I noticed that the crowd had grown considerably in size, and from every direction more people were arriving. We drove back to Livingstone under a full moon with the drive back taking two hours longer than our journey out the previous day.

Later that morning I was able to talk with Mr Hanna and explain what had occurred. I also acquainted him with the state of health of the doctor. After the post-mortem, when the body was released to them by the court, the relatives collected it and thanked the police for bringing him back safely. A date for the inquest was fixed and the relatives informed.

Now armed with the registration number of the vehicle involved in the death, we were in a position to find it. However, we were saved the trouble of doing so when the lad who had been driving the vehicle at the time of the accident drove it into the station yard and offered himself up for interview. To say that he was upset and sorry for what had happened would be an under-statement.

He explained that his friend had been standing in the open back of the truck and had been firing at the animals they were hunting. He had been leaning against the back of the driver's cab when a rifle inside the cab had discharged and killed him. He cried as he recounted how his friend had bled to death and he hadn't been able to stop the bleeding or help him.

He was even sorrier when we confiscated all the guns that had been carried in the vehicle or used that day. I submitted written evidence, which I went through with Mr Hanna in his office as I would be back in England on the day set for the hearing.

The verdict eventually was "death by misadventure".

In a separate court hearing, also conducted when I was on leave in England, the vehicle involved in the death was confiscated as well as all the weapons and ammunition. Finally, a large fine was imposed upon the truck owner for illegal hunting in a restricted area and without a licence. I almost felt sorry for the lad.

As I started to pack my belongings for the following day's departure to England I suddenly realised that by the morning I would have become an inspector. I also wondered where my next posting would be. There was little or no chance that I would remain in Livingstone. The force, like most others, had a policy of moving officers to different areas every few years. It made sense to provide officers with fresh challenges every so often, and each new posting provides different opportunities.

52

Home Leave

On the 26th October 1961 I travelled on my first jet aircraft from Livingstone to Paris, where I was to spend the night in a small hotel near to the airport.

Although I was tired I found that it was difficult to sleep because of noise on the streets near to the hotel and the constant sound of police vehicles and their sirens. There was still a lot of unrest after the failed coup earlier in the year, when an attempt by a number of generals to take over control of the country and establish a military government had been defeated.

The following morning I flew from Paris to London and took a taxi to the house of Anita's parents in Ealing. Here I was greeted by her mother, who was Jewish, and her father, who was Italian. I took to them immediately and found them to be very welcoming.

The following day I went by bus to Performance Cars Ltd, and after looking at a number of cars bought a Jaguar 2.4 mk.1 1957 model for £700. This car, when new, had cost £1,532. It had a top speed of over one hundred mph but only managed to achieve just over eighteen miles to the gallon. I felt that it would be ideal for driving on the new motorways, which had no speed restrictions at that time.

That evening I said goodbye to Anita's parents and set off to locate the new motorway, which would take me from the north of London to somewhere near to Birmingham. On finding the motorway I drove at a steady eighty miles per hour until it ended abruptly near Birmingham. It then took me several hours to find my way through the Midlands and drive into a part of the country that was familiar to me. I stopped for an early breakfast and took my time over coffee to avoid arriving home before the family had got out of bed.

Eventually I stood at the front door of the house I had last seen three years before and rang the bell. When she opened the door to me, my mother took a step back. She said afterwards that she had not immediately recognised me as my skin was so dark. And so my six months' leave began.

*

I could not have chosen a worse time of year to come home. When I first arrived I found it hard to adjust to the low temperatures, but as the winter set in and we moved towards Christmas I really felt the cold. I spent much of my time driving around the country in my Jaguar, visiting friends and burning petrol. I decided that I would not take the car back to Africa with me but would buy a new, more sensible car which would suit African conditions. I eventually settled for a Volkswagen.

I managed a visit to my sister Jill and her husband Joe in a bitterly cold part of Norfolk, and although it was great seeing them again I was glad to leave the icy east winds behind me when I returned to the less cold west of the country.

My brother John was at that time working in a hospital across the Pennines and found it hard to get time off to come over to see me. I managed a visit to see him and we had a meal out together but that was the only time we were able to meet.

Just before Christmas, accompanied by my young sister Jane, now seventeen years old, I drove to the Lake District in search of Lorton, a village to the east of Keswick. Brian Parnaby, an assistant inspector in Livingstone, had asked me to call on his parents who lived just outside the village. We eventually found the Parnaby residence and were made very welcome by Brian's parents. Our visit resulted in me renting a small cottage in the grounds of their house for a week in late January.

A few weeks later Jane, Ann (home from university) and I enjoyed a snow-filled winter holiday. We climbed Helvellyn in knee-deep snow and we all felt that we had achieved something worthwhile. I found that driving every day on snowy and frozen roads improved my driving. All in all we had an excellent holiday.

As spring approached I met up with Anita and Roy and we had a holiday together, staying in Bovey Tracey on the edge of Dartmoor. Later in the year we managed a second holiday, this time in a wet and blustery Lake District, where Anita and Roy taught me how to handle a small sailing boat in a force six to seven wind. Although the boat was small it handled well and soon I was able to steer it well enough to allow my companions to retrieve a sealed empty bottle which they kept throwing overboard in various directions, forcing me to turn the boat into or across the howling gale-force wind.

Another day of my leave was spent at the house of Pete Jameson's parents with his mother and father and other members of his family. We gathered on the day Pete got married in Livingstone. As the time for the wedding approached I was able to describe everything that would be happening. I went on to describe the church as the ceremony was taking place and the reception venue later. I was also able to talk about police work and life in general in Northern Rhodesia.

Eventually April arrived and with it the end of my home leave. Now it was time to return to Africa.

53

Back to Africa

My home leave was due to expire on the 26th April 1962, and I had booked my passage by sea to Cape Town. I was taking my new car with me, of course, and had estimated that I could drive from Cape Town to Fort Rosebery in the three days remaining of my leave after disembarking at Cape Town. It would be a tiring drive of about 1,900 miles but with little traffic, except for that in the large towns, I felt that it could be done.

On my drive down to Southampton I began to feel unwell. By the time I had handed over the car for loading and had found my cabin I was feeling extremely unwell and I knew that the dreaded malaria was back again. Shortly before we were due to leave Southampton there was a knock on my cabin door and a young coloured man entered and introduced himself as the steward who would be looking after the occupants of several cabins in the area, including mine. He had come to see if I would like a drink, but began to look concerned when he saw me. I told him that it was only malaria and that I had tablets that I would take. He asked if I needed a doctor but I told him that I didn't think so. I asked if he would make sure that I always had a supply of cold drinking water and come in occasionally to see that I was alright.

As it happened, that bout of malaria was one of the worst that I had ever suffered and we were approaching the equator by the time I could get up and walk around again. During the time I was confined to my cabin the steward, whom I discovered was called Joe, was in constant attendance. I lost count of the number of times he changed my sweat-soaked bedding and brought ice-cold towels to wipe me down. Needless to say he received a large tip from me at the end of the voyage. I also wrote a letter to the shipping company commending what he had done for me, often when he was officially off duty. I made sure that he had a copy.

Once I was fit enough to go on deck I rapidly regained my strength. We had crossed the equator by this time and I had made some new friends and enjoyed, with them, watching dolphins and flying fish swimming in front of the ship.

After another three days my recovery was almost complete. I was eating well again and recovering my strength. It was then that the captain announced that we would be delivering mail and goods to St. Helena.

The map showed that the island was situated about a third of the way west across the Atlantic on a line drawn from the Angolan coast in West Africa to Brazil. We had been travelling a long way from land for some days and I had not realised it.

We were told by a ship's officer that there were no docking facilities on St. Helena and that anyone wishing to go ashore should be agile and able-bodied enough to jump from the ship's launch on to the quayside without hurting themselves. He warned that there was quite a heavy swell and recommended that only younger and fitter passengers should attempt the landing. Not wanting to miss the chance of seeing the island, I joined the party going ashore.

None of us had anticipated the height of the swell. As we drew up alongside the harbour wall the boat was dropping five feet below and rising five feet above the wall. Of those who had hoped to go ashore there were only three males including me, and also a very fit young lady of about twenty years of age, who were willing to make the jump. We jumped, one at a time, anticipating the rise or fall of the boat, and all of us made good landings. One other guy then decided that he would try as well and also made a good landing. Nobody else fancied the jump. Having been given a time when we would be picked up, we set off together to explore.

We started our exploration by climbing up a set of stone steps known as Jacob's Ladder. There were 699 steps set at forty-five degrees to the horizontal. The ladder was nine hundred feet long. It was used in two directions. It joined the coastal area to the high farming area inland. Farm produce came down from the top to the populated coastal area, and manure for fertilising the fields was sent upwards. We didn't ask where the manure came from or whether it was human in origin.

Our main interest was centred on a visit to Longwood House, where Napoleon was incarcerated after losing the Battle of Waterloo. It was also here that he died. We visited every room in the house and looked out on to a very pleasant view of open fields and jagged mountains.

The most remarkable thing we saw on that visit, however, was the oldest and largest giant tortoise in captivity. His name is Jonathan and he is still alive today. In 1962 when I saw him he was 129 years old. Today he is 182 and reportedly thriving. He has four other tortoises living with him, all younger than he is, but still old.

We left St. Helena that evening and arrived in Cape Town two and a half days later.

54

Cape Town to Fort Rosebery

On arrival in Cape Town I waited for a couple of hours for my car to be unloaded and in the early afternoon set off to drive northwards towards my first target, which was Johannesburg, 868 miles to the north-east.

I filled up the car with petrol before leaving, having been warned that petrol stations were few and far between. Having cleared the area of small towns and villages surrounding Cape Town and finding the road in good condition, I eased the car up to seventy miles an hour and relaxed. There would be no need for map-reading. This road would take me all the way to the Southern Rhodesian border at Beitbridge and then continue through that country to the Northern Rhodesian border at the Victoria Falls.

Shortly after covering 230 miles I sighted my first petrol station. Not knowing how far the next one would be, I stopped the car to top up my tank. As my car was being filled I wandered into the building and was happy to find that food was being served. As I was eating, a young white lad, about twenty years of age, approached my table and addressed me in Afrikaans. I did not understand what he was saying and he immediately switched to English. He told me that he was a student and was studying in Cape Town, but was trying to get home to see his parents in Johannesburg. I told him that I would welcome his company. He told me to call him Davie.

The drive to Johannesburg proved extremely tiring. I found that I was in danger of falling asleep so I developed a routine to keep myself awake. Every hour, on the hour, I stopped the car and sprinted back down the road as far as I could in one minute. Breathless, I then trotted back to the car. This drove away some of my tiredness for the next part of the trip.

After nine hours of hard driving and eight runs back down the road, we eventually arrived at Bloemfontein, the largest town so far on our trip. I had covered the first 624 miles of my journey. It was now about two o'clock in the morning but coffee and breakfast were being served at the petrol station. I had two cups of black coffee and a large breakfast and treated my passenger to the same. He didn't want black coffee but I insisted he drank it as it was his job to keep me awake if I showed any signs of falling asleep.

With Johannesburg still 247 miles away, we set off. I felt refreshed and the coffee was working to keep my brain active. I aimed to reach my passenger's house by 7am at the latest. As it happened it was nearer 8am when we arrived, due to the morning traffic in the area. Davie navigated and finally we arrived at his parents' house, which was large and situated in what appeared to be a wealthy area.

I was invited in and introduced to his parents, who insisted that I should have a few hours' sleep before continuing my journey. By this time I was feeling near to exhaustion and was happy to agree. I was shown to a spare bedroom and slept until midday, when I was wakened by my friend, had a quick shower and was then given a light meal. Davie's father later led me out of Johannesburg in his car so I was able to join the N1 quite quickly.

The drive to the Southern Rhodesian border at Beitbridge was about three hundred miles, which took me a little over four and a half hours. At about five o'clock that afternoon I crossed the Limpopo River and entered Southern Rhodesia. The drive through Southern Rhodesia via Bulawayo to the crossing at the Victoria Falls covered a distance of 481 miles, which I completed during the night, arriving in Livingstone in time for breakfast the following morning. I now had one day left in which to reach Fort Rosebery.

As I had breakfast with one of my Livingstone friends I gradually came to the conclusion that it would be impossible to reach Fort Rosebery that day. I might reach the point where I would have to cross the Katanga Pedicle which crossed the Congo, but there was no way that I would attempt that journey at night even if I was allowed to pass through the customs posts. I decided that I would have to report to my new station one day late.

I drove through the rest of the day, covering the 497 miles to Ndola on the Katanga border. Here I booked into a hotel for the night and after a good dinner, slept like a log until I was awakened by the alarm clock the following morning.

The drive through the Katanga Pedicle was made easier by the fact that I picked up two African women shortly after passing into Katanga. They, together with their luggage, ensured that there was no room for additional hitch-hikers. The drive itself was over a sand road notable for its potholes and deep ruts. I drove carefully, mindful of the heavy additional load that I was carrying. I dropped my passengers off just before I arrived at the Luapula River and its ferry, which was hauled from bank to bank by chains driven by machinery. Once over the river and back in a civilised country, I drove the rest of the way to Fort Rosebery in a couple of hours on a better-graded road.

55

Fort Rosebery

The town was smaller than I had anticipated. There was a small main street with a few shops and I saw houses scattered about in no discernable pattern.

I noticed what appeared to be a fairly large public works department with several buildings and many vehicles inside a large fenced area. I asked for directions to the police station and found it in a wooded area on the edge of the town. It was a small station compared to Livingstone and I entered it to find two African officers manning the enquiry office. As I identified myself they started smiling.

'We have been expecting you, *bwana*,' said the senior officer, a sergeant.

'Where is everybody?' I asked.

They both started chuckling as if at some private joke.

'They are playing golf, *bwana*,' said the sergeant, 'and they will be searching in the long grass for many lost balls.'

His companion roared with laughter.

'My son will also be searching for lost balls. He carries the sticks for the same *bwana* each weekend but spends most of the time looking for balls. He often finds a ball that is not his *bwana's* ball so he keeps them and sells them back to other *bwanas* who have only a few balls left.'

Again, both officers were convulsed with laughter. Leaving my car outside the station, I followed their directions and walked to the final hole of the nine-hole golf course.

A group of three players approached. There was one ball on the green, one about thirty yards short and one missing. The three went to search for the missing ball and quickly found it. The bush was not too deep near to the last hole. I watched as they completed their round and then came over to me. None of them were police officers but they invited me to accompany them to the club, where lunch was available and where scorecards would be checked.

The club was already half-full when we arrived and I was quickly seen and collared by one of the golf-playing police officers who welcomed me to

Fort Rosebery. He told me that my servant, Crispin Sakala, had arrived some days earlier and had been given access to my room, which he had cleaned and polished for me. He had already found some suitable accommodation for himself. I thought to myself, I bet he has found a woman. And so he had, the first of many.

I later found the house which I was to share with three other officers. We each had our own bedroom and shared the bathroom. I found that everyone did their own thing, although we would often sit in the lounge and chat or listen to the radio. Television had not yet reached the Luapula Province.

As I settled in, I quickly became aware that life in the evenings was largely centred on the Fort Rosebery club. The club was the place where the single police officers mixed with guys from the civil authorities, the public works departments and with various business people. There was a dartboard, which was in use throughout the evening, and there were a number of very good darts players. The main activities, however, were drinking and talking. There was always something to talk about or news to pass on in such a small and tight-knit community.

56

Fort Rosebery CID

My first few days in CID were spent getting to know the staff and reading through active files which were now my responsibility as criminal investigation officer at Fort Rosebery. Assistant Superintendent Robby Jones was commanding officer and Superintendent Brian Coase, who had very recently arrived in the Luapula Province, was also stationed at Fort Rosebery and was divisional commander. I had a European detective assistant inspector and several African CID officers as my staff.

At this point I must say that I intend this part of the book to reflect the sort of life that we lived at Fort Rosebery. I shall not dwell on the cases we solved or struggled with. There were many and we worked hard, although life was a little less fraught than it had been in Livingstone. At least it was for me.

Luapula Province covered an area of 19,489 square miles at that time. Since I left Zambia it has become larger due to reorganisation of boundaries. One of my aims as I settled in was to get to know the area. Fort Rosebery had originally (in 1900) been situated in the Luapula Valley, where most of the African population lived at that time. After an outbreak of sleeping sickness in the valley some years later it was moved to the present site in the belief that the higher plateau would be healthier. The town now lies on a featureless plateau situated between the Luapula River to the west and Lake Bangweulu to the east.

57

The Valley

In early May, shortly after my arrival, I decided that I would take a look at the Luapula Valley and its people. I had arrived at the best time of year for exploring. May to September produced only one single rainy day, which was in May. The coolest months of the year were May, June, July and August. It was a very good time to explore, with good, freshly graded roads and pleasant weather.

My visit to the valley introduced me to one of the main Ushi tribal areas. I found that the Ushi people we met were watchful and withdrawn. They exhibited no desire to enter into conversation with my driver, and certainly not with me. Their main language appeared to be Chi Bemba, which I of course could not speak or understand.

As we drove through the area near to the Luapula River I saw a line of people walking along the side of the road towards us. I stopped the vehicle. There was something unusual about the way they were walking, one behind the other. At the front of the group was a young boy, probably about ten or eleven years old. He was holding something in his right hand. On closer inspection I realised that it was the end of a stick, which I then saw was long enough to reach all the way back to the last person in the line of people following him. Each of these people was holding his own part of the stick in his right hand.

They were all men, and I was just wondering if I was witnessing some form of ceremony when my driver said, 'These people are all blind, *bwana*, except for the boy of course. He is their leader and will be taking them somewhere, maybe to work or maybe to be seen by a doctor. There are many such people in this valley.'

Later that morning we saw a similar group further along the valley. In the weeks and months that followed I became more and more familiar with the Luapula area. It was not the healthiest place in which I had ever lived. Malaria was rife among the people living along the valley and was common among the African population even on the plateau and in Fort Rosebery.

I had seen evidence of the blindness which, although also found in other parts of Northern Rhodesia, was almost endemic in the valley tribes in the Luapula area. Rabies was, throughout the province, common enough to cause considerable concern and bilharzia was common among the tribes living along the edge of the Zambezi.

58

A Brief Encounter

Daily work in CID often required me to travel long distances, just as it had in Livingstone. I always had one of my officers with me and learned quite a lot of useful facts about any area we were travelling to or across. On one occasion, with a detective sergeant for company, I was driving the vehicle on our way to Samfya, situated on the shores of Lake Bangweulu, when in the distance I saw a log lying across the road.

Feelings among the African population concerning the move towards independence had been stimulated by local African politicians. Local people were very aware of what was happening in the Congo across the river and there was a tangible air of excitement wherever you went. We had arrested a number of local members of the United National Independence Party (UNIP) for making speeches advocating violence.

Taking all this into consideration I stopped well short of the log, suspecting an ambush. As I considered what to do I suddenly realised that the log was moving slowly across the road from left to right. I drove the vehicle closer and as we approached it I realised that I was looking at a snake. I had not seen the head but I could see the hooked tail, which had just appeared from the bush on the left-hand side of the road. I got out of the car and went to the snake. It was larger than any other snake I had ever seen in the wild or in captivity. The road, which I measured afterwards by striding across, was approximately eighteen feet wide. When we had first spotted the "log" there had been no head or tail in sight. I reckoned that the snake was at least nineteen feet long. It was so large that it had to be a constrictor of some kind.

No longer fearing a possible poisonous bite and wanting to look at the snake's head to identify it, I took hold of it by grasping the hook at the end of the tail. Leaning back, I exerted my full force to hold the snake in position but, finding poor footing in the sand, was slowly pulled to the far side of the road. Here I found good footing against the raised edge of the road and halted the forward movement of the reptile. We had arrived at an impasse.

After about a minute had passed I heard a rustling noise to my left, and then, as I had hoped, the head of the snake appeared about six feet away from where I was standing. The head was triangular in shape and marked on the top with the shape of a dark brown spearhead, and I knew that I was looking at an African rock python. It was not just any old rock python. It was enormous, and it gazed at me with unblinking, expressionless eyes. It remained perfectly still and silent. I had seen enough and gently released my grip on its tail. I was happy to watch the snake as it silently withdrew into the bush.

Excitedly, I turned to speak to my sergeant but found that he had stayed in the vehicle and was sitting there shaking his head. He remained silent for the rest of the trip until we reached Samfya.

I had a good meeting with the officer in charge there and the sergeant went to talk with the African officers. As we left to return to Fort Rosebery I noticed that several African officers were looking at me and shaking their heads.

I mentioned what had happened to a couple of the people I lived with and word soon got around. "Bloody idiot" was the most common comment that was addressed to me. I received strange looks from the African officers. Word had spread quickly amongst them about this new, mad CID officer. I felt that I had never been in any danger and that the experience had been well worth having.

Although I visited Samfya on a number of occasions in the line of duty I never had the time to drive south-east to the site of the death of Dr David Livingstone, the great Scottish missionary and explorer. He died in Chief Chitambo's village at Ilala on the edge of the Bangweulu Swamps in 1873, and his heart was buried there under a *mpundu* tree, which is no longer there. In 1899 the tree was decaying and was cut down and sent to the Royal Geographic Society's museum in London. It was eventually replaced by a memorial plaque.

After he died Dr Livingstone's body was eviscerated before being carried to the east coast of Africa for return to England. The monument to him in Zambia now has four bronze plaques. The latest plaque was added in 1973.

59

Golf at Fort Rosebery

Possessing no golf clubs of my own, I could not enter the weekly golf tournaments so I followed various friends around the course each Sunday. I became more and more frustrated and longed to have a try myself. I asked in the club if anyone knew of clubs for sale.

Nobody did until one evening in late June when one of the golfers approached me in the club and offered to sell me his old clubs. He had ordered a new set and had received them that day. His asking price was very reasonable and he offered to include a lesson in the price. I duly bought the clubs, had my lesson and received as a gift a book on how to play golf. The book contained the main rules of golf as well as coaching tips. He also sold me a box of old balls to use for practice.

I started to practise after I finished work for the day. European officers did not work night shifts but took it in turn to be on call. The town was so small that should the officer on call need assistance, he would receive it almost immediately. There was enough light to allow practice and recovery of balls up to about seven o'clock each evening, and I took advantage of it.

Within a few days I was hitting the balls straight and easily up to about a hundred yards. I had the swing and the power to hit them much further but found that if I applied it, the balls would not go straight. I decided to play careful, controlled golf on the coming weekend.

When Sunday finally arrived I found that I was very nervous. During the week I had, with the help of the sergeant whom I had first met on my arrival at Fort Rosebery, hired two young boys to carry my clubs, scraper and sand. I arrived at the first tee to find about thirty golfers assembled there. Most were chatting and laughing but a number were obviously nursing hangovers. I found that I was due to tee off in the last group.

'It's so that you won't hold the rest of us up,' laughed one of the PWD guys. I took comfort from the fact that the sun, which was just showing above the trees, would not affect me as much as it would those who went before me.

The drive from the first tee was directly into it. It seemed to take forever until it was my turn to drive off. I was paired with a shopkeeper and a guy from the PWD. I was soon to find that neither were competent golfers. When my turn came to drive off I selected a seven iron. I hadn't practised with the woods yet. I hit the ball straight up the fairway about ninety yards or so, unlike my companions, who had both found the rough about fifty yards beyond where my ball had finished up. The hole was a par four and I was on the green in three. Two putts later I proudly entered my score on my card. My fellow golfers, having struggled to extricate themselves from the rough, both scored two over par. There was something to be said for going carefully on this course. At this point I must mention that the "greens" we played to were not grass greens but sand mixed with a binding substance. The scrapers our caddies carried were used to flatten footprints and other marks in the sand.

The third hole was, if I remember rightly, another par four. The tee looked down what was ostensibly a long fairway, which sloped fairly steeply down to the green at the bottom of the hill. To call it a fairway would be a contradiction in terms. Rocks jutted out from the sparse grass and even using preferred lies it was hard to find a place upon which to tee up the ball on sand from the bucket.

I hit a decent drive of about 120 yards and watched as the ball hit one of the many rocks and disappeared at a right angle into the bush on the left of the fairway. Despite both my boys searching with me we could not find the ball. I dropped and then teed up another ball on sand and this time got a good bounce and ended up near the green. One chip and three putts later I holed the putt, and so the day continued.

My companions were faring no better than I was. We went on to lose balls steadily. Later I lost two in the river. When I finally hit my third across the water I hit it into the bush beyond the green and never found it. I felt thankful that I was using the old balls that I had been given when I bought the clubs.

By the time we had completed our round and reported back to the club I had one ball left. Fortunately there were balls on sale in the club. I bought some second-hand balls and a pack of new ones. I handed in my card rather sheepishly and when the marker loudly announced my score there was a loud cheer followed by extended clapping.

One of the players shouted, to loud laughter, 'Did you find the balls snaking around a bit?'

After lunch we did it all again. This time I improved by avoiding some of the mistakes that I had made in the morning. I ended up with a total of one hundred and twenty-something but was not last, and there were quite a number of people who had not beaten one hundred.

*

As time passed and I gradually improved my game I began to use all of the clubs in my bag and to iron out the pulls and the slices. I now used new balls and had a stock of them, but still practised with used balls.

Over time I played with most of the people who were regular players in the Sunday competitions. Apart from a few notable exceptions they were decent people. I found that one could form a fair idea of a person's hidden character by playing golf with him or her. Some pleasant people in everyday life turned into unpleasant, self-pitying moaners on the golf course. Golf also had a way of exposing cheats.

There was a member of the civil administration who was popular and well liked by most people in the town, but I never fully trusted him on anything important when I found out that he cheated on the golf course. I first learned about his methods when I was playing with him one Sunday. He had hit a ball into heavy rough and went to find it. My bag carrier came up to me and told me that the man would cheat and that his ball would fly out of the rough on to the fairway. I waited, and then heard the sound of the club being swung through heavy grass. The ball appeared high in the air and landed in the middle of the fairway. My playing partner appeared through the bushes, sweating but smiling.

'That was a hard one,' he said.

'Well played,' I replied, and we proceeded down the fairway.

'He always does this, *bwana*,' my caddie said quietly. 'Sometimes we caddies go to help him find his ball but if we find it we put it in our pockets, and he will still find his ball when we are not looking and he will always find it in a good place.'

I never thought of the man again without thinking about golf, and never fully trusted him with any kind of sensitive information.

60

Father Tomley

I never saw the name of Fort Rosebery's Catholic priest written down, so I have spelt it as it sounded. Father Tomley was a regular attendee at the Fort Rosebery Club, and would arrive every evening, entering the club with the same blessing.

'God bless all assembled here, and mine's a large whisky, if you please.'

A large whisky would quickly be handed to him and would rapidly disappear down his throat.

'Ah, that's better,' he would say. 'It's been a busy day.'

A second double whisky would appear from a different buyer, but this one would be slowly savoured, and so the evening would progress. Father T, as I shall call him, because most of us knew him by that name, was a learned man who would often enter discussions or tell stories, which would be listened to by attentive groups of us. He was well liked and respected. Yes, he drank to excess but he held his drink well and never made a fool of himself. Occasionally someone, not necessarily of the Catholic faith, might ask his advice about a personal problem and this would be quietly given in the corner of the room he always frequented.

Father T had an unusual way of finding his way home after his night in the club. If we were in the dry season and the weather was fine he would not accept a lift back to his house. He preferred to walk, but his walk home was by a route he had worked out especially for himself and no matter how many whiskies he had consumed it would lead him, without fail, back to his house. He travelled in the large open storm drains. He had an entry point where he could slide into the drain and an exit point near to his house where the drain went round a bend and the side nearest to the house was lower as it was on the inside of the bend.

I liked Father T very much and was one of the many who would take turns to collect him and bring him to the club in the wet season and drive him back to his house at the end of the evening. When I left Fort Rosebery he was still going strong.

61

Fort Rosebery Hospital

The hospital catered mainly for the African population and was staffed by nuns. During the time I served at Fort Rosebery the head of the hospital staff was a nun called Sister Didicus. The good sister was a strict disciplinarian and ran a tight ship, but she was loved by everybody who spent any time with her. Her staff adored her.

The nuns played rounders, which helped to keep them fit, and they played the game very enthusiastically. Sister Didicus was very fit for her age and a great wielder of the rounders bat. She kept her fellow nuns fit by hitting the ball all round the field.

One evening towards the end of the year I was on duty and sitting in the lounge of our house with a couple of the lads. It was a wet night and we were wondering whether it was worth getting soaked by going to the club when the telephone rang. As I was on call, I answered it. It was an emergency call made by one of the nuns at the hospital. A male patient had armed himself with a knife from the kitchen and was running amok through the hospital.

As soon as I told the others what was happening they jumped up to go with me. I broke all records driving to the hospital and we ran into the building expecting to see all sorts of carnage, but everything seemed to be as peaceful as usual. There were no cries for help or screams of fear or pain.

We moved cautiously through the building only to be greeted by Sister Didicus striding round a corner and walking towards us. She greeted us with a beaming smile and thanked us for getting to the hospital so quickly. In her right hand she was gently swinging a rounders bat and she explained that the unruly patient had been subdued by a single tap to the side of the head. He was now sleeping peacefully, having been injected with a quietening medicine.

Later, as we were all enjoying a cup of tea and some excellent cake made that day by one of the nuns, I asked whether she had used paraldehyde to subdue the patient. She looked at me keenly.

'Why do you ask? Are you familiar with it?' she asked.

'I am, as matter of fact,' I answered, and told her the story of it being used on me in Livingstone.

'I use a gentler sort of sedation,' she said, and so the evening progressed. Eventually, as we were sitting alone, my two friends having taken the vehicle and returned to the house, Sister Didicus started to talk about the Ushi people as a tribe.

'They have some barbaric customs,' she said.

She went on to tell me that many of the tribe still believed that the husband was to blame if his wife died in childbirth. Some had even killed husbands in the past by dragging them through fires lit for the purpose.

'These days they usually extort money or goods from the husband. If I suspect that a wife is probably going to die during childbirth, I warn the husband. It gives him a chance to run if he wants to, before the relatives catch him.'

I had not personally come across any cases concerning the deaths of husbands whose wives had died in childbirth, but I had not then been long in the area.

62

A Chance Encounter

Late in 1962 I was returning from a trip to the Copperbelt in continuous heavy rain. Lightning flashes filled the sky, which was so dark that I looked at my watch to check the time. It was only four o'clock in the afternoon.

I had covered barely fifteen miles of the distance to Fort Rosebery after getting off the ferry and leaving Katanga when I saw a figure ahead of me, standing at the side of the road with his arm outstretched. I could see that he was asking for a lift. I could also see that he was a white man and that he looked to be at the end of his tether. I beckoned him into the car and he gratefully sat down, water dripping everywhere.

I asked him where he was going and if his car had broken down. He told me that he had no car and that he was an insurance salesman trying to prove himself. I began to think that I had picked up someone who had escaped from a lunatic asylum.

'Who do you work for?' I asked.

'Legal & General,' he replied, and started to open a briefcase that he was carrying.

'Don't show me now, I need to concentrate on my driving.'

'It's a sort of trial.'

'Bloody hell, some trial,' I said.

To cut a long story short, I bought a Legal & General policy from him the following morning, having found a bed for him overnight. I was in the habit of taking out new policies every so often in those early years so that they would mature over set periods when I needed them later in life. Of all the policies I ever bought, that Legal & General policy paid out the most money and gave me the best return for an investment that I ever received.

63

Sting

In February 1963 on a warm, sticky, rainy night, I climbed into bed and lay on my back, pondering the lack of progress in an ongoing investigation. As I did so I was suddenly struck by such a severe pain in the back of my right leg that I shouted out in agony. I threw the sheet off me and rolled out of bed. Something had stung or bitten me, and I could see that my leg was already swelling. The pain began to make me feel sick but I had to find whatever had bitten or stung me.

By this time one of my friends, who had heard my shout, had come into the room. He told me to go and sit in the lounge and called on a second officer to get the local doctor urgently. He then scoured the room for any sign of my attacker. By now the whole of my leg had swelled to an alarming degree and I was gritting my teeth to avoid shouting out in pain. There was no trace of any snake or insect that could have caused the bite or sting.

When the doctor arrived and examined me he came to the conclusion that I had been stung by a scorpion as he could only find a single puncture wound. A snakebite would have produced an altogether different wound. He gave me an injection and some strong painkillers and ordered me to remain in bed until he passed me fit for duty. I returned to work about four days later but had pains in my leg for a further couple of months. From that night onwards I always stripped and remade my bed every night before getting into it.

64

Drama on the Tee

In early April 1963, as the rains were beginning to taper off, I was, one Saturday afternoon, practising on the golf course ready for the following day's competition. I was playing with a chap from the public works department. Playing ahead of us on the same hole were Brian Coase, my commanding officer, and Helen, the daughter of a senior civil administration officer.

We were all playing the worst hole on the course. It was the third hole, the one with the long, rocky, downhill fairway with thick bush close in on both sides.

Helen was accompanied by her two dogs. They were beautiful animals. I think that they were Labradors. They were very well trained but when following Helen around the golf course they explored the bush on both sides of the fairway, appearing and disappearing, but always remaining within calling distance.

We waited until Helen and Brian left the green and started to make their way towards the next tee before playing our second shots to the green. The fourth hole was a short par three, about 120 yards in length. The area in front of the fourth tee flooded in the wet season to a depth of about two feet, and it was almost at its deepest that day following a very wet rainy season. When the area was flooded and badly hit balls ended up in the water the ball boys would wade in and locate the balls with bare feet and pick them up with their toes. This was the day when all that changed.

My partner and I had just arrived at the green and were within chatting distance of the two ahead of us when a number of things happened in quick succession. I heard Helen shout at the dogs to come out of the water in front of the tee. This was followed by two separate screams. One was Helen screaming and the other a dog screaming.

I started to run towards the tee and was in time to hear Brian shout, 'No, don't, Helen!'

But he was too late. Clutching her golf club she had jumped into the water towards where there was splashing and the sound of the dog screaming. It all happened in a flash. I saw her bend forward and grab the dog and start to move to the edge of the water. She had dropped her club and held the dog, which was bleeding heavily, in her arms. The other dog was running backwards and forwards along the edge of the water and was crying.

We all raced to her and as she stumbled out of the water she kept repeating over and over again, 'Crocodile, crocodile.'

My partner offered to run for help and transport and set off as Brian and I started to work on the dog, which was crying. It had been slashed along its side and was bleeding copiously. Fortunately the wound didn't expose any interior organs so our main aim was to stop the bleeding. We took towels from our golf bags and stemmed the flow. Our caddies, who had always been in the habit of wading to collect balls, were very quiet and upset.

We were using the raised tee as a place to work on the dog when there was a huge splash and a scream from Helen. She saw what was happening before either Brian or I did. Out of the water lunged a large crocodile. It had propelled itself forwards over the soil upon which the tee was built and crouched there with its head and lower jaw resting on the tee. I took the dog and carried him away from the tee as the beast obviously wanted him for its lunch. Helen helped me to carry him. I turned to speak to Brian but he hadn't come with us. He was standing on the tee holding what I suspected was a one iron in his hands.

I shouted, 'For Christ's sake, come away from there, Brian.'

He took no notice of me. Club raised, he moved slowly towards the crocodile and then with one swing cracked it on the head with the club. I had run from Helen and the dog and was almost next to him, ready to drag him away should the enraged crocodile decide to attack, but it blinked and slowly slid backwards into the water and disappeared.

I looked at Brian standing there, still holding the club at shoulder level, and said, 'Bloody hell, Brian – I mean sir – what on earth did you think you were doing?'

'I was paying it back for what it did to the dog and to Helen.'

As we talked and went back to Helen, two vehicles approached at speed. In the distance I saw another vehicle approaching. Later the vet confirmed that the dog, although still shivering with fright and feeling very sorry for himself, would recover.

Brian Coase went back to the station to prepare a leaflet to be distributed around the town and African areas, instructing that care should be taken because the area had now become dangerous. In the past, as far as anyone knew, crocodiles had stayed in the Luapula River and had not ventured up our little tributary. But now we knew that they had. Brian and I agreed that the crocodile was about eleven to twelve feet long and certainly big enough to kill and eat a human being. An order was issued to golfers to stop ball boys from going into the flooded area in the wet season.

Helen's dog made a full recovery, but she stopped taking the dogs around the course in the wet season. Even in the middle of the dry season both dogs avoided the area and waited up the hill, well away from the river. The only danger they were exposed to there was being hit by a golf ball.

65

Incident on the Katanga Pedicle Road

As I mentioned earlier, I travelled along the pedicle road across Congolese territory for the first time on the day of my arrival at Fort Rosebery.

Only later did I begin to learn what a dangerous crossing it could be. United Nations troops had first been deployed in the Congo in July 1960. With the Katanga government virtually at war with the Congolese government and murder, rape and pillage occurring on a fairly large scale, the mass flight of thousands of mainly white civilians had taken place, as I had witnessed in Livingstone.

From late 1960 onwards numerous clashes occurred between pro-Tshombe loyalists and Baluba tribesmen who supported the Congolese government. By mid to late 1961 almost seven thousand Balubas had been killed and were now attacking both sides in the conflict. After I arrived at Fort Rosebery, fighting continued in various parts of Katanga and went on until January 21st 1963 when Moïse Tshombe conceded defeat and allowed UN officials into his last remaining stronghold in Kolwezi. Officially this ended the fighting and the country was now united as the Democratic Republic of the Congo. However, this was not to say that it was a safe place through which to travel.

I made three return trips through the pedicle before January 1963 and I found each one an uncomfortable experience. When a group of people stood in your way to force you to stop the car and take on passengers and their luggage, it was asking for trouble to refuse. This stopping of the car occurred on every trip and always resulted in an overloaded car.

On one occasion, however, when driving to the Copperbelt I saw nobody waiting for a lift and noted that the villages along the road were empty. There was no sign of life anywhere. I came upon the cause about forty minutes later when I saw a large cloud of dust ahead of me. As I approached it I realised that I was following a heavily armed United Nations convoy, transporting at least one but maybe two battalions of infantry. They were possibly Indian troops by the look of them. I didn't try to overtake and they turned off the road just short of the customs posts into Northern Rhodesia. The post on the Congolese side of the border was empty. Everyone appeared to have fled. I carried on to the Northern Rhodesian side where I was greeted by questions about what was happening. I told them what I had seen.

Later in 1963, after the end of the rainy season, I had work to do with the CID people in Mufulira in the Copperbelt. I decided that whilst I was down there I would treat myself to some new golf clubs and stock up on golf balls. I was really getting a taste for golf and I felt that I would improve my game with new clubs. The dry season had arrived and things were starting to become competitive again. I spent half an hour selecting my clubs and a new golf bag and then set off on the journey back to Fort Rosebery. It was a journey that I shall always remember and made a great impact upon my life at that time.

The road was in very poor condition and little had been done to maintain it during the rainy season. I had been driving slowly and carefully for about an hour and had covered about twenty-five miles when I saw a crowd of Africans, mainly men and boys, standing in the road. One of them signalled me to stop. I had no option but to do so, and slowed the car until I came up to them. I wound down my window, expecting a request to give several of them a lift.

Before I could react, one of them reached into the car and removed the ignition key. I was told to get out of the car by one who spoke English. I asked why and was told that they were going to search the car for weapons. As I was about to tell them that I had no weapons, the door was wrenched open and I was pulled out. Two men dragged me to the side of the road and threw me, face down, on to the sand. One of them knelt with his knee in my back, and by twisting my head I saw that he was pointing a handgun at my head. The other man placed his foot on my leg behind my knee and moved all his weight on to it.

Eventually there was a shout from the direction of my car, followed by excited talking. I felt the handgun press hard into the back of my neck and I closed my eyes. My life didn't flash before me. I did not think about loved ones or my life so far. I came to the conclusion that there was no way of escaping becoming yet another statistic in the number of murders carried out in the Congo, and I felt a profound, helpless sadness come over me. I closed my eyes and waited.

Suddenly, the man who had told me to get out of the car spoke to me.

'We have found guns in your car. You have lied to us.'

'I have no weapons!' I shouted. 'I don't carry weapons in my car.'

'You are lying,' he said threateningly, and threw my new golf bag down alongside me. I forced myself to laugh loudly, although it was the last thing I felt like doing.

'Those are not guns. They are golf clubs. If you let me stand up I will show you,' I said.

'We have also found bombs, boxes of them,' he shouted.

'They are not bombs. They are golf balls, which you hit with the golf clubs. It is a game that we white people play. Let me show you, and then you can try the game for yourself.'

Eventually, after talking among themselves, they hauled me to my feet. I was shaking and felt sick. I found a patch of sandy soil and marked a circle about twice the size of a golf cup on a golf course. I dug out the sand with my hands. I then measured twenty paces and placed a ball on the sand. I took my putter and in four putts had the ball in the hole. A boy brought the ball back as I handed the putter over to my captor. He had watched me intently and had the ball in the cup in six putts. He demanded to try again, and did so several times until he finally beat my score with a three.

Things progressed over the next half-hour, with more people trying different clubs. I was able to observe the hierarchical structure of the group mapped out before me. The stronger took balls and clubs from the weaker and put down objections violently. They in turn were sometimes subjected to similar violence from those superior to them. I watched impotently as those without golf balls hit stones instead and I saw my new clubs ruined before my eyes. I said nothing.

It was now a case of getting out of the place alive as soon as possible. I offered advice on how to play golf to the man who spoke English and he listened intently. By now he was in possession of two clubs and several balls. Eventually I told him that it was time for me to leave or I would be in trouble for being late. I asked him if he would like to keep the clubs as a gift and he smiled at me and offered his hand. There was no apology for the way I had been treated. It was as though it had never happened.

As I got into my car, the keys already back in the ignition, I turned to wave, and they all stood and waved back as though they were waving to a family friend. I set the milometer to zero before I pulled away to enable me to give an accurate location of the incident when I arrived back in Fort Rosebery. I had driven a couple of miles when I had to stop and vomit at the side of the road. I heaved and retched and then vomited until I thought my stomach lining was being ripped out of me. I stayed bent double until I was sure that there was nothing more to bring up; then got back into the car. My body was shaking uncontrollably and I sat there for about ten minutes before I recommenced my journey.

When I reached Fort Rosebery I found the CO and told him that the road through the pedicle was dangerous, and mentioned that I had been stopped and seen others stopped and that the people stopping the vehicles were violent and unbalanced.

He asked if my car had been searched and I told him that it had, and that the people doing the searches were thugs. I did not mention what had happened to me. I decided to keep that information to myself, but I recommended that a bulletin should be put out warning drivers of the risks involved. He said that he would do so and added that he would inform Lusaka. He looked at me keenly.

'Are you sure that you are alright, David?' he asked.

I told him that I was, but I wasn't.

As the days passed I concentrated on my work, and although I went to the club most nights I didn't stay as long as usual. I tended to stay in my bedroom more than I had in the past, and gradually I became more and more depressed. I felt that I needed to talk to someone about my depression and inability to sleep for any length of time, but I couldn't talk to anyone in the police force or they might decide that I was unfit for duty. If I spoke to the local doctor he would probably give me tablets, which would reduce my ability to do my job properly. I could think of only one person in whom I could safely confide. I would talk to Father Tomley, but not in the club.

A few nights later I stayed in the club until I saw Father Tomley stand up and prepare to leave. I waited for him to put on his coat and went across to him.

'I am leaving now, so I'll take you home, Father,' I said.

He thanked me and we went to my car.

'I wonder if I could talk with you, Father, in private?'

'You have something which is troubling you, my son. I have been aware that you have not been yourself recently. Are you in trouble, by any chance?'

I told him that I was not in any trouble but that something had happened to me which was affecting me. When we arrived at his house he invited me inside.

'Come in and we'll have a drink together. Orange juice for you, I believe?'

He busied himself pouring the drinks and I noticed he poured himself a small glass of what appeared to be a very expensive Scottish whisky. He smiled at me.

'A grateful constituent gave me this bottle. I keep it for when I have problems to solve or people to help.'

He sat back and fixed me with his eyes.

'Now tell me what is troubling you, my son. I know that you are not of the Catholic faith but that doesn't matter. I will help if I can.'

That evening I told him about what had happened to me on the road in the Congo. I told him about my feelings as the gun was pushed hard into the back of my neck. I spoke of the sadness I felt and how I had become resigned to the bloody ending of my life, and had then shut out all thought. I explained what had then happened and my sickness on the way back after I had been allowed to leave. I ended my account by saying how I had been feeling since I had returned to Fort Rosebery that day.

We talked long into the night and by the end I felt much better. He felt that I had been saved by God for service later in my life.

When I smiled, he said, 'I know you are not of the faith, but God watches over all of us and has plans we know nothing about. One day you will serve the greater good without realising how you were guided into it.'

I bid him goodnight and went back to my room. I slept soundly that night and gradually, over the following days, began to feel better. I delivered a very expensive bottle of whisky to his house a couple of weeks later and thanked him for his help.

'I only listened as you voiced your feelings and sorted them out yourself,' he said.

'No, you did more than that,' I replied.

We had a drink together; I with my orange juice and he tasting the whisky I had brought for him.

66

A New Taste for Fort Rosebery

As the dry season set in and the winter of 1963 began I introduced a new taste to the residents of Fort Rosebery. The food we were served by our cook was quite acceptable by African standards but the menu was limited and repetitive. At times I longed for meals and treats such as those my mother produced when I was at home. I longed for something sweet, but at the same time full of flavour. My mother was a genius in the kitchen and had a fantastic memory for recipes for all sort of dishes and things to eat. She stored this knowledge in her head and rarely consulted a cookery book. My thoughts and longings turned towards lemon cheese.

Most people today are used to seeing jars of lemon curd for sale in the supermarket, and only occasionally will you find lemon cheese. There is a difference between them and I have always preferred lemon cheese. I wrote to my mother and asked for the recipe. Her reply took time, as always. She wrote that because she always cooked instinctively, rarely measuring the ingredients exactly, she had had to make some lemon cheese and note down the ingredients and amounts as she did so. She had enclosed the directions for me. All I had to do now was to buy the ingredients I needed and produce a trial jar or two. Eventually everything I needed was assembled.

I waited until everyone was at the club and began the process. Everything went well and the aroma in the kitchen as I worked brought back all the right memories. I had produced enough to fill three jars. All I had to do now was to be patient and let the contents cool and settle. I hid the jars in my bedroom and waited for three days before I opened one. I stuck my finger into the jar and withdrew it coated in pale, yellowy, sticky delight. It smelled and tasted exactly as it had when I had last tasted it at home several years before.

That evening as we sat down to dinner I produced a jar of my lemon cheese, together with a plate upon which I had assembled a number of slices of buttered bread. I invited my three housemates to try my creation after dinner was concluded. When they did so, they demolished the bread that

I had prepared and cut and buttered more. Very quickly most of the contents of the jar had been consumed, with much licking of lips and many compliments.

I took the remaining two jars to the club and first invited the ladies present to try the lemon cheese, followed by Father Tomley and then any other members of the club. The following day I had several visits to my office from ladies asking if I had copies of the recipe for the cheese. It was all, of course, a one-week wonder, although months later when I finally left Fort Rosebery many of the residents of the town had a few jars on their shelves.

67

Moving On

Time moved on and we approached the wettest part of the year. I happened to be on call one night and had gone to the station after receiving a call for help. An arrested African male was giving the African staff problems by claiming that he could not be arrested as he was a senior official of the United National Independence Party.

When I arrived I could see that the man was very drunk and could hardly stand. The officers on duty were obviously worried about arresting him because he had been threatening reprisals if they did. I turned to the drunken man and told him that I was going to give my officers an instruction to arrest him.

'They have to obey me as a senior officer, so if you want to complain then you can complain about me. I shall see the district UNIP official for this area in the morning and complain about your behaviour. You are a disgrace to your party. When you take over the government of this country you will need a loyal police force to assist in keeping the country safe. You should be ashamed of yourself.'

I then instructed a constable to put him in a cell, which he did without any protest from the drunken and now subdued man.

I turned to the African officers and said, 'Never consider how important an accused person is when dealing with him. Just do what you were taught to do in training school. Your president will rely upon you to do this. Never be afraid of some local bully. Just do your duty and nobody can accuse you of doing wrong.'

As I shook off the raindrops and entered the lounge back at the house I sensed a tension in the air. My three housemates were clustered around the radio and were listening intently to an American voice. The radio volume was turned up high.

As I entered one of my friends said loudly, 'President Kennedy has been shot dead.'

I quickly sat down and joined them in listening to the news as it came in.

The date was the 22nd November 1963, and yes, I will always remember where I was and what I was doing at the time. We listened intently for some time until the news became repetitive and we had had enough.

The following morning I went to the local UNIP office and spoke to the official in charge. I gave him the details of what had happened and what had been said and told him that his party would need the goodwill of the police if they wanted a settled country.

'And the police will be directly answerable only to the president and his chief of police,' I added.

The official surprised me when he nodded and said, 'I will talk to him. The drink does him no favours. I hope that you made him think.'

We parted with a handshake and I felt a small feeling of hope rise in me.

On Christmas Eve 1963 I was called into the commanding officer's office and told to pack my belongings and report tos Lusaka Central CID. I was to be transferred. By the time I had gathered everything together and said my goodbyes to friends and other acquaintances it was late afternoon. I certainly wasn't going to attempt a crossing of the pedicle at dusk. I would have a few orange juices in the club and say a few more goodbyes.

68

Lusaka Central Police Station

On Christmas morning I was up early. I had my final breakfast in Fort Rosebery, gave the cook a Christmas present and went to the car. Crispin had already loaded it with my luggage and his own and was sitting in the front passenger seat. I was glad to see that we had no room for further passengers. The other three with whom I shared the house were still sleeping off the previous evening's drinks, so I left my house key for them on the breakfast table.

Our journey across the pedicle was for once uneventful. When hitchers saw how heavily loaded we were they just shrugged and waved us through. I stopped briefly in Mufulira for petrol and sandwiches and then we continued on our way. We had 240 miles left to drive to reach Lusaka. I estimated that it should take us about four and a half hours of steady driving. The rest of our journey was now on the T2 and passed relatively quickly. We met little traffic and eventually reached the northern outskirts of the capital.

After about ten minutes I found that I was driving south down Cairo Road. Eventually I saw the sign indicating Church Road and followed it over a bridge, which crossed the main north-south railway line.

After driving a few hundred yards I saw my new workplace. It was an impressive building which extended for some distance behind an imposing façade. It stood four storeys high with single officers' living quarters commanding the top floor. There were several vehicle entrances which led to the rear of the building and the vehicle yard beyond.

I selected one of these and drove through it. I found a parking space for my car and went to find the main entrance to the building, which I expected would lead to the enquiry office. As I entered I saw that the desk was manned by two African officers. One was wearing the uniform and headwear of an assistant inspector. He looked up and saw me.

'Good afternoon, sir. May I help you?' he asked.

I noted that his manner was friendly and businesslike. I was impressed. Apart from the great and good Michael Mataka, with whom I had worked in

Livingstone and who was destined to become the first African officer to rise to the rank of Chief of Police in 1965, this was the first African officer holding assistant inspector rank that I had met. I identified myself and he welcomed me warmly.

'You are the second new officer to arrive here today, but I'm afraid that it is not a good day to be arriving here.'

I asked him why that was.

'Apart from the place being empty except for the officers on duty, the kitchen staff have been given the day off and the bar is also not open. All the unmarried officers who live at the station have been invited by married officers and their families to spend part of the day with them when not on duty. I'm afraid that you will have to go into the town to find somewhere to eat.'

After being shown my room, which was the last room on the top floor at the far side of the building, I helped Crispin to unload the car and we carried all my belongings up the top floor and dumped them in the room. Crispin then left and said that he would see me in the morning. As he was leaving I gave him two weeks' extra wages to help him to find and settle into his new accommodation. I didn't ask where he would go. Knowing him as I did, I was confident that he would soon find a suitable temporary place to occupy until he found something permanent.

Later that evening, together with the other officer who had arrived that day, I went in the car down Cairo Road looking for somewhere to eat. Everywhere was packed, mainly with Africans all noisily celebrating Christmas. All the tables in every eating-place we tried in the centre of the city had been taken. We eventually found a small café away from the main streets and had dinner there. We didn't linger over our food, as we were both tired after long journeys.

69

CID Lusaka

The following morning I wakened early and went down to the enquiry office to check on shift changeover and breakfast times. I then went in to breakfast and chatted to a couple of the uniformed staff, who told me how things were run at the station and how to open a bar account, which had to be settled each month. We chatted about the numbers of people leaving the force and the constant European staff turnover. Both seemed rather depressed by events. I learned where the CID offices were located and I set off to find them.

I eventually found the CID area, which was home to twenty-five or so officers. They ranged from aides to CID to a detective chief inspector, who was in charge but had already applied for retirement. About twenty officers had arrived for work. I introduced myself and was told that the superintendent in charge of the Lusaka District CID wished to see me when I arrived.

I was directed to his office. I knocked on the door and heard a distant call to come in. He had a large office and sat looking out of the window with his back to me.

'Sit down, David, and make yourself comfortable.'

I knew that voice very well, and my pleasure in hearing it was confirmed when Don Bruce, now superintendent in charge of Lusaka Division CID, swung his chair around and observed me with a wide grin on his face.

I spent the next half-hour listening to him laying out duties and what he expected from me. He had planned that I should spend three or four weeks familiarising myself with the duties and progress of each individual section of the department.

With his well-known smile, he gave me my first assignment, which was to work on the "crimes against business" section. This was a small section dealing with complaints mainly from Asian shop and business owners. The complaints were invariably concerning theft of stock or unfair trading practices, many of which were not police concerns.

He then went on to list the order in which he wished me to tackle the other sections. I took notes as he spoke. My last task would be to work on sudden and/or unnatural deaths, violent assaults and all interracial assaults of a serious or political nature. As Lusaka Central was the largest and the most senior police station in the division, all serious and or sensitive crime that the satellite stations could not handle came to us.

He confided in me that he expected legislation in the immediate future to facilitate the departure of a large number of European police officers from the force. This would hasten the rapid promotion of suitable African officers, who would move into the vacant positions. It would be an important part of our job to steer the right people towards promotion.

'The boss', as I called him in Livingstone and would now do so in Lusaka, told me to take the day off to sort myself out and locate where everything was in the building.

The New Year of 1964 had arrived almost unnoticed and I had quickly settled into the hard-working routine of a large city CID force. I found that on the whole I was working with a good set of officers. The African officers formed the larger part of the squad and varied in ability and enthusiasm. I started to keep private notes on individual officers who showed ability and enthusiasm for the job and who did not need to be pushed or reminded too often.

I mentioned what I was doing to the boss, who replied, 'Well, I expected that you would do so.'

70

The Winds of Change

Early in January 1964 a scheme was introduced to allow serving officers to retire. The scheme would become effective from the 1st May. Officers would be allowed to retire at any time upon giving six months' notice. Any officer giving notice within a month of the 1st May would not be required to remain in the country after independence. On the 24th October 1964, Northern Rhodesia would be granted independence as the new state of Zambia.

The new ruling had included information relating to pay and pensions and their calculations, and formed the main talking points for discussions in the mess for several weeks. It became apparent that for those of us staying on after independence there would be no more six months' home leave on full pay every three years, and more importantly, salaries would be paid by the Zambian government and not the Crown Agents for the Colonies. Very few found the new terms attractive although we all realised that they were to be expected.

71

A Rude Awakening

As the weeks passed and I got to know everyone, I found that I slotted easily into life at Lusaka Central. I was placed on the rota for call-out at night and did my share of evening shifts. There was a steady stream of cases for officers on call and life was much busier than it had been at Fort Rosebery.

Nights when one was not on duty were usually spent in the lounge, drinking, reading or more likely just chewing the fat about resignations, pensions, promotions and all the latest rumours about what was happening in the country as a whole. I stuck with my orange juice, and on nights when I wasn't on duty or call generally left the lounge early and tried to get a good night's sleep.

On one such night I was awakened suddenly by a strange sound. It was a distant sound, but was steadily getting nearer. My first impression was that it was a train travelling at high speed, but trains didn't travel through Lusaka at high speed. As the sound came nearer it became louder and the glass on the ledge above the sink began to vibrate and jiggle about. By now whatever was causing the sound was almost upon us, and I opened the bedroom door on to the corridor.

Other officers started to appear from their rooms and the noise of smashing glass and falling objects could be heard all along the corridor. The building started to tremble and I felt the floor vibrating. The noise level seemed to reach a peak and then the rumbling sound started to move away into the distance.

It later transpired that we had experienced an earth tremor. I thought that I would not like to experience a proper earthquake. No major damage had been done, but one officer who happened to have had his girlfriend in bed with him at the time was able to boast that she had said that she had felt the earth move.

72

The Police Ambulance

Parked in the yard of the station there was always a police ambulance fuelled up and ready to go. There was no dedicated driver on standby for the vehicle. A number of officers who were qualified to drive force vehicles were allowed to drive the ambulance. Anyone in this position had also to have a current first-aid qualification, as did those who were travelling as passengers. I was qualified and was happy to take out the ambulance if needed. Some qualified officers preferred not to do this kind of work unless there was nobody else available.

During my first few months I went out to several serious accidents, one of which had resulted in the death of three young European men in a car which had been in collision with a vehicle driven by an African man. Both vehicles were wrecked and traffic officers were at the scene when we arrived. Normally we wouldn't have transported bodies in the ambulance, but would have sent another vehicle for them.

I was arranging for the bodies to be moved as quickly as possible from the scene when a voice said, 'Good grief, have some respect for the dead. Take care how you handle them.'

I turned round and saw that it was Pete Saffin, who had been in the same squad as me at training school. I had last seen him at the Northern Rhodesia Football Finals in August 1962.

'Sorry, Pete. Look behind you.'

Coming up the road towards us was an angry crowd of African people. Pete had been intent upon examining the scene and had not yet seen them.

'Oh, bloody hell,' he said. 'You'd better get going then.'

'I'll send backup for you,' I replied, and set off back to the station.

73

Blooding the Staff

Attending accidents always carried a risk. African crowds could be very volatile and easily roused to violent action. The worst accident I had so far attended had occurred outside the city and was at a railway crossing on the T2 north of Lusaka.

I had begun to take out the more senior and experienced African officers in CID whenever there was something particularly horrible to see or a particularly difficult scene to deal with. Some of them could distance themselves from the horrors around them, but others were affected and distracted. I had begun to build up a picture of the various characters in the section.

The traffic officers were already at the scene, and I was not involved but I wanted to see how the two officers I had with me would react. It would have been hard to envisage a more upsetting scene. The train had stopped quite some distance beyond the impact area, which had been at the road crossing.

The car, containing what was left of an Asian family, was hardly recognisable as a car and was smouldering high up on the top of an anthill at the side of the crossing. It transpired that an entire family of three or four adults and I think four children had been wiped out instantly. All that was left of them and the car was a bloody mess and I didn't envy the traffic officers their job.

My companions had turned pale, but both gathered themselves together and started to answer questions I put to them about what they thought might have happened. I then asked what they would do if they came upon such a scene and help was not likely to arrive quickly.

As they answered, I questioned them further based on their answers and asked for alternative ways of approaching problems. I could see that they were beginning to think more carefully and take into account various options. When I finally felt that they had thought through the problems thoroughly enough and had benefited from the exercise I decided it was time to leave.

As they had concentrated on the problems, they had also gradually begun to separate their feelings of horror from the need to think clearly, form an action plan and organise the protection of the scene. As we drove back to the station they continued to discuss the problems connected to the scene and I didn't interrupt. I would make further notes on each of them that evening.

Independence Day was on the 23rd October 1964 and the build-up to it was a very busy time for all members of the force in every part of the country.

The actual handing over control of the country to the new African government took place in Lusaka in front of representatives of most of the world's nations. The police were faced with a multitude of tasks aimed at ensuring that everything went smoothly and safely.

In the end everything passed peacefully and with great rejoicing from the thousands of Africans who assembled for the ceremony as the Union flag was lowered and replaced by the Zambian flag.

I was now a member of the Zambian Police Force.

74

Restlessness

There had been few feelings of not being welcome in the country, as some had predicted. There had been no mass rape of white and Asian women, as others had predicted. Early in the life of the new government the maximum penalty for anyone found guilty of rape was changed from death by hanging to possible life imprisonment. I imagine that the new government had been worried about the possibility of a large increase in sexual assaults by Africans on European and Asian women.

There had been no mass seizure of farmland, as was to happen later in Southern Rhodesia. Although many white people had left the country, many others had remained. Jobs which had previously been carried out by white people but were within the ability range of the less experienced Africans were gradually being handed over, so all in all the transition was taking place quietly and mainly peacefully.

We continued training our African police staff in a way which tested not only their ability but also their stamina and their desire for promotion. Only the best would be good enough to take over. Everything was progressing as I had hoped. Some of the promoted officers were very quickly lost to us, as they were sent to other stations in the Lusaka area and beyond to establish or take over small CID units.

Eventually 1965 arrived and work continued apace to help the African staff take increasing responsibility. As the year progressed I began to feel restless and wondered about leaving the force, but I was undecided. My current three-year term would end on the 22nd April. I had listened to a number of the African CID officers expressing alarm and despondency about the numbers of white officers who were already leaving. I started to scan the various newspapers for advertisements for police jobs abroad and one afternoon I found one for police officers needed in Borneo.

I found out as much as I could about that country and learned that there existed a confrontation, which had started in late 1962, between Indonesia and Malaysia. Elements of the British Army were deployed, together with other Commonwealth forces, in support of the Malaysians against the Indonesian forces.

I telephoned the contact number given in the advert and was asked a few questions relating to my present job. We then agreed a date and time for an interview, which would take place in Salisbury in Southern Rhodesia. Having taken no local leave for almost two years, I applied for a week's leave and said, without mentioning my real reason for taking it, that I was going down to Livingstone to visit some old friends, which was partly true. My leave was scheduled for the first week in March. I felt that after the interview I should have a much clearer idea of where my future would lie.

On the first day of my leave I arrived in Livingstone. I visited the police station and was amazed at the changes. I recognised hardly any of the European officers, but was greeted warmly by a number of African officers whom I knew. I had a drink at the bar with a couple of officers with whom I had originally served, and found the same unease about the way things were going. Later I visited some of my other friends from the equitation and saddle club.

75

Interviews

The following day I drove to Salisbury, the capital of Southern Rhodesia. My interview was scheduled for the next day and would take place in one of the government buildings in the city. I found a good hotel, had dinner and went to bed. My interview was scheduled for early the following afternoon.

The next morning I spent walking around the city. I returned to my hotel for lunch; then took a taxi to the building where the interview was due to take place.

Having taken a lift to the top floor I was directed to a room in which a secretary was working. She offered me a cup of coffee, and shortly after this she invited me into an adjacent room where three men were seated. They all stood up, shook hands with me and introduced themselves. There was a senior police officer from the local police force, a representative from the British Embassy and a third man who gave his name but did not reveal what his position was.

The interview lasted for about forty minutes and was very interesting. It was obvious that they were keen to recruit experienced officers with a view to using them to improve the effectiveness of the local police force in Borneo. Not much different to what we were doing in Zambia, I thought.

At the end of the interview I was offered the position. They told me that it would remain open if I was serious about taking up the offer. I promised to let them have my answer in writing within two weeks. We all shook hands and I left the room.

As I walked out of the office and along a corridor towards the exit, I heard my name called. A door in the corridor had opened and a well-spoken white man with a local accent asked me if I could spare him a couple of minutes. He held the door open for me and we went inside into a well-furnished office. He offered me a chair and sat down opposite me.

A lady who appeared to be his secretary sat to the side of us. She had a file open in front of her and started to read aloud from it. What I was hearing

213

amazed me. She had details of my name, my date of birth, details of my education and, most interesting of all, my full national service history including promotions and details of work in Eritrea, Sudan and Egypt with the South Lancashire Regiment. Then she started to read details concerning my work so far for the Northern Rhodesia Police in Choma, Livingstone, Fort Rosebery and Lusaka. She even had a copy of the letter I had received from my CO upon leaving Livingstone. I was then staggered to hear her read out the marks I had received in the various examinations taken to achieve promotion to inspector level. It gradually became apparent that they were mainly interested in my law examinations results.

'You are remarkably well informed,' I said.

'Yes, we are. We have a number of good friends in the civil service and of course in the police force and the army in Zambia.'

'Well, I am very impressed, but why are you showing me this information?'

'We know that Zambia, now that it is independent, has good, experienced officers who are presently working for the Zambian government but who will soon be leaving the country,' answered the man opposite me. 'We are making lists of such officers who interest us, with a view to offering some of them positions in this country when they leave. You are such an officer.'

'And what sort of position would you be offering me?'

'Well, your profile indicates that you are very much at home when working in court, either as a witness or acting as a prosecuting officer. Your law examination results show that you have an excellent knowledge of the criminal law that our two countries mainly share. We feel that you would fit nicely into our legal system as a resident magistrate. We have several vacancies and there will be more to follow. You would, of course, be assisted in court by assessors and have legal and secretarial backup.'

'I shall have to think about your offer over the coming couple of weeks,' I said.

'Of course, but let us know your decision as soon as you can.'

We shook hands and I left the building, rather dazed by the afternoon's events. There would be much to think about in the next week or two and I was really in need of some advice, but I could not think of anyone whom I knew well enough to approach.

76

Promotion

I returned to Lusaka three days later and at the end of my week's leave, returned to duty. On the morning of my return I was told that the boss would like to see me when I arrived for duty. I went to his office and knocked on the door. He called me in and waved me to a seat.

'How did your leave go, David? Did you see the people you went to meet? Did they ask you to work for them?'

I was shaken. How the hell did he know where I had been? He saw my confusion and embarrassment, and smiled.

'Who do you think supplied them with much of the information they had on you? We all help each other, and have good links between forces. Did they offer you the position in Borneo?'

'As a matter of fact they did, sir. They also offered me a job as a magistrate in Southern Rhodesia.'

'Yes, I thought they would. Did you accept either of the positions they offered you?'

'No, sir, I didn't. I told them that I would think about their offers and let them know as soon as possible.'

He nodded and looked thoughtful. 'What made you hesitate?' He looked questioningly at me.

'I have a problem, sir. You know that I have been taking some of the more promising African staff to tricky situations, and have been challenging them to give me their ideas for dealing with them.'

He nodded. 'Yes, I heard that you took two of your staff with you to that railway crossing tragedy.'

'How did you come to hear that, sir? I didn't tell any of the staff where I had been or what I had put the African officers through.'

He chuckled. 'I have members of the African staff, just as you do, who tell me things. The two officers whom you took out couldn't stop talking about it and what you had asked them to do. They quite sickened some of the other members of staff. Did you know that they have a new name for you, and that they all call you by this name, though not in your presence, of course?'

'No, I had no idea that they had a name for me. In the Southern Province my nickname was "Bodies", and that followed me from Choma. Please tell me what they call me here.'

He grinned. 'Your name here is "Teacher", and I believe that the name is used in respect and the hope that you will continue with this work.'

I was left without words, and sat quietly for a few minutes. The boss didn't interrupt my thoughts, but sat patiently looking out of the window. I finally came to a decision.

'I have decided not to accept either of the offers made to me last week. I'll carry on here, and even though the staff don't enjoy the situations I expose them to, I'll be satisfied if some of what I try to teach them sticks.'

I stopped and looked at the boss, who was grinning.

'So you are staying?'

'I am, sir.'

'Then congratulations, David, or rather, congratulations, Detective Chief Inspector.'

And with that he extended his hand and we shook hands.

77

Workload

I spent part of the morning with the boss going over my new duties in detail. I would no longer work shifts but would always be on call for serious cases, not necessarily to lead the investigations myself but to allocate teams to deal with them and to maintain an overview. Serious cases included murder, attempted murder and assaults occasioning grievous bodily harm, all serious interracial crime and serious politically based crime.

I would, from about half past six each morning, receive calls from each division in the country reporting serious crime and other incidents that had occurred during the previous twenty-four hours. I would then organise the information into a single document, which would have to be ready by the time the commissioner arrived at his office each morning. My coaching of the team was to continue and a full appraisal of each member of the CID team was to be written up in a file prepared by me.

I was to keep a strict overview of all the current cases being dealt with by the team, making sure that a backlog of unsolved cases did not build up.

All this I knew, and I had my own ideas about how I would run the section but I didn't say so at the time. I now had an office of my own and a secretary to call upon. The boss told me that the appointment would be posted on the information board so that all members of CID and uniformed officers would be kept informed.

As promised, a letter confirming my new position arrived two days later and on the same day the news appeared on the main noticeboard. I received congratulations from most of the people I regularly talked with, and also from some people whom I hadn't yet really spoken with. Several of the African staff came up to me with big grins on their faces and said that they were pleased that I was now their senior officer.

The first thing that became apparent to me as I assumed my new position was that the composition of the morning national crime report should be taken over by another officer, possibly an assistant superintendent who would be more office-bound than I was. This became apparent following two mornings when the report reached the commissioner very late in the day. I had not been back in the station to prepare it, having been out at a serious crime scene since the early hours of the morning. It was with some relief that I handed over that particular part of the job to someone else. On average I was being called out at least three times each night, usually a couple of times before midnight and once or twice in the early hours of the next morning.

We had by now several African detective assistant inspectors in the squad, and they were facing levels of responsibility that they had never encountered before. Consequently they needed a guiding influence from more experienced members of the squad. We had a number of excellent European officers up to inspector level and they would take the lead if they were available.

If a new African officer was faced with a serious crime of a type he had never managed before and there was nobody available in the office to help him, I was informed. With several of these new officers I was able to talk them through what they needed to do and they were able to manage their teams without my presence. Most, however, needed more reassurance, so I went out with them and worked them through the necessary procedures. Those I helped in this way I instructed to provide me with a full written report the following day covering everything they had done under my supervision the previous night, and to make an extra copy for themselves to keep as a guide for future occasions.

In my notebook I now had the names of several confident and competent officers who could work largely on their own initiatives.

78

The Inspectors" Mess

My promotion had automatically made me mess president, which was more of a title than a job. However, there were certain duties attached to the position. As in police messes throughout the larger towns in the country, there was an established bond between police officers and hospital nurses. In Lusaka there was also a bond with young ladies who worked, usually as clerical officers, for the civil administration. These "sunshine girls", as they were called, were invited, together with nursing staff, to our functions and we to theirs.

Some of our functions were full dress affairs where all officers wore dress uniform. Badges of rank were worn on the shoulder straps, with chief inspectors wearing three bars, senior inspectors two bars and inspectors one bar. Assistant inspectors wore no badge of rank. Our invited guests used such occasions to dress up in their most alluring dresses, and each function was one of relaxed enjoyment.

An important part of the dinner was the loyal toast, when glasses were raised in honour of the Queen.

When the moment arrived, I, as mess president, would rise, rap the table and in a loud voice say, 'Mr Vice, the Royal Toast.'

The most junior member attending the function would stand and say, 'Ladies and gentlemen, raise your glasses.'

Everyone would rise to their feet.

'Ladies and gentlemen – the Queen.'

Everyone would echo the toast, with most adding, 'God bless her.'

Following independence and with single African officers now living in the station and attending functions, the Royal Toast had been replaced by the Loyal Toast to the country. Fitting though this was, it didn't seem quite the same to those white officers remaining, but it was honoured just the same.

Once the dinner was over, officers and guests would retire to the bar for an evening of relaxed conversation and drinking. It was from such evenings as these that many friendships grew. Several marriages also blossomed from these gatherings.

79

Friends

Being the most senior member of the inspectors' mess and therefore mess president, I came to know most of the members quite well. There was a constantly changing set of officers, with African members increasing in number as the European numbers steadily declined.

I became close friends with a number of officers, both in CID and in the uniformed branch. I was honoured to be asked to be best man at both Dick Stacpoole's and Paul Lancaster's weddings. Both were young officers, at least seven years younger than me, but we were good friends. I shared boating experiences on the Zambezi with Paul, who had a boat, and I furthered my horse-riding training with Dick, who was a good rider himself.

He had access to a rather frisky horse and offered me a ride one day. The animal took me by surprise when he suddenly stopped dead in the middle of cantering around the field. I went over his head and landed in an untidy heap. I looked up to find the animal looking down at me as though wondering how I got there.

Dick was convulsed with laughter, and came up and said, 'Make much of your horse, Dave. Make much of your horse. Tell him that it is not his fault, but your lack of anticipation.'

He couldn't stop laughing. I had to join in as I went up to the horse and stroked him and told him it wasn't his fault. As I remounted him and continued my workout I had lost my complacency.

Another friend I remember well was Jim Carmody. At about the time that I first got to know him I had started to play bridge in the mess. We played for money, not huge amounts but on a good night, winnings and losses could add up. Regular players would only accept a beginner as partner on the understanding that the novice would pay all debts for that game. If you played well enough you could always find a partner.

Eventually Jim and I teamed up and were quite successful. We even went as far as entering a big tournament held in Lusaka over a full weekend.

There were thirty-two pairs, I think, and we finished about twenty-second, or somewhere in that region. There were several Asian pairs playing and one of these was warned against talking in their own language during the game. Their game deteriorated following the warning.

Another member of the CID team, and a good young officer, was Len Norman, who joined the team as a detective assistant inspector in 1965, I think. He was about nine years younger than me, so I kept a watchful eye on him. He didn't disappoint and had the makings of a good officer. In 1968, the year after I left the force, he was promoted to detective chief inspector and went on to serve until 1987 when he retired from the force. He was decorated with the MBE for his work and his loyalty.

80

Skydiving

It was Martin (always referred to as Taffy) Linnette who got me interested in skydiving. He was an assistant inspector at the station and had made some jumps himself.

I decided to go down to the airfield and talk with the people who ran the Lusaka Skydiving Club. I met Eric Rule, the founder of the club, and Ian, his second in command. They welcomed me and offered me a jump the following day. I was shown how to complete a good landing by jumping off a low wall, and practised rolling after hitting the ground. It was also explained to me what to do if I had a chute malfunction. Today one would have to successfully complete an intensive course over at least three weeks before being allowed to jump from a plane.

On the following day, a Sunday, I was fitted with a chute and a reserve, which was a much smaller chute and worn on the front of the body. I was then talked through the process of leaving the aircraft and the position to adopt upon leaving. I would be attached to the aircraft by a static line, which would open my chute for me. All I had to do was await the order.

When the plane reached 2,500 feet I was told to stand at the door, which was opened. The noise of rushing air came as a shock to me. As the pilot throttled back the engine I received the instruction to step out on to the wing. The aircraft we were using was a de Havilland Rapide, and was a two-winged plane. One of the vertical struts joining the two wings made a good hold for my left hand. My right hand held the side of the doorway, and I now stood balanced, my left foot on the wing, my right foot on the edge of the doorway. It took all my strength to hold on.

On receiving a wave of the hand from the dispatcher I kicked backwards with my feet and pushed off with my hands a moment later. Fixing my eyes on the aircraft as instructed, I saw the gap between us rapidly increase as the aircraft become a small speck in the sky. I pulled the ripcord as instructed on the count of three although it was not attached to the chute, and suddenly felt the shock of the chute deploying.

As instructed, I checked everything that I had been told to check and then searched the ground below for my landing area. I turned the chute towards our airfield, but soon became aware that I was making no forward progress towards it. I was instead being blown backwards away from my landing strip and towards Lusaka International Airport.

I realised that if I did nothing, the wind would carry me on to the runway and maybe even into the path of a commercial aircraft. I came to the conclusion that the only thing I could do was to turn the chute and, using the wind, drive across the runway as quickly as possible. By this time there was quite a breeze getting up and I crossed the runway at a good speed at about two hundred feet above ground level. My thoughts now turned to my landing.

I was approaching the edge of an African village and was finding the chute difficult to control. I didn't have much of a choice about exactly where I would touch down, but had the luck to make perhaps the softest landing of my skydiving career. I landed in a newly dug back garden where a high ridge of soil awaited planting. As my feet hit the soil they sank in until it was covering my ankles and lower legs. It was the first of only two stand-up landings I ever achieved.

As I started to unclip the chute prior to rolling it up I was surrounded by a crowd of excited African children. It was all I could do to stop them grabbing hold of the chute. As I was sorting everything out a car raced up. In it were Eric and Ian, looking anxious. There had evidently been a complete change in the wind's direction and an increase in wind strength between the time it was last tested and the time of my jump. The control tower people at the airport were not pleased with us, and the club received a warning.

The following weekend I managed three more jumps, after which Eric asked if I would like to try my first free-fall jump. I would not be attached to the aircraft by a static line, but pull my own ripcord to open the chute. I said that I would be delighted, and up we went.

I must admit to feeling a little tense, but everything went well and I had a good exit from the plane, this time from four thousand feet. Having opened my chute, I looked around and saw that I had had a very good dispatch. I was in line to try for a landing fairly close to the target marker in the centre of our landing area.

As I drove the chute closer I realised that I could possibly land in the centre of the target. Here I made a serious mistake. I was concentrating so hard on the target that I forgot the fundamental rules about safe landings. I failed to turn my feet and legs to the correct landing position and made what I learned later was called a toe-knee landing. In doing so I felt severe pain in my right foot and a pain in my right leg below the hip.

I had little time to worry about the pain. As I had been about to land I had noticed a police Land Rover followed by a police truck speeding towards the airstrip. In the van were three of my African officers, and I was quickly informed that there had been a double murder at an African village about thirty miles away. Handing my parachute and other gear to one of the club members, I hobbled to the Land Rover and got in.

As we set off I decided to remove my boots, but the pain was so severe that I couldn't remove the boot from my injured foot, so I left both boots on. Eventually we found that a stream stopped us from approaching the village in the Land Rover and we were left with a two-mile walk, which I found to be extremely painful.

On arrival at the village the case turned out to be fairly straightforward, and had involved a bitter argument between several men of the village who had all been drinking. The argument had eventually developed into fighting and the use of weapons. One of the men had used a knife and killed two of the others before being overcome by several villagers, who had tied him up and placed him in a hut to await the arrival of the police. There were a number of injured villagers who needed attention, as well as the bodies to be taken back to Lusaka.

I handed over the crime scene and the taking of statements to the African inspector who was the senior African officer with me, and left him with two men and the Land Rover. I returned to Lusaka with the bodies and the injured villagers. After visiting the mortuary we went straight to the hospital where the villagers were treated for their injuries and then driven to the police station to be questioned and to give statements.

I asked to see a doctor and told him of my bad landing earlier. It took some time and a lot of pain before my boot could be removed. By the time my sock was cut off, the cause of the pain I was suffering had been revealed. Four of the toes of my right foot had been badly dislocated and had swelled so much that the doctor had great difficulty in relocating them. The pain involved in him doing this was extremely severe. An examination of my right leg then revealed a large swelling which, when drained the following day, produced over a pint and a half of fluid and an area of flesh which even to this day has no feeling in it as the nerves appear to have been destroyed.

On my return to the skydiving club later I received a telling-off from Eric and Ian for attempting to make a landing beyond my capability at this stage of my training. It had been a hard lesson to learn, and it took some weeks before I was fit to jump again.

*

Skydiving as a sport was in its infancy. In developed countries such as the USA, Britain and some of the countries in Europe, advances in equipment and techniques were taking place, but in large areas of the world the sport was in its infancy. Admittedly we had reserve parachutes and altimeters, which indicated our height above ground level, but our parachutes were ex-army surplus and exactly the same as those used by airborne troops in the war. These chutes had been developed for troops being dropped from relatively low levels, and were limited in their steering ability.

Eric was envied by all of the club members. He had managed to buy a ParaCommander, the latest sports parachute, from a firm in South Africa. It had only been in existence for two years and it was at least twice the size of our army surplus chutes. It was very steerable and landed at a much lower speed. Jumping with our army surplus chutes resulted, over time, in injuries caused usually by the speed at which we hit hard ground. The club landing area was surrounded by, and dotted with, numerous thorn bushes, and on occasions a chute would end up in a bush, sometimes accompanied by the parachutist. Small holes ripped in the chutes were sealed by burning round the edges of the rip with a cigarette. When a chute had too many mended areas it had to be scrapped.

As my training progressed I jumped from higher and higher altitudes. My favourite height was twelve thousand feet. Jumping from this height it was possible to free fall for about fifty seconds or so, and one could use this time to try different manoeuvres. It was on a visit to Southern Rhodesia one weekend that trying manoeuvres in free fall almost cost me my life. I was also given a warning as to my membership of the club.

I was free falling from ten thousand feet and decided to practise a series of flat, face-down spins. I was spinning slowly clockwise; then anticlockwise, and controlling the various speeds of spin, and was enjoying myself when a glance at my altimeter showed that I was just under a thousand feet from the ground. I pulled my ripcord at once, but saw the ground rushing up to meet me. I also saw that I was heading towards water in the form of a lake. Everything happened simultaneously – the loud crack as the chute opened, the splash as I hit the water and the sudden pain in my ankles as my feet hit the bottom of the lake.

I realised that I was still alive. My heart was beating so strongly that when I opened my mouth to take a huge gulp of air I could hear it beating through my open mouth. I was standing on the muddy bottom of the lake about forty feet from the bank. The water was up to my shoulders and the chute was fortunately drifting with the waves towards the bank. As I started to slowly wade towards dry land, two vehicles appeared from behind a low line of hills which lay between me and the airfield. They drove towards me and arrived just as I staggered on to dry land.

Eric and Ian jumped out of their vehicle and ran towards me. They were followed by two local skydivers. They all looked pale and were breathing heavily. Eric came up to me and asked if I was alright.

'We all thought that you were dead when you disappeared behind the hills. What the hell happened to you, did you have a malfunction?'

I could see how upset he was. He was shaking and sweat was running off his face.

'No, Eric, I didn't have a malfunction. I got lost in the manoeuvres I was carrying out and nearly killed myself. I will resign from the club immediately. It's taught me a lesson I'll never forget. If I hadn't landed in the water I would probably not have survived the landing.'

'Yes, and I would have been hauled before the coroner and the club would probably have been subject to inspections, or possibly have been shut down. You have been improving steadily since you joined the club and I have high hopes for you. We all make mistakes and you have been very lucky. Let it be a lesson learned. Now let's get back to the airstrip. You've just time for one more jump before the light goes.'

From that day until I stopped jumping due to gradual deterioration of my lower spine, I became a safe jumper.

In our group I became close friends with Yvonne Sinclair, a lovely Scottish girl. Yvonne was a sunshine girl, as girls coming to the country on short-term government contracts were called. She was the girlfriend of Detective Inspector Dave "Chalky" White, who was one of the more senior CID officers in our team.

Yvonne had made a number of static line jumps before I joined the club, and I was told in confidence by Eric that he could not visualise her ever free-fall parachuting as she always jumped with her eyes closed, never tried to demonstrate a ripcord pull and never attempted to assume a stable position. However, once her chute opened she took command of it, steered it well and usually made a good and safe landing.

After each day's jumping we all gathered at the club for an evening's get-together. Yvonne was a popular member of our group and the life and soul of the party. She loved the fun and teasing and everyone loved her. Even though she would never be allowed to free fall and just waited for the chute to open on the static line, she got so much enjoyment from the sport once the chute had opened that it was felt that she should be allowed to continue jumping.

81

Progress

As we progressed through 1965 and entered 1966 I pushed more and more work and responsibility on to those African officers who could accept it without crumbling under the strain.

This resulted in several of the best officers being promoted to the rank of inspector. We lost a couple of them to other, smaller stations, but retained the best. With these officers I now shared on-call duties at night and this lessened my workload. If they came upon a situation that they found difficult to handle without help I was always ready to go out to help them. Their pride stopped them asking for help too often, but they always sat down with me the next morning to go over any case which had been difficult for them. This allowed them to build up a confidence in their own abilities.

During 1964 seventy-seven European officers holding the rank of assistant superintendent and above had been retired from the force. Three hundred and thirty-nine officers up to and including the rank of chief inspector had also left the force. I awaited with interest the inevitable promotion of one or more of my top African officers to my rank of detective chief inspector.

82

An Old Enemy

In mid-1965 I was at my desk one day when I received a phone call instructing me to report to Force Headquarters. I had no idea whom I would be meeting, but dutifully reported and on arrival was given a guide to show me to a room.

I knocked on the door and an African voice called for me to come in. When I saw the owner of the voice my mind went back to Livingstone and a UNIP political meeting. The man in front of me had been a speaker at one of the meetings where it had been my turn to record what had been said. At that stage of the country's political development, what was said at political meetings was routinely recorded with the intention of preventing speakers from rousing crowds to commit unlawful and possibly harmful actions.

On that occasion in Livingstone the man now sitting behind a desk had been carried away by his own oratory, and I had stopped him and warned him about his language.

He had carried on ranting about driving the white people out of the country, and turning to me, had shouted, 'And this white *sheet* will be the first to go.'

I had closed the meeting and taken the recording together with my report back to the station, where it was handed to Special Branch. Now here he was, sitting, together with an assistant, in an office at Force Headquarters and obviously in a position of some authority. He smiled at me. It was not a friendly smile.

'Well, Inspector, we meet again.'

'Detective Chief Inspector,' I replied.

He continued as though he had not heard me, and gave me instructions to go to the airport and arrest a senior member of the Zambia African National Congress who would be arriving that afternoon on a flight from England.

'On what charge do I arrest him, sir?'

'I am sure you will think of something, Inspector. Your sort always do.'

'As this is obviously a political case, sir, I shall need an order from a senior court officer before I can carry out any arrest. To obtain the order we will have to show just cause, which obviously you will have to provide.'

He looked at me and sneered. 'Get out of my office, Inspector. You always were useless.'

'Gladly, sir,' I replied, and walked out. As I closed the door behind me I heard loud laughter.

On my return to the station I ran a check on passenger lists for aircraft due to arrive that day and found that there was no trace of any ZANC officials travelling on any of the flights.

83

An Unexpected Visitor

By late July 1965 the excitement following the independence celebrations had died down. I was in my office one morning checking through the previous night's crime reports when a uniformed constable knocked on the door and reported that there was an African man in the enquiry office who wanted to see me. He would talk to no other officer and would not give his name. I told the constable to bring him up to my office.

A few minutes later the constable brought in a man who had obviously fallen upon hard times and had been living rough. I looked carefully at him as he stood with his head bent forward and averting his eyes. He looked vaguely familiar.

Finally he slowly raised his head and looked at me and said, 'I see you, *bwana*.'

'And I see you, Samene William Mwape. The last time we met you kicked me in the stomach and I ended up in hospital.'

On hearing this, the constable quickly moved closer to Mwape.

'It's alright, Constable, leave him with me. Go back to your duties. Samene is not going to attack me.'

After the constable had left the office I closed the door and told Mwape to sit down, which he did with some relief.

'Where are you living now, Samene?' I asked.

'I have no home and can find no work, *bwana*. I have only a few friends and they also have no work. I have come to you because you may know where I can find work.'

'And why would I want to help a man who kicked me in the stomach and put me in hospital, Samene?'

'Ah, *bwana*, I was drunk. I did not know what I was doing and I am sorry for what I did.'

He looked as though he was going to cry.

'When did you last eat, Samene?'

'I have not eaten for two days, *bwana*.' His head dropped forward again and he looked genuinely exhausted.

'Do you know the main market in Lusaka, Samene?'

'Indeed I do, *bwana*. I am there all the time looking for work, and sometimes I am given food which they have not sold by the end of the day.'

'I can't give you a job, Samene. You have a criminal record. But there is a way you can earn money from me. There are many thieves who use the market as a place to sell the things they have stolen. People in the market will not tell the police who these people are because they are afraid, but maybe you could tell me who they are and where they keep the things that they have stolen. If you can do this, and if we make arrests because of information you have given us, I will pay you for telling us. Only I and one other officer will know you are helping us and you will not have to give evidence in court.'

He immediately started to offer me names of people who were selling stolen goods on the market. I told him to stop.

'I am going to give you some money now out of my own pocket so that you can buy food, Samene. Go away now and have a meal. Don't eat near the market. Always beg in the market. Don't change anything about your behaviour. Don't go to the market in new clothes even when you are earning money from me. Live two lives. When you have earned enough money to pay for somewhere to stay and are able to buy new clothes and other things you need, make sure that that part of your life is lived somewhere else in Lusaka, well away from the market. Of the two lives that you will lead, one will be as a beggar who begs in the marketplace and one as a respectable man who lives in another place. Do we understand each other?'

'Indeed we do, *bwana*.'

I went out of the room and called my senior African inspector. He was a man in whom I put great trust. I explained that he would control and look after Samene and would meet up with him at places well away from the market, and at arranged times. Samene would supply him with information which he would bring to me, and we would, together, decide how to use it to produce the best outcome from our point of view. He was not to discuss this with any other members of staff or any friends.

We used the first two pieces of information from Mwape as a test. Both proved to be valuable and we were able to convict two minor criminals after obtaining warrants, raiding their houses and finding a number of identifiable stolen items. One of them asked the court to take into account several other offences and I was very encouraged by the outcome. I was able to reward Samene by paying what to him was a large amount of money for his efforts. I had decided to keep the reward side of the arrangement under my control until I was happy with the way my inspector was handling this new part of his work.

Whenever what appeared to be a good piece of information was passed to us by Samene, I sat down and talked everything through with my inspector. The passing of money was organised by me, but was eventually carried out by him. By now all transactions were recorded in the official record book and Samene, who could read and write, signed to acknowledge that he had received the rewards. We always made sure that we also got his thumbprint in addition to his signature. He signed under a false name, which we had given him. He never approached the police station again, so I never saw him again. All transactions took place in other parts of Lusaka.

The police relationship with Samene grew throughout the time I remained in Zambia and it yielded a number of excellent successes against important targets. He turned out to be the best asset I had ever recruited or had dealings with. His handling officer was subsequently promoted to the rank of detective chief inspector. I was at the same time promoted to acting assistant superintendent, which allowed me to remain in charge of the Lusaka Central CID.

By this time I had decided that there would be no real future for me in the force beyond the end of the minimum two years that I had signed up for when I had been promoted to chief inspector.

84

Lecture Time

One morning, shortly before Christmas, the boss invited me into his office and asked me if I could do him a favour. He looked anxious.

'I am due to give a talk to a meeting of the Central African insurance societies, who are currently meeting in Lusaka to discuss the current situation in newly independent countries and those awaiting independence. They are very worried about implications for the insurance business as a whole. I have another appointment that I had forgotten about and was wondering if you could take over the talk for me?'

Yes, I bet you have, I thought.

'Alright, I'll do it for you, sir, but I'll confine myself to the situation in this country. I am not going to give opinions of what may happen in other countries. When is this meeting due to take place?'

'This evening,' he replied, looking very uncomfortable.

'Bloody hell, that doesn't give me any time to prepare.'

'Take the rest of the day off, and thank you. I owe you one.'

To cut a long story short, my talk just dealt with how independence had affected life in Zambia. I could not say how life might be after independence in other countries, but I gave them a picture of hope, drawing on crime statistics from before and after independence in Zambia. I received prolonged applause when I had finished and made my escape as quickly as possible.

85

Convoy

One weekend in February 1966 as I was working in my office I received a phone call from a "friend" in the north of the country. He was not a police officer but was in a position to monitor suspicious movements of people or items of interest crossing into Zambia from Tanzania. He told me that a European customs officer had let him know about a small convoy of cars from Tanzania. The cars and their occupants had been waved through the border control point by the African officer in charge without having to produce any form of documentation or evidence of identification.

The person giving me the information had checked later with friends on the Copperbelt and was informed when the convoy had passed through and was heading towards Lusaka. I felt that it was worth checking before it got to Lusaka.

Having attempted to get in touch with the boss without success, I decided to put together a mixed team of uniformed officers and my own CID officers to lie in wait on the T2 north of Lusaka. Following a wait of about two hours, three cars appeared and we duly stopped them. There were three African men in each of the two leading cars, and just a driver in the rear car.

All of them, when questioned, refused to speak or answer any questions. We took them to our police vehicles where they waited under guard as we searched each car in turn. In the two front cars we discovered a number of automatic weapons and a large amount of ammunition. In the third car there were boxes, which we did not open at the time. Judging by their size and weight I suspected that they probably contained explosives or some sort of explosive devices.

I instructed two senior members of my party to formally arrest each member of the group on suspicion of conveying weapons and ammunition through Zambia without authority to do so. No replies were forthcoming from the accused men. We then returned to Lusaka where the arrested men were all placed in separate rooms under guard and the weapons and ammunition were set out in a downstairs office. I noted down full details of the arrests in the occurrence book and tried to phone the boss.

Before I received a reply, a senior African officer from Force HQ arrived. He told me that the prisoners were to be released. Everything seized from them was to be placed back in their cars. This was done, and they then drove away. I later found that the page upon which I had made entries in the occurrence book had been removed. When the boss came to see me later he told me that I had stirred up a hornets' nest and that plans to defuse the situation were ongoing.

The following day, the 19th February 1966, I was handed a letter of introduction signed by the assistant commissioner of the CID, Mr GD Patterson. I was also given a large, bulky envelope of sworn written evidence. My mission was to locate and extradite an African male, thought to be in Washington DC. I was to return with him to Zambia, where he was wanted on several serious charges. I think the hope was that during the time I was in the USA everything would calm down in Lusaka.

I boarded a plane to London that afternoon.

86

Extradition from the USA

My plane left Lusaka for London in the early afternoon, making its first stop at Luanda International Airport in Angola. From the airport I could hear heavy gunfire, which I estimated was probably about ten to fifteen miles away. I had no way of knowing that the sounds I could hear were in fact heralding the building up of the troubles which were to disrupt that country for many years to come.

The rest of the flight to London passed slowly and uneventfully. We arrived early the following morning and I quickly crossed the airport and managed to catch a flight to Manchester. Here I hired a taxi to take me home to Stockton Heath. A six-hour visit with my surprised parents, a reverse journey to London to catch my flight to Washington DC, and by nightfall I was in the air again, heading for the USA.

There were only eight passengers in our section of the plane and to our delight we were all invited to move forward into first class to help balance the aircraft. I spent most of the journey playing bridge with two of the stewardesses and a male passenger.

About an hour before we were due to land I began to plan what I should do when I landed. I had my passport, a letter of introduction "to whom it may concern" and my force identity card. The accused was a relative of the Zambian Ambassador to the USA so I decided that I would present myself to the Zambian Embassy and take it from there.

As we lost height on our approach to the airport I looked out of the window and saw to my horror that the ground was covered by snow. My clothing was suitable for African temperatures but I realised that I would have to buy a new set of winter wear very quickly or I would freeze.

When we landed we were not allowed to disembark until cards that we had had to fill in whilst in the air had been scrutinised. As we finally left the plane and walked towards the customs and immigration area, a large black man walked along the queue of passengers holding a board upon which, I saw to my astonishment, my name was written. As he walked along the line, he was calling my name. I quickly made myself known and he identified himself as a driver for the Zambian Ambassador. He told me that there was an embassy car in a diplomatic car park near to the customs and immigration area in which the ambassador was waiting. He asked for my passport and then showed me to the car, where the ambassador welcomed me to the USA.

As we waited for the driver to return he engaged me in talk about Zambia and what was happening there. We were soon joined by the driver, who was carrying my suitcase and stamped passport.

'I am going to take you to my home where you can relax while I arrange accommodation for you,' the ambassador said. 'I will also send for your week's allowance to cover your expenses. While you are in America our government will pay you a weekly sum to cover the cost of your daily expenses, such as the cost of your accommodation and any travel costs you may incur.'

We eventually arrived at his house, which was large and well furnished. I was introduced to his wife and then shown into a large lounge in which two very young children sat gazing at a television set. It was my first sight of American TV, and it was awful. The colours were garish and the picture unfocused. The youngsters hardly gave me a glance, for which I was grateful as it allowed me to sleep for about three hours until I was awakened by the ambassador, who was holding a cup of coffee for me.

He told me that he had arranged accommodation at the Dupont Plaza Hotel on Dupont Circle, and that the embassy car would take me there. He handed me a wad of money, which was to cover my expenses for the coming week. When I counted it later I realised that it worked out at about $45 per day, a very generous amount in 1966. I later found that I could buy a full breakfast including coffee for $1.

When I arrived at the hotel in the late afternoon I was very tired. I was shown to my room, which was fairly small but had the usual coffee-making facilities and television. I wasn't interested in these as all I wanted to do was to lie on the bed and catch up with some sleep.

I had been asleep for about an hour when the telephone in my room rang and a reception clerk told me that a US deputy marshal was waiting to see me in reception. I got dressed and went down in the lift.

As I approached the reception desk there was only one man waiting there. He was tall and well built and possessed a rugged face. He would have been perfect for the hero's part in a Western film. As I enquired about my visitor at the desk he stepped forward with a smile, extended his hand and introduced himself as Warren Emmerton. I introduced myself in turn and asked him if he would like a drink. He politely declined and we sat down together.

What he told me revealed just how quickly things had moved that day. Warren had been assigned to the case and after talking to the Zambian Ambassador had visited an address in a downtown area of the city. In a room at the top of a high building he and an accompanying deputy marshal had found the accused hiding in a cupboard. Warren had arrested him on a warrant obtained earlier from a district judge. He told me that the accused would appear in court the following morning, and that he would take me to the hearing in his car. I told him about my clothing being unsuitable for the cold Washington weather and he offered to take me shopping after the preliminary hearing was over.

When we arrived at the court the following morning I was astonished at the size of the building and the hall in which the remand hearing would take place.

As we entered I was almost overcome by the noise. I looked around and saw that there were four docks, and four judges were taking their seats. We sat in the first row opposite judge number one. It soon became apparent that he was rapidly disposing of newly arrested prisoners and either allowing them bail or remanding them in custody. He was also accepting guilty pleas from some prisoners accused of lesser crimes. Very few prisoners seemed to be represented by counsel. Out of interest, I started to time how long he was spending on each case and worked out that it was about one and a half minutes on average.

When our prisoner came into the dock he was escorted by two prison officers. The prisoner was remanded in custody to appear in seven days to answer the charges which would then be put to him.

Now it was time to buy some more suitable clothes.

That afternoon, dressed comfortably for the cold weather, I ventured out to explore my surroundings. Warren had dropped me off at the hotel and said that he would call in to see me that evening. I decided to take a taxi and was pleased at the small amount that it cost to travel around Washington DC, which measures just over sixty-five square miles. One driver explained to me that the prices were controlled by the government in favour of government workers.

That evening, as promised, Warren arrived and said he would show me some of the city by night.

'Are you carrying?' he asked.

'Carrying what?'

'A firearm, of course. You do have a firearm, don't you, Dave?'

When I said that I didn't have one with me and wouldn't carry a gun in

Zambia unless I had a good and specific reason for doing so, he shook his head. As a man who felt naked without his gun he found the British way of policing extraordinary, but he soon got over it.

The first place we visited was another hotel on the circle. As we walked into the large lounge where a number of people were drinking and chatting, I commented upon the number of beautiful girls in the room. He started to grin.

'Out of our league, I'm afraid,' he said.

'What do you mean?'

'If we put all the money we are carrying together we might buy a smile, but that's all. You must realise that Washington has some of the most beautiful and costly prostitutes in the world. Their targets are mainly senators and the higher grades of civil servants.'

I shook my head and offered him a drink. He had a beer and I had my usual orange juice, which I had, as usual, to explain. We went to a number of interesting places that evening, which I enjoyed. I felt quite safe in Warren's company, especially when he told me that he competed each year in the White House Police combat match. He also competed in the White House Police/US Secret Service revolver matches annually, and had won one of these.

During the following five or six days I was left to my own devices. I became used to travelling around Washington on my own, but grew bored having nobody to talk to. I partly compensated by agreeing to share my table with another diner for my evening meal whenever the restaurant was busy.

On one occasion I dined with the attorney general of Mexico, a very interesting man. He invited me to stay at his house if I ever visited his country. Another guy who joined me for dinner told me that he was undercover and an agent for a European country, but would not say which one. I dropped a few questions into the conversation and it soon became obvious that he was making it all up. I amused myself by asking questions and watching him squirm. He excused himself as soon as he had finished the main course as he had a secret meeting to attend. I wished him well.

During my travels I visited a number of places of interest such as the Smithsonian Museum, the Library of Congress and the Arlington National Cemetery, which was a huge and sad place. Perhaps the most interesting place was the Smithsonian Air and Space Museum, but all the endless walking about was beginning to depress me. I looked through the telephone directory one evening and discovered six pages of McCues, but I had no wish to meet any of them. I decided that the following day I would visit the British Embassy. Maybe there would be a British girl who would fancy showing me round the interesting night places after I had treated her to dinner at a restaurant of her choice.

As it happened, two very attractive young ladies from the embassy staff turned up at my hotel the following evening, and after an excellent dinner we set off on a tour of the nightspots. We went to several well-known nightclubs and visited several small bars. At some of them there were musicians playing various types of music. My new friends seemed to be known and were welcomed at many of our stops. The night came to an end early the next morning, and looking back, it was one of the best nights out I had had for a very long time.

Eventually the day of the court hearing arrived, and again Warren picked me up and we went to court together. The hearing was in a smaller and quieter court, and I saw that the defendant was this time represented by a defence counsellor. The prosecutor had already supplied the judge with a copy of the evidence, which contained affidavits sworn before a judge in Zambia. Everything seemed straightforward until the judge asked how the accused pleaded.

'Not guilty, sir,' replied the accused.

Before the judge could say anything, the defence counsel was on his feet.

'Sir, the defence case is that there is no extradition treaty in existence between Zambia and the USA. Zambia is a newly independent country and has not as yet arranged such a treaty with this country.'

'Ask for an adjournment and I'll sort this out with the embassy,' I whispered to the prosecutor.

This he did, and the hearing was adjourned for another week.

Later the same day I went to the embassy and saw the ambassador, who agreed to make an urgent call to Lusaka for clarification. He also told me that he had arranged a number of things for me to do and places to visit whilst I was in Washington. He handed me a list, which was very comprehensive. It appeared that starting from the next day, I would be fully occupied.

I don't intend to give a detailed account of the visits and activities arranged for me, but they included two lunches hosted by congressmen where several invited guests, including myself, were introduced to the assembled diners. Both of these events were boring and I would rather not have been there. More interesting activities included a visit to FBI Headquarters, which included handling the gun that had been used to kill President Kennedy. I spent one afternoon with border control officers who specialised in the US-Mexico border, and was taken aback when I heard the details of the number of their officers killed on duty. I also took a trip on the underground rail system, which serves the people who work in the various parts of the capital. For this trip I was photographed and was accompanied by a member of the underground railway staff.

On all of these trips I was introduced as Chief McCue. When I had first arrived in the US I had been asked about my rank, and had answered that I was a detective chief inspector. Americans, being Americans, latched on to the word "chief" and thereafter I was always addressed as "chief". I felt that it was not necessary to explain that there existed several ranks of commissioned officers senior to my rank in the Zambia Police.

On the day of the next appearance of the accused, the prosecutor informed the judge that the Zambian government had sent written confirmation that a treaty existed between Zambia and the US in relation to extradition. The defence objected and demanded proof. They also requested once again that the accused be granted bail, and once again were refused. The accused was remanded for two weeks, but the prosecution was warned to produce tangible evidence of an extradition agreement or the accused would have to be released.

I returned to the embassy and informed the ambassador that tangible evidence that an agreement existed between the two countries was required by the court. A certified photocopy of the agreement signed by a high-ranking judge in Zambia would be acceptable. The ambassador looked exceedingly uncomfortable.

'They are searching all their files, but so far have not been able to locate it,' he said.

A few days later I received a call from the embassy which informed me that two people, a man and a woman, both about twenty-five years of age, had been found to show me more places of interest in Washington. They would call for me at the hotel that afternoon and show me some of the sights I had not yet seen. They proved to be excellent company and we had a good time. They were very interested in my work and asked me many questions. I asked them what they did and they said they were both at university studying for masters' degrees, but had plenty of free time.

The following day it started to snow and a strong wind began to blow. This was the day they had chosen to take me up the Washington Monument. Because of the weather, there were not too many tourists there. They asked if I was fit. Well, in those days I was and carried very little extra weight.

'Good, we'll go up the stairs. We need to keep fit,' said the girl.

I didn't ask why. The stairs comprised 898 steps. The monument, the world's tallest stone structure, stands 554 feet and a few inches high, and we went all the way up the stairs following the girl, who never stopped or slowed her speed. I was breathing heavily by the time we reached the top. My two friends hardly seemed to be affected. The girl laughed.

'You must be fit. You kept up with us and we do this regularly. Come on, we'll go down by lift after we have had a good look at the city from up here.'

And off she went. When we left the monument she called a taxi and told me that the next place we would go to was in another part of Washington.

We eventually arrived at a large building in a street of similarly sized buildings, and they led me in. We walked down several corridors and then came into a large hall. At the far end was a stage, upon which stood a man. Seated in front of the stage in rows of chairs were about sixty or so young men and women. My two friends sat down on two end seats.

'Welcome, Chief Inspector,' the man on the stage said. 'I hope my two students showed you some worthwhile sights. I know you are here from Zambia and I wondered if you would talk to us about that country and how it has changed since independence.'

I was taken by surprise and felt that I had been set up. I was annoyed, but tried not to show it. Why had my two friends not prepared me for this? Here I was facing a silent audience of what I supposed were graduates like the two I had been accompanying for the past two days, and I was not prepared. I didn't like it, and was quietly fuming inside. I decided to give them the same talk that I had given to the insurance people in Lusaka, but to expand on it in places to suit the audience.

As the talk progressed I was interested to see that many of the audience were taking notes. I was impressed by the attention they were all paying. All I saw were interested faces. I spoke for about forty minutes, and when I finished I was surprised at the sudden and prolonged burst of applause. Even so, I was still seething at the way I had been set up.

The man who had welcomed me on to the stage came forward to thank me. He congratulated me on presenting such an interesting and informative talk without preparation, and asked if I would now be prepared to answer questions from the audience. I said that I would. I turned to the audience and saw that several hands were raised. I was still annoyed at the way I had been treated and told them to put their hands down.

'Before you ask me questions, I have a few to ask you,' I said. 'How many of you would be able to locate Zambia on a map of Africa if the names of the countries were removed?

A few hands were raised.

'Who knows what Zambia was called when it was a British colony, before it became independent?'

Two hands were raised.

'Who knows what Zambia relies upon for its main source of revenue?'

No hands went up.

'That's very interesting. It makes me wonder what interest anything I may say will have for you. As you can see, I'm pissed off about the way this visit was set up. As the head of a large criminal investigation department I can usually see through people who are trying to pull the wool over my eyes, but I have to admit that I was taken in by my two friendly guides. What I don't understand is why. Well, ladies and gentlemen, I have said my piece. If you would like to ask questions I shall answer them if I can.'

There was silence. Most of the audience seemed to be studying their notebooks, but some were looking at me with what appeared to be keen interest. I waited, slowly letting my eyes travel along the lines. Eventually they were all looking at me and the room was silent. I sensed a movement behind me. A glance to the side showed that the man who had greeted me was slowly walking to the front of the stage where I stood. It was obvious that he was going to bring the affair to a close. I glanced at him and waved him away. I continued to look at individual members of the audience, attempting and often succeeding in meeting their eyes.

Eventually it was one of the men who asked a question about the structure of the Zambia Police Force. As I answered I had already marked the girl who would ask the next question. I could tell by her body language as she listened to my answer to the first question.

And so the afternoon progressed. After about half an hour of questions and answers, the man in charge, who I learned later was named Dr Columbo, brought proceedings to an end. There were still hands in the air when he did so. As he thanked me the burst of applause was even louder and more prolonged than the previous one. The students were all standing and everyone was smiling. I began to feel sorry that I had been so bad-tempered earlier.

As I left the hall the two who had been my guides came up and shook hands with me.

'We were acting under orders,' the girl said. I took it that she was referring to orders from Dr Columbo.

Later that evening Warren came to the hotel and we settled down for a chat. When I told him of my afternoon adventure he listened intently as I gave him a full blow-by-blow account. He asked about the location of the building and I told him as best I could, giving him a description of the street and the other buildings nearby. He was silent for a couple of minutes and then turned to me with serious look on his face.

'You don't want to have anything to do with that crowd,' he said.

'Why, what's wrong with them?'

'You've been a guest of the CIA, and that's always bad news,' he answered. 'By the way, I've been talking to Helen, my wife. We have agreed that we would like you to come and stay with us for the rest of the time you are in the country. After what you have just told me I think that it is imperative that you come. You're not safe to be let out by yourself.' And he grinned.

The following morning, I informed the ambassador of my new arrangements and gave him Warren's address and telephone number. He told me that there was still no news from Lusaka. Warren picked me up later in the morning when I had packed my belongings and settled the hotel bill. He drove me over to the main office of the US Marshals, where I was introduced to the chief. As the day progressed I met other deputies, and as the days went by I would develop an increasing understanding of and admiration for the work they carried out.

That evening Warren drove me to his home, which was located in the town of Indian Head in Maryland. The town lay almost due south of Washington DC and was about a one-hour drive once you had managed to get out of the city. Helen, Warren's wife, welcomed me to their home and showed me to my bedroom, where I unpacked. For the remaining time that I was in the country they treated me as a member of the family, and I got to know their young son and also many of their friends and neighbours.

I quickly adapted to leaving for work at 6.30 each morning and arriving back at the house at about 6.30 each evening. At weekends we went for drives into the mountains and examined the contents of shops selling Civil War relics, especially guns, in which Warren took a great interest. I insisted on buying lunch whenever we went out, despite the argument that invariably arose. The two things that I found were common among all the Americans whom I met during my time in America were their unconditional welcome and their boundless generosity.

On the 27th March, just two days before the next court hearing, I was called to the embassy. The ambassador was looking more cheerful than on the last occasion we had met.

'We have solved the problem of the new agreement document,' he said.

'Where did they find it?' I asked.

'There isn't one. The original agreement between Northern Rhodesia and the USA is still valid. Our two countries agreed that the existing extradition agreement, as well as other existing agreements, would remain in force following the statement by the Zambian government that any agreements not abrogated by Zambia or the other country upon independence would be considered still to be in force. This is all well documented and the court hearing has now been rescheduled for the 30th March to allow time for all this information to be prepared for the court.'

On the due date, after a relatively short court hearing the accused was ordered to be deported to Zambia. I now needed two things. I had to have an order from the Secretary of State ordering his removal from the country, and I needed an airline that would be willing to take me and the prisoner on one of their planes.

The first task was accomplished after I had waited for over an hour in the outer office of the US Attorney General. The meeting was brief and ended with a handshake. I left with an envelope containing the extradition order, which I would need when I landed in London.

The second problem, which I requested the ambassador to solve, was to book a flight for me and the prisoner from Washington to Lusaka via London. This proved difficult, as none of the large carriers wanted a handcuffed prisoner on one of their planes. No US or British carrier would even consider it. I began to think that a sea journey, with the prisoner locked away in one of the cells with which all large cruise ships are equipped, would be a pleasant way of travelling back to England.

My hopes were dashed, however, when the ambassador phoned to inform me that an Italian company would fly me back to London on condition that the prisoner and I would sit in two bucket seats in the very rear of the plane, and that we would remain handcuffed together for the complete journey. He had then arranged for a British company to take me from London to Lusaka.

In the late afternoon of the 31st March 1966 I met with Warren and two other deputy marshals at the airport and took over the prisoner, who was acting in a very lethargic manner. Warren explained that they had given him something to calm him on the flight. I handcuffed him by his right wrist to my left wrist. I said my goodbyes and thanks to Warren and the others and we boarded the plane ahead of the other passengers.

The flight to London seemed to take forever. My prisoner slept almost all the time and never needed the toilet. I had emptied my bladder before boarding the plane, and so neither did I. I refused drinks and food and just sat through the night as other passengers slept.

On arrival at Heathrow we left the plane after the other passengers had disembarked, but still had to queue to pass through the immigration control. As soon as we came to the immigration desk the prisoner immediately demanded asylum. I explained the position to the customs officer and produced the extradition documents. A few seconds later two officers arrived and took my prisoner away. He would stay in a holding cell located a few miles away, until the following afternoon when he would be returned to me at the airport.

I left the airport and took a taxi to Ealing, where Anita's mum and dad were still living. They were delighted to see me and offered me a bed for the night. Having had breakfast with them, I took a long shower and went to bed where I slept through until the following morning. We then caught up with the latest news, chatting until I had to leave for Heathrow in the afternoon.

Having received custody of my prisoner once again, I boarded a British Airways jet and settled in the very back of the plane as I had the previous day. I shall not try to describe the journey back to Lusaka. It seemed to take forever and this time the prisoner was wide-awake. He assured me that at every stop he would apply for political asylum, and this time he was sure that a black country would allow him to stay.

We stopped several times on that journey, and every time the rest of the passengers got off to stretch their legs and have a coffee or whatever. I kept my friend on the plane despite his objections. We used the time to walk around the aircraft and use the toilet and wash ourselves.

Eventually on the afternoon of the 2nd April we landed at Lusaka and I thankfully handed over the prisoner to three waiting prison officers. I felt half-dead and all I wanted to do was to have a shower and then sleep, but I knew that I should see the boss first.

'Where the hell have you been for the past six weeks?' he shouted.

'I've been working my guts out trying to extradite Chummy. I've not been on a fucking holiday.' I paused. 'Sir.'

He looked at me and seemed to slowly relax.

'I suppose you want to go to bed now to sleep. There's a mountain of work on your desk.' He smiled. 'Anyway, it's good to have you back, David. Go and get some rest. Take the morning off tomorrow and come and see me after lunch.'

The following afternoon I duly reported to his office and was waved to a chair and handed a cup of coffee. Before he could say anything I apologised for my outburst the previous day, and he, in turn, apologised for the way he had greeted me. He looked at me for a while and then spoke to me in a considered and serious manner.

'Firstly, David, I have to say well done on your American trip. The result was good even though it took so long, but that was through no fault of yours. Secondly, the furore caused by your interception of the weapons convoy has largely died down, but you have made a number of new enemies, some of them well placed to do you harm. However, you also now have certain people in high places who are indebted to you. These are people from whom the convoy was kept a secret. You still have a year of your chief inspector's position to fulfil, although I'm sure that if you applied to leave the force right now your resignation would be accepted with some relief in certain quarters.'

'I have no intention of resigning, even if my status and pension of a chief inspector were to be guaranteed. There is still a lot of hard work to be done.'

He smiled and looked relieved. 'I was hoping you would say that. There's a lot of work to be done as you have said, but I want you to let your team get on with it and act more as support for them rather than leading so many investigations yourself. They'll make more mistakes, of course, but you will be in a position to correct them after they occur. If a mistake is a serious one you will not be held responsible. You can't afford to give any of your enemies an excuse to move against you.'

I nodded. What he said made sense. It meant that I would be taking up the role of consultant rather than director.

'I still must retain the right to take over any case that falls in the area of my personal experience, and I include in that European-on-European crimes and certain interracial crimes. I would of course consult you first.'

He nodded rather reluctantly.

'I'll keep you fully in touch with how everything is going, sir, and I will always let you know if anything tricky turns up, or if I feel that I need advice. I'll also draw up a formal training programme for all ranks, but with extra training for the high-flyers.'

He smiled. 'Just the sort of answer that I'd hoped for.'

87

Adviser and Consultant 1966

I was no longer leading enquiries, and was therefore not spending nearly so much of my time advising and coaching staff on procedure at the sites of crimes.

However, this did not really reduce my workload. My door was always open to all my own officers as well as other officers in the station who wanted advice. Problems were not always work-related and could be personal. These types of questions I usually dealt with in the afternoon or after the shift had finished. Questions about work in progress were always dealt with first thing in the morning.

Many questions dealt with later in the day involved education and the best ways to work towards advancement. The brighter members of staff understood that successfully qualifying in higher educational studies was one of the pathways towards promotion. If this was linked to hard, uncomplaining and careful work then the way was opened to a successful career. We were fortunate to have a number of officers who ticked all the boxes, but, as usual lost many of these on promotion to posts in other parts of the country.

Because of my open-door approach I was at times swamped by officers waiting for advice on work in progress. I solved the problem by using my newly promoted detective chief inspector, now in the next office to me, as a fellow problem-solver. He turned out to be very good at it, and as he had sat in with me and watched me dealing with officers asking for help, he also adopted my quiet and usually supportive role. He had also watched me close the door of my office before tearing a strip off a member of staff who had produced a lazy or unacceptable piece of work, and he adopted similar tactics.

I didn't ask him how Samene William Mwape was getting on. Samene was his concern now and not mine. In this job you had to know when to let go, however hard that might be.

There were a number of times in Lusaka when several serious crimes occurred at the same time and the section was stretched to breaking point. On such occasions I could not stand aside and watch the team struggle, and

I happily took the chances offered and joined in. When we were stretched to the limit the high-achievers stood out and I wrote up my notes accordingly. I always noted how such officers dealt with officers of lower ability than their own. If they dealt supportively with lesser souls this was noted as a big plus on their reports.

Because of the role that I now had, there was much more time to liaise with people in other parts of the station, and I got to know many more of the uniformed officers. I decided that I should give up the job of mess president, although nobody had raised the subject. Now that I had the acting rank of assistant superintendent it was hardly fitting that I should continue, even though I was still accepted as full member of the inspectors' mess. The role was now passed to a uniformed African inspector.

88

A Box of Tricks?

One morning in early August there was a knock on my office door. A constable stood at the door holding a large cardboard box. From the way he was holding it I could see that it was heavy.

'*Bwana*, this box was found on the steps at the front door when the shifts changed this morning. It is addressed to you.'

I thanked him and told him to put it on my desk. After he had left the room I examined the writing of my name on the box for clues, but it was in block capital letters. I cut the sticky tape which bound the box and lifted the lid. What I found caused my heart rate to accelerate. I quickly locked the box away in the safe, planning to look at it in my bedroom later that evening.

Later, when I carefully opened it and surveyed the contents I found that they comprised a large number of files. There were a number of large, bulky files but on average most appeared to be fifteen to twenty pages thick. Each file was contained within a strong binder carrying a number. There was no writing on the binders. I spread the contents of the box on the carpet and selected one file at random to look at. As I opened it several photographs fell on to the table. They had been included loose within the file. They showed an Asian man in several different places in the city, and at first glance appeared quite innocuous. It was, however, obvious that these were surveillance pictures.

I had just started to read the reports in the file when I was called to give advice on the handling of a new case. Locking everything away in my room, I went down to the enquiry office. I had no further time that night to continue my reading.

Eventually it took me almost a month to examine all the contents of the box in my spare time. They mainly comprised basic surveillance reports largely relating to people who meant nothing to me, but there were exceptions. There were several subjects who were known to me as targets. These were people whom we knew were carrying out criminal activities, but against whom we had not yet found enough evidence to warrant an arrest and arraignment in court.

This information was, in itself, not enough to warrant an arrest, but would be invaluable when we did eventually manage to bring them in.

There were also some interesting photographs of several married, well-known, upstanding local citizens in compromising situations with partners, not always members of the opposite sex and not related to them. Much more interesting were several photographs of prominent African officials meeting people whom I didn't know but who were obviously important enough to be followed and photographed. The written notes were confined to information relating to date, place and time. I began to wonder why the files had been sent to me and who had sent them.

There were several possibilities. To begin with, it was highly unlikely that the person or persons compiling the files could be CID officers. The photographs had been taken in many cases over a continuous period of time. The absence of a member of staff would have been noticed and commented upon. They had been taken by an experienced person. It could have been a police officer of a specialist department such as Special Branch, or a freelance photographer. The photographs themselves were obviously dangerous to or embarrassing for the people in them. Who would take such photographs and for what reason, and why would they send them to me? It was a puzzle.

I began to wonder if I knew the person who had sent me the box. Was he or she stationed at Lusaka Central? Was this person still in the country, or was my benefactor, now an ex-member of the force, sunning him or herself on a South African beach? Was the gift a "This may be useful to you" type of gift, or a "Watch your back" type? I had no way of telling.

I pondered the problem for several days and then made my decision. I went through the papers again and extracted those items which I felt could be useful to me in interrogation situations at some point in the future. I then took the box to the boss' office, minus the items I had kept, and placed it on his desk. I explained the circumstance under which I had received the box but didn't mention that I had retained any material.

'Did you find anything useful among all this?' he asked.

'One or two things,' I said.

He raised his eyebrows but said nothing. I gave him one of his types of smiles back, and also said nothing.

'I'll get these over to HQ and see what they want to do with them,' he said.

I nodded, and that was the last time we ever referred to the files. Some of the information did become useful on a couple of occasions and resulted in the removal of a drugs merchant and one of our other targets from the streets.

89

"Bwana, I Have Keeled My Flend"

In October 1966 I was called down to the enquiry office one evening just before midnight. Two African men stood at the desk. One of them, who was elderly, appeared to be the complainant. He had refused to talk to the African duty staff, but demanded to speak to a *bwana*. I asked him why he had come to the police station.

'*Bwana*, I have keeled my flend,' he said.

'Where is your friend now?' I asked.

He turned to the man with him and nodded to him. The man bent down and reached for a box on the floor, which he put on the desk in front of him. I nodded to the African duty assistant inspector to open the box. As he did so he suddenly jumped back with a loud exclamation and a horrified look on his face. I moved over, and peering into the box, saw an African head whose eyes seemed to be staring back at me.

'Is this your friend?' I asked.

'Indeed he is,' was the reply.

I called the duty detective inspector to come down from the office and handed the case over to him.

Further investigation revealed that the two friends had been drinking at the beer hall and had returned home together. They had fallen out over a trivial matter and ended up fighting and insulting each other. The outcome was the beheading of the deceased.

The court, taking into account "the primitive nature of the accused" as it had to, and his genuine grief for the death of his friend, sentenced him to three years' imprisonment.

90

Increasing Tension

As 1966 drew towards its close there was a significant increase in criminal activity in Lusaka and the surrounding districts. Not only was the number of crimes increasing, but the violence used by some of the criminals involved was also escalating. Gangs of criminals from outside Lusaka had begun to appear within the city and the surrounding areas.

On a number of occasions uniformed officers of the rank of assistant inspector and above had been instructed to carry their service revolvers fully loaded when patrolling certain areas of the Lusaka district. Lower-ranking officers were to carry batons on these patrols. It was on such a patrol that one of our new African assistant inspectors was attacked and severely injured. In the course of the attack his loaded revolver was taken by the assailants. We had little to go on. An African constable had been nearby but could only give rather vague details of the number of assailants and hadn't been close enough to be able to provide a useful description of any of them, as it had been late at night.

When I was informed about the attack I went into the enquiry office to check the details. I was told that there had also been an attack on an old nightwatchman earlier in the evening, and that gratuitous violence had been used against the old man. He had been tormented by a gang who had beaten him and stolen the meagre meal he had been about to eat. Not content with eating his food, they had then thrown him on to his fire and left the area, laughing as they heard him screaming for help. The watchman was now in hospital and I accompanied my detective chief inspector to the hospital to speak with him.

We found a thin old man wrapped in dressings over much of his body. He was in a bad way but was eager to tell us what had happened to him. He added little to what he had told the attending officers who had taken him to hospital. I asked him how the assailants had been dressed and he told us that much of their clothing had looked new, and was of the type worn by people who had money and wanted to show off. I asked about the sort of things they were shouting when they were molesting him and I saw a glint come into his eyes.

'They were not from this country, *bwana*. They used words I have never heard before. I could not understand what they were saying to me.'

When we returned to the station we found that there had been a new development. A man had been arrested by one of the many patrols that had been put out following the attack upon our assistant inspector. The prisoner had been handed to CID for questioning on suspicion of being one of the gang we were looking for. So far he had not said a word and was refusing to answer any questions, but it was obvious that he had some knowledge of the English language. I could tell by the way he concentrated upon what we were saying to each other.

I asked my chief inspector to step outside the room with me and suggested that we could use the man to lead us to the other members of the gang.

'But we don't know that he is a member of this gang.'

'I know that, but if he *is* a member of this gang we are looking for he may be willing to tell us where they are living and where the revolver is. He knows that we have two witnesses, the people who were attacked. If he does show signs of cooperating with us we can then mention the possibility of him becoming a state witness. If he doesn't want to help us you can tell him that we will put him on an identification parade. You must ask yourself why he was wandering by himself and not with the gang. Maybe their violent acts have made him uneasy.'

We returned to the room where our prisoner sat in a chair. I told the constable who had been guarding him to wait outside the room. I then quietly discussed the condition of the constable and of the watchman. I was aware that the prisoner was listening intently.

'This could soon turn into a solved case, Chief Inspector,' I said.

'Indeed so, *bwana*. We have good identifying witnesses.'

'Well, I have some work to attend to. I'll leave you to it. Come and see me when he has decided what he wants to do.'

With that, I left the room.

Following a discussion between my chief inspector and the suspect, a raid was carried out on a house in the outskirts of Lusaka. This resulted in the capture of several members of the gang, but not all of them. The assistant inspector's revolver was recovered and my chief inspector received a commendation for his work. Both victims of the gang made full recoveries and were able to give compelling evidence at the trials.

In February the following year, the case was finally dealt with and the culprits were sentenced individually to long terms of imprisonment. I didn't attend the hearing. Our chief witness, who, as a witness for the state, had given evidence for the prosecution, was released and quickly left the Lusaka area. My DCI was destined for rapid promotion but I had left the country by the time he received it.

91

The Lusaka Rapist

Towards the end of 1966, after a discussion with uniformed colleagues I met with the boss to discuss the steadily rising number of break-ins in certain European areas of the city. European and Asian houses were being targeted and mainly small, easily disposable but valuable items were being stolen. Patrols had been increased but the number of break-ins had continued to rise.

During the Christmas period several houses had been broken into and in one of these the female owner had disturbed the burglar when she had got up in the night to check on one of her children, who was unwell. The person she disturbed was small and agile and had made a rapid escape through the window that he had earlier forced. As she had only caught a glimpse of his back she could not say what he looked like but she was sure that he was a black man or boy.

As January arrived the number of break-ins continued to rise and a worrying change in the behaviour of the thief manifested itself. If discovered, as he was on two occasions, he no longer fled but produced a knife with which he threatened his victims. On each occasion these had been women. The police showed them photographs of known criminals who had been arrested for crimes of this nature in the past but they had failed to pick anyone out. They were able, however, to provide general descriptions of the man when interviewed separately. It became obvious that we were dealing with just the one man.

Despite increased patrols the break-ins continued. The most worrying thing was an escalation in the violence employed by the man carrying them out. On two occasions he had been disturbed by male householders and had used his fists to subdue them. This was a further indication of his willingness to use whatever means he considered necessary to achieve his ends.

In CID we put together the behavioural pattern of the man. His method of entry was usually through a window and was silently achieved. He worked quietly during his time in a house but was careless and left his fingerprints everywhere. Unfortunately none of them matched any of those in our records.

If discovered during his time in a house he showed an increasing tendency to use violence in order to subdue the householder. He took small, valuable and easily sold items, none of which we had been able to trace despite having questioned market traders and shopkeepers dealing in such items. We had contacted all of our informers but had drawn a blank. We produced lists of items stolen in break-ins which we had connected to him and circulated them widely but received no feedback.

Time passed and we moved into February. We now had a number of artist's drawings of the man we wanted to arrest. The main problem was that the people aiding the artist to produce the drawings were European or Asian, and to most of them one African face was much like another. All of our witnesses did, however, agree upon the man's build and fitness. All said that although he was not very big he was strong and muscular and moved in the easy manner of a person trained in some sort of sport.

Eventually in early March the crimes committed by our man escalated in an alarming manner. I was called out at about two o'clock in the morning to a case of black-on-white rape. The victim was the matron of the Lusaka General Hospital and she had been raped in her own home. I immediately took charge of the case, collected a team of my officers and called out the force forensic team to attend the scene as a matter of urgency. I took with me a European female officer to gather the details from the victim of the attack, a maiden lady of about sixty plus years of age.

On arrival at the scene I found several European and African uniformed officers already there. They told me that they had secured the scene and had assigned a European female officer to look after the victim pending our arrival. The victim had summoned one of her female hospital doctors to attend her. This doctor had already treated her injuries and had taken swabs to check for any sexually transmitted disease. My own female CID officer now took over the task of obtaining a written statement, with the uniformed officer remaining in the room and continuing her comforting and supportive role for the victim.

I turned to the crime scene, which I found to be upsetting. Lying on the carpet were the bodies of two small dogs. Both were covered in blood and both had been stabbed and had their throats slashed. It was obvious that they had been trying to protect their mistress, and this was later confirmed in her statement.

As I was completing my notes I asked the African servant who worked for the matron to bring me two pillowcases. The forensic team had by now completed their work and all the photographs had been taken. When she returned with the pillowcases I told her that we would put the dogs in them after cleaning them up as far as possible, and this we did together.

We had just completed our task when a uniformed inspector rushed into the room and breathlessly reported that a second rape of a white woman had just been reported. Leaving the uniformed female officer with the matron, I collected my female officer and my senior detective and we set off to the second scene. The second victim lived not far away and we arrived there just as a Land Rover containing several uniformed officers drove up.

The second victim turned out to be about twenty-five years old and was in a deeply shocked condition. Her description of her assailant was the same as the matron's description, and without any doubt we were dealing with the same man. It was almost certainly the man who had been plaguing us with his break-ins for so many months. I immediately sent an officer back to the original crime scene with instructions to ask the matron for the name of the doctor who had treated her, and a request for her to ask this doctor to attend the second victim.

Now having two victims and two crime scenes, it was essential to call back the same experts who had processed the first scene. They arrived quickly and rapidly got to work. They proceeded to carefully but quickly process the scene, but this time also looking for similarities between the two attacks. My female officer came out of the room where she had been quietly taking a statement from the victim and confirmed that everything the second victim had said tied in exactly with the evidence of the first victim. As she was telling me this, the doctor arrived and was shown into the room where the victim was waiting.

When she eventually came out of the room she came over to me and said, 'You have got to catch this bastard quickly. He is a sadist and enjoys hurting his victims. These are not just sexual attacks. There is a large element of sadism involved. He enjoys terrifying and hurting people and this gives him his greatest pleasure. From what you have told me he is escalating as well. I would say that if he carries on for much longer he will kill someone.'

With that, she left. My female officer had by this time located two of the victim's friends and they were on their way to come and stay with her. We also left two uniformed officers to guard the premises. Other people who lived in the same building had heard nothing. The victim had been warned to keep quiet and threatened with dire consequences if she tried to shout for help.

On my return to the station I decided to get the boss out of bed. I knew he was deeply concerned about the crimes committed by this individual, and that he would be furious if he had not been kept informed, especially now two rapes had occurred. He came down to the station immediately. We went over everything that had occurred and the steps we had taken over the months we had been searching for this criminal. He said that he would have to arrange an urgent meeting with the Assistant Commissioner Crime later that morning. As it happened, this proved to be unnecessary.

I was early into the office next morning, as were many of the team. At about eight o'clock as I was checking statements and going over evidence connected to the two rapes a constable from the enquiry office arrived with an envelope. It was addressed to the officer in charge of the station CID. The writing on the envelope was in large, badly written capital letters. When I carefully opened it the writing on the paper inside was in the same hand and obviously written by the same person.

I asked the constable if the person who had brought the letter into the enquiry office was waiting for an answer. He told me that a young African boy had handed in the letter and then had run away before anyone could question him. He had not said anything to the officers on duty.

The letter was very brief but went directly to the point, stating that the man we wanted for the rapes was a well-known professional boxer who was often to be found in the main market in the city. It also said that he would be carrying stolen property with him. It ended with the words, "He has gone too far".

I made several copies of the letter by hand and then photographed it. Together with the envelope that had contained it, the letter, now in a plastic sleeve, was sent by hand to the forensic boys. I included a set of my own fingerprints for elimination purposes. I then took a copy of the letter to show the boss and told him what I intended to do. I had questioned the staff to find out if any of them knew of any local boxers who fought in the lower-weight groups in boxing matches in the Lusaka area. Several of them did.

I chose two of these officers and told them to dress in casual clothes. I explained that I had reason to believe that our man was a boxer and that he would probably be found in the main market area. They were to arrest for searching and questioning any boxer that they could identify who fitted our rapist's description in regards to size, age and muscular development. I also instructed another pair of my younger officers to distance themselves from the arresting officers, but to stay within sight of them, ready to move in should an arrest be made.

When it happened it was an anticlimax, really. A man was arrested without any fuss and was transported to the station in a car which had been waiting a few hundred yards away from the market. The accused, when searched, was found to have items from the first raped woman's home and from a couple of other burglaries. He then, surprisingly, offered to show us all the houses from which he had stolen items after breaking in. There were a number of houses that he showed us where the offence had not even been reported. He accounted for all the ones we knew about as well. He seemed to take pride in showing us how he got into each house. When he was fingerprinted, everything slipped into place and there were smiles to be seen throughout the station.

When he appeared before the court a few weeks before I was due to leave the force, he pleaded guilty. The judge told him that had the maximum punishment for aggravated rape not been reduced from death by hanging to life imprisonment, he would have been sentenced to death. Instead, he was, I think, sentenced to thirty years' imprisonment without remission and twenty strokes of the cane, the maximum number allowed. These were to be spread over time to be dictated by a doctor.

We never did locate the writer of the letter which had given us the lead we needed. I have always felt that it was probably the man or woman who fenced the stolen property for the accused who wrote it.

92

A Shattering Blow

As time moved on and April arrived I was now in a position where I only advised my chief inspector if he asked for help. Other officers requiring advice were directed to him. I had watched him grow into a confident and effective officer, but he didn't have all the answers and he still came to me when he needed help or advice. If I couldn't give him the answer he needed I took him along to the boss and left them to sort things out.

This weaning process left me with more time to engage in activities such a skydiving and tennis. My trip home by sea from Cape Town was already booked on a Dutch liner and I looked forward to the rather expensive luxury trip.

I was playing in a tennis competition on the first Sunday in April. My partner and I had reached the semi-finals of the men's doubles. I had been skydiving the previous day but the tennis took first place on the Sunday. The doubles match proved very enjoyable but we lost it narrowly after three fiercely contested sets. I was sitting with friends and was enjoying my usual orange juice when an African uniformed inspector arrived and asked me to return immediately to the station. All he could tell me was that there had been a very bad accident, and it involved a friend of mine.

I jumped into my car and followed him back to the station. As I walked into the enquiry office I was aware that a number of officers were looking at me. I picked up the occurrence book and checked the most recent entry, which showed that a call had been received from the airport reporting that there had been a skydiving accident with one fatality recorded. The body was being removed to the autopsy department at the hospital for a post-mortem examination, which was scheduled for the following morning. The name and details of the deceased had not been entered. I told the officer on duty to record that I had been informed and was going to the skydiving club to find out what had happened.

*

When I walked into the clubhouse I was met by the sight of many of my skydiving friends and acquaintances sitting silently, some holding their heads in their hands and others leaning back in their chairs with their eyes closed, or just staring ahead. I heard a sound of quiet sobbing but didn't look to see where it came from. I saw Eric Rule and beckoned him to follow me outside.

'Tell me what has happened, Eric. This will be off the record, as I will take no part in the investigation.

'It's Yvonne, Dave. She's dead. She was jumping your chute. She just went straight into the ground. The chute never opened.'

I felt bile rise in my throat and for a moment thought that I was going to be sick. Tears started to well up, and I blinked rapidly.

'But my chute is rigged for free fall. How the hell did she come to be using my chute?'

'I don't know, Dave. I didn't check her.'

'Who did?'

'I don't know.' He looked almost ready to burst into tears.

'Christ almighty, there's going to be all hell let loose. What's happened to the chute she was jumping with?'

'They took it with them when she was taken away.'

'Well, the hospital can't have it. I'll send an inspector down there to take custody of it. The police will hold it until a board of enquiry needs to look at it, and they will obviously find that it is rigged for free fall. Bloody hell, what a mess. The coroner will open the case tomorrow and will then immediately adjourn it pending the findings of the board of enquiry. God knows when that will convene. They may have to bring experts up from South Africa.

'After the post-mortem the coroner will release the body for disposal. I imagine that the British consul will contact the family in Scotland and discuss with them what they want us to do with her. I'll check with them to find out what is happening. If it is a funeral here in Lusaka we had better start collecting money to help towards covering the costs involved.

'I advise you and the rest of the group jumping here today to make no statements to anyone about the incident, especially to the newspapers. You and Ian get yourselves legal representation immediately and wait for the official enquiry. If you are questioned by the police about the incident, have your solicitor with you. He will tell them that you will wait for the official hearing before saying anything.'

In the end, Yvonne's funeral was held in Lusaka with a large number of friends in attendance. The police force added to the considerable presence, many officers still in uniform having just completed their shifts. The skydiving communities were fully represented, with a number of members from clubs in several neighbouring African countries swelling the ranks of the locals. The church was decked with flowers sent by members of the community and by many friends. The service was just about as bearable as most funeral services are. We all returned to our homes later that day saddened by the loss of such a young and vibrant life. Yvonne's body was later cremated, and the ashes sent to her parents in Scotland.

Some weeks later, after returning home from Africa, I contacted Yvonne's parents and travelled up to Scotland to meet them. They were a charming couple but were obviously deeply affected by what had happened to their only daughter. After I arrived at their house and was sitting and having coffee with them, Mr Sinclair suddenly jumped up and abruptly left the room. He was shaking his head and looked very unsettled.

When he had left and the door was closed Mrs Sinclair turned to me and told me that she wanted me to tell her exactly how Yvonne looked after her death. I will never forget her face as she waited for me to answer.

I thought quickly and said, 'Mrs Sinclair, you have asked me a terrible question.'

'But I must know the answer, whatever it is.'

She had begun to shake, and there were tears in her eyes. I thought that whatever I said would form the picture she would carry in her mind for the rest of her life.

'Do you really need to know how she looked? Can't you just remember her as she was when you last saw her?'

She shook her head, and tears streamed down her cheeks.

'I have tried to remember her as she was but I can't, I just can't. I have nightmares about her hitting the ground and what that did to her. Please tell me.'

'I will, but this will not be easy. Shall I ask Mr Sinclair to come in and sit with you?'

'No. No, you mustn't,' she sobbed. 'He wouldn't be able to bear what you might have to say. It would destroy him.'

Good grief, I thought, how am I going to do this? I sat silently for a while and then moved my chair closer to her and took her hand in mine.

'Mrs Sinclair,' I said, 'what I am going to tell you is awful. If you find that you can't continue to listen, please tell me to stop and I'll gladly do so.'

She nodded, but I could see that she was shaking violently and was transmitting her tremors through her grip on my hand. I began.

'Firstly I must tell you that her fall, from the moment she left the plane to the time that she hit the ground, took only about twenty-eight seconds. I have spoken to a doctor and he feels that, as she had never reached such speeds before, she would almost certainly have lost consciousness in the first ten seconds of the fall. Death was instantaneous.'

She looked intently at my face and then she nodded, and I continued.

'Her dispatcher watched her all the way down to the ground. There was nothing he could do. Even if he had dived out after her when he realised that she was unresponsive it would have been physically impossible to reach her. He told me that she did not struggle or move in any way, and he also came to the conclusion that she had lost consciousness.'

As I paused for a few moments to think about what I would say next and how I would say it, I saw that she was plucking up courage to ask the question which I had, I suppose, been avoiding. I drew a breath, ready to continue, but she had found the courage and spoke before I could start.

In no more than a whisper she said, 'Please tell me what she looked like.'

I felt sick. It was no good asking if she really wanted to know. Her eyes were pleading and she had now become very still. She seemed to have stopped breathing. I drew a deep breath and started to tell her.

'Your little girl landed on her back in fairly soft earth,' I said.

She shuddered, and her face, which had been pale before, was now turning a dull grey colour.

'The post-mortem showed that she had broken virtually every bone in her body. She died instantly. There could have been no pain.'

I felt the hand I was holding crushing mine. I had never felt such a grip before.

'Her face.' The words were almost inaudible. 'What about her face? Please tell me the truth.'

Her eyes were unfocused and looked almost dead.

'Amazingly, her face was untouched,' I said. 'She still had her helmet on and this had protected her head. She just looked as though she was sleeping. Her eyes were closed and her face was peaceful.'

Hearing this, she started sobbing loudly and put her arms around me and pushed her head against my chest, the tears running down her face and soaking my shirt. I found tears running down my own face and continued to hold her tightly for what seemed to be a long time. I hoped that I would one day be able to justify to myself the lies that I had just told her.

Following this meeting my hosts both seemed to relax. Mr Sinclair, or Bill as he asked me to call him, took me for walks to show me his favourite fishing spots. His wife, whom I now called Margaret, seemed to regain some of her colour and vitality. I even heard her laugh once with a customer who had come to collect clean clothes from the laundry which the Sinclairs managed. I noticed that a number of photographs of Yvonne had now appeared in the lounge where there had been none when I had first arrived.

Before leaving Africa I had sent a cheque representing money collected to help in the purchasing of a stone for Yvonne's monument, which would be situated in the main cemetery in Aberdeen. I had suggested that the Sinclairs might wish to use some of the money to commission a carving of a skydiver to be mounted above the words:

She Died Pursuing the Sport She Loved

It would form an appropriate monument to a much-loved young woman. I made it clear, however, that it was entirely up to them how the money was used.

On a second visit some months later I was taken to the cemetery and shown the stone with the words carved into it just as I had hoped they would be. There, above the words, was the figure of the skydiver, obviously carved with a great deal of care. Beneath them were Yvonne's name and date of birth, and words expressing the family's grief at their loss. Mr Sinclair smiled as he pointed at some new flowers beside the monument.

'Not ours,' he said. 'Other people put flowers here as well. We find it very comforting.'

93

A Last Skydive

On the morning of Saturday 22nd April 1967, the day I was scheduled to leave the country for the last time, I joined a group of friends from the skydiving club to have one last jump and link-up over the farm of Mrs X (name withheld). Her husband had died some years before and she ran the farm herself in his absence.

Eric and Ian would not be there as they were taking part in the Rhodesian Skydiving Championships, which were being held at the Borrowdale Racecourse in Salisbury, Southern Rhodesia.

I had previously discovered that the farm was being used by a small group of like-minded young white men as a meeting place. Here the group assembled information relating to the movement of terrorists who were trained mainly in the Middle East and were regularly entering the country from the north. Such people invariably ended up in a camp in the bush to the south-east of Lusaka. After resting there they would travel south through the bush until they came to the Zambezi, where a boat would be waiting to take them across to the Southern Rhodesian shore.

The men I had stopped on the road north of Lusaka in February 1966 had been such people. Their job was to pick off soft targets in Southern Rhodesia. These were often shopkeepers, who were usually Asians, and white farmers and their families. The object was to spread fear and despondency among the non-black community.

Several of the men jumping that day were members of the group passing information to the authorities in Southern Rhodesia. Such information was vital in helping to stop the atrocities which were being committed across the Zambezi. Unfortunately a group is only as strong as its weakest member, and the weakest member had been arrested the previous week after being heard drunkenly boasting of the group's work. The members of the group consoled themselves by reassuring each other that he would not talk. I had serious reservations.

We took off from our normal airstrip and were soon climbing. Our aim was to jump from twelve thousand feet and do a five-man link-up if the cloud permitted. Over the farm, however, there was plenty of high cloud, which was to prevent us from completing our objective.

I was last to leave the plane and quickly lost sight of the others as they disappeared into the clouds below. As I eventually emerged from thick cloud I picked out the rest of the jumpers scattered far below me. As I was considering going head-down to join them, something caught my attention. I saw a flash of light from the bushes that circled the fields belonging to the farm. I then saw further flashes from two other areas of the bush. I immediately pulled my ripcord and opened my chute.

As I slowly glided down the other jumpers were almost on the point of landing. I didn't think that I had been noticed. As I got lower I began to notice movement in the cover around the farm. I realised that I was looking at a police or military operation, and that it was aimed at the farm. The intermittent flashes of light were coming from sun reflecting off various metal objects they were carrying or wearing.

I realised that I had been seen when the sudden movement of the watchers into better cover took place. There was only one thing to do. I joined the rest of the jumpers in the farm lounge.

Two of them had seen movement in the bush, but the others had not.

I looked at them all seated on chairs and a settee and said, 'I think that some of you could be in trouble, gentlemen. This farm is surrounded by observers and I suspect that your member who was arrested recently has been telling the authorities about you. If you are not arrested as you leave here this afternoon they are probably waiting to see if anyone else joins you. If they don't arrest you I would advise you to leave this country at once.'

There were immediate arguments about this and no definite conclusion was reached. Two of the men had businesses which they felt they could not leave. Mrs X felt that she could not leave the farm and her farm workers.

'Well,' I said, 'I had intended to leave Lusaka on Monday, but I shall now leave as soon as I can pack a case when I get back to the station.'

Mrs X told all who needed a lift to get into her large car, which was parked outside. She then instructed her main farmhand to put all the skydiving gear into a van and deliver it back to the skydiving club. We set off, and one by one she delivered us to our homes. I got out at the station and wished her luck. She shrugged her shoulders in reply and drove away.

On return to my room I packed my two large cases with as much as I would be able to carry and then wrote a short letter to my servant Crispin Sakala, telling him that I had to leave early as the boat was sailing early. (Little did I know!)

In the previous week I had given him the money I had saved for him during the years he had worked for me. For every month's pay that he had received I had put the same amount into a savings account without ever letting him know. The week before, I had helped him to open an account in his own name at the bank where I had banked, and had explained to him how a bank account worked. He showed that he understood and, as he thanked me, he told me that he would now be able to be the headman of his village. He was almost overcome by his sudden change of fortune.

In the letter I had written to him I gave him permission to take for himself any of my property remaining in my room when I had left. He was to show this letter to a senior police officer.

94

Leaving

I quietly left the police station, loaded my car and prepared to leave. I found one of the remaining European officers on duty and told him to say goodbye to everyone for me. I explained that I would be hard-pressed to get to Cape Town in time to catch my ship. We shook hands and I drove away.

I crossed the border into Southern Rhodesia without any trouble that evening, so I assumed that the authorities were not looking for me. I got out of my car on the Southern Rhodesian side and went into the customs office and asked to talk with the Special Branch officer. When he arrived I identified myself and told him to get on to his boss in Salisbury as I needed to speak to him urgently. He looked at me doubtfully.

'I am talking about assets of yours who are in great danger in Zambia,' I said.

His attitude changed immediately and he picked up the phone. He eventually connected with the top man and handed me the phone. I quickly mentioned a few names to the man at the other end of the line and heard a quick intake of breath.

'I need to speak with you face-to-face,' he said.

I told him that I was travelling down to Cape Town and was in a great hurry to catch my ship, but I could see him in Salisbury as soon as I could get there.

'This is urgent. I'll drive down to meet you,' he replied.

I gave him a description of my car and its number and set off towards Salisbury. As there was only one main road and I was on it, we would have no difficulty seeing each other. I was just over a third of the way to Salisbury when I saw a car driving at high speed towards me. Its lights were in continual flash mode. I flashed my lights and we both stopped alongside one another. We got out of our cars and shook hands as we introduced ourselves.

Our conversation lasted about ten minutes, during which time I told him everything I knew and answered his questions. After a warm handshake and an expression of thanks he jumped back into his car, which took off at high speed back the way he had come. I followed, but it very quickly disappeared into the distance.

I made good time to Salisbury and stopped there to have a meal and a rest. It was late afternoon when I found a restaurant. Near to the front door there was a boy selling the local newspaper. I bought a copy, hoping that it might contain a report of the skydiving championships. It would be something to read as I waited for my meal.

After ordering my meal I turned to the paper. I didn't need to look inside for a skydiving article. Across the whole of the front page were headlines. I can't remember the exact words but the words "skydiving" and "horror" and "sickening" were all there in ultra-large print. There were pictures of two men, and I felt sick as I recognised Eric Rule and Terrance Daly who wasn't a member of our club but who had done some jumping with us. The article said that they had collided at high speed in the air, and both had plummeted to the ground and had been pronounced dead at the scene. Their parachutes had shown no sign of opening.

Rather theatrically, the article went on to talk of women and children turning their heads away, and the screaming of the crowd just before the two men hit the ground. It went on to liken the sound of the bodies hitting the ground to shots fired by heavy rifles. It stated that the sounds had been heard over two miles away. In sombre tones it announced that the skydiving championships had been immediately cancelled and that no further skydiving would take place on the following day, as had been planned.

My dinner was not as tasty as I had anticipated but I ate it just the same. I had a long journey ahead of me.

I don't intend to write about the journey down to Cape Town except to say that it seemed to last forever. When I arrived there I drove down to the main harbour and found the ship. I found the loading crew and handed over the car, keeping a suitcase with me for my stay in a hotel in the town overnight.

The following morning, refreshed by a good night's sleep, I had breakfast and then went out for a walk. I found a newsagent's and bought a newspaper. Wondering at what time my ship would leave the following day, I turned to the page showing all the shipping arrivals and departures. To my horror, in the column listing departures I found the name of my ship. It had sailed during the night. I set out to find the shipping company offices.

When eventually I walked into the busy shipping office the whole place suddenly became silent as about twenty or so people stopped working to stare at me. A man who was obviously in charge came out of his office and walked up to me.

'Mr McCue, I presume?' he said.

I nodded. 'Well, I'm not David Livingstone.'

'We've been expecting you.'

'Why has the ship sailed early?' I asked.

Eventually everything became clear. Letters had been sent out to all passengers well before the new date of sailing. I was the only one who had not received my notification. The postal system was obviously not working quite as well in Zambia as it had been before independence.

I was offered a sincere apology and invited to dinner that evening at the manager's house. A flight had been booked for the following evening and I would be travelling first class at the shipping company's expense.

I took the opportunity the next day to go to the top of Table Mountain by cable car and enjoyed watching several climbers scaling the sheer rock.

The flight back to Manchester was comfortable and the service was excellent, but I couldn't help thinking about the missed sea trip.

Postscript

Despite efforts made by the Southern Rhodesia Special Branch, the members of the group supplying information about the movement of terrorists across the Zambezi were arrested. Mrs X lost her farm and the others lost their businesses or jobs. All of them were held in close confinement in a guarded camp on the Zambian border with one of the neighbouring countries to the south. This is second-hand information and only what I have gleaned in discussions over the telephone.

As far as I know I don't think that any of them were ever brought to trial. It would have been very embarrassing for certain members of the government. I believe that eventually all of them were expelled from Zambia and moved south. I heard that Mrs X had been given a farm by a grateful Southern Rhodesian government to replace the one she had lost. I doubt that she could have held on to it for more than the few years during which the country moved towards its own independence.

On my return to England I spent a year studying and then took and passed sufficient A Levels at the required level to allow me to take the four-year Manchester University degree course in education, which I passed with honours.

My degree equipped me to teach children of both junior and secondary age. I chose to teach at junior-school level where the children were aged from seven to eleven years. I felt I would be more able to influence and inspire children before they reached the cynical teenage years.

I was always given eleven-year-olds to teach, but eventually I was promoted to deputy head teacher without a class of my own. I made sure, however, that I could, in addition to my other duties, teach one or more fourth-year classes at least once each week and other classes in rotation.

During the four years of my degree course I had founded the Didsbury College fencing club and coached young men and women in fencing. I had passed my fencing coach's examinations and had qualified to be an instructor in Foil, Epee and Sabre several years before I joined the police. After a year's

272

coaching I took my team of students down to London where we won the British Colleges Championships.

During this period I did some work outside college hours at the Margaret Barkley School for severely handicapped children. One of the older boys had suffered badly from spina bifida. His legs were completely wasted so he spent his life in a wheelchair. His name was Howard Wardle. He worked out and had a marvellous upper body, but he was very frustrated and this led to problems.

I took several of my own weapons along one afternoon and started to teach him how to fence. In Howard's mind it was how to fight, not fence, but I gradually calmed him down. I sat in one wheelchair and he in another. He was very aggressive, sometimes turning his chair over and crashing to the floor in an attempt to hit me.

Eventually he represented Great Britain in two Paralympics. In Toronto in 1976 he won the bronze medal in the men's individual foil novices. In Arnhem in the Netherlands in 1980 he won silver in the men's team sabre event.

Acknowledgements

My thanks are due to Tim Wright, author of *The History Of The Northern Rhodesia Police*. I found Tim's book most helpful when checking names of fellow officers, dates of various events, and changes to conditions of employment etc. As well as being interesting, his book was a source of information that I would otherwise have found almost impossible to locate.

9 781781 326329